Sustainable Tourism as a Factor of Cohesion Among European Regions

CoR Studies E-6/2006
Brussels, March 2006

A great deal of additional information on the European Union is available on the Internet.
It can be accessed through the Europa server (http://europa.eu.int).

Cataloguing data can be found at the end of this publication.

Luxembourg: Office for Official Publications of the European Communities, 2006

ISBN 92-895-0378-5

Printed in Belgium

PRINTED ON WHITE CHLORINE-FREE PAPER

SUSTAINABLE TOURISM AS A FACTOR OF COHESION AMONG EUROPEAN REGIONS

Contents

Executive Summary 1

Introduction 5

SECTION A: 7

TOURISM IN THE EUROPEAN UNION 7

1. Tourism in the European Union: an Assessment 9
    1.1   The Key Issues 9
        1.1.1   European Tourism in Figures 9
        1.1.2   Strengths and Weaknesses 21
        1.1.3   Risks 23
    1.2   The European Tourism Facing New Challenges 25

SECTION B: 29

CONCEPTS AND PRINCIPLES OF SUSTAINABLE TOURISM 29

1. Sustainable Tourism: Definition, Principles and Objectives 31
    1.1   What is Sustainable Tourism? 31
        1.1.1   The Sustainable Tourism Definition 32
    1.2   Respecting General Principles 33
    1.3   Matching Strategic Objectives 34

2. Sustainable Tourism: Policies and Strategies at International and European Union Level 38
    2.1   Recent Developments of Sustainable Tourism Policies 38
        2.1.1   General Framework: Sustainable Development, Environment and Sectoral Integration ... 38
        2.1.2   The European Union Tourism Policy 41
        2.1.3   The Committee of the Regions and Tourism 46
    2.2   Initiatives to Support the Development of Sustainable Tourism 49

3. Characterization of European Regions with respect to Sustainable Tourism 59
    3.1   Tourism Environmental Indicators 59
        3.1.1   The Development of Indicators 59
        3.1.2   Problems and Constraints in Developing Sustainable Tourism Indicators 63
    3.2   The Clustering Process 65
        3.2.1   Assessment of Sustainable Tourism Development in the European Regions 65
        3.2.2   Identified Tourism Typologies 76

4. Recommendations 80

SECTION C: 83

SUSTAINABLE TOURISM AND TERRITORIAL COHESION 83

1. Sustainable Tourism and Territorial Cohesion Policies 85
    1.1   Concept and Rationale of Territorial Cohesion 85
    1.2   The Dimension of Sustainable Tourism within Cohesion Policies 88
        1.2.1   Cohesion Policies and the European Spatial Development Perspective 88
        1.2.2   Sustainable Tourism and the Services of General Economic Interests 90
        1.2.3   The Trans-European Networks 93

2. Sustainable Tourism as a factor of Territorial Cohesion 100
    2.1   Co-operation with Border Regions and Sustainable Tourism 103
    2.2   Outermost Regions and Regions with Natural Handicaps 105

2.3   Sustainable Tourism and the Lisbon Strategy..107

2.4   General Measures for Harmonisation to foster Sustainable Tourism Development and Regional Cohesion 110

3.   Tourism types regions and cohesion indicators 113

3.1   Tourism Types Classification, GDP per Capita and Unemployment Rates............113

      3.1.1   Type 1- Most Visited Regions...114

      3.1.2   Type 1.1. - Densely Populated Regions 115

      3.1.3   Type 1.2. - Mass Tourism Destinations..115

      3.1.4   Type 2 and 2.1 - Traditional Regions and New Tourism Destinations 116

      3.1.5   Type 3 - Less Visited Regions 117

      3.1.6   Sparsely Populated Regions and Peripheral Regions 118

3.2   Fostering Sustainable Tourism in the Identified Tourism Types.............................119

4.   Conclusions and Recommendations 122

4.1   Conclusions...122

4.2   Recommendations...123

      4.2.1   Recommendations related to the Cooperation with Border Regions...............126

      4.2.2   Recommendations related to the Outermost Regions...126

      4.2.3   Recommendations related to Identified Tourism Types......................................127

SECTION D: GOVERNANCE AND SUSTAINABLE TOURISM 129

1.   Governing Sustainable Tourism: the Background..131

1.1   Targeting Good Governance..131

      1.1.1   The Definition and Basic Principles of Good Governance 131

      1.1.2   The Dimension of Multi-level Governance and the Subsidiarity Principle....................132

1.2   Structural Characteristics of the Tourism Sector: Actors and Policies in Europe....................134

      1.2.1   Key Features of the Sector and its Stakeholders 134

      1.2.2   Links to European Union Policies..137

1.3   The Crucial Level of Governance for Economic Development: the Territorial Authorities.......139

      1.3.1   Potential of the Territorial Authorities 139

      1.3.2   Functions and Role of the Territorial Authorities in the Tourism Sector......................141

      1.3.3   Barriers to a more pro-active Role of Territorial Authorities...........................142

1.4   Conclusions on the Principles of Good Governance in the Tourism Sector and its transformation into a Sustainable Strategy..146

1.5   Recommendations...147

2.   Models of Governance in European Tourism...148

2.1   Experimenting with Typologies..148

      2.1.1   A Classification based on the Level of Decision-making Autonomy and Capabilities....149

      2.1.2   A Classification based on Tourism Relevance 150

      2.1.3   Path Dependencies: introducing the Level of Sustainability 152

2.2   Main Conclusions on the Clustering Process...154

      2.2.1   High Regional Strategies for Tourism..154

      2.2.2   Tailored Regional Strategies for Tourism 155

      2.2.3   New Regional Strategies for Tourism 157

2.3   Funding Needs, Constraints and the Relevance of Public- Private Partnerships 157

2.4   Conclusions...159

3.   The Role of ICT in Sustainable Tourism 162

3.1   Key Features of the ICT revolution 162

3.2   The Influence of ICT on Tourism 163

      3.2.1   The Role of ICT for Tourism: Ways of Influence...164

      3.2.2   Evidence on ICT Penetration in the Tourism Industry.......................................166

      3.2.3   Striking a Balance between Centralised and Decentralised Systems 168

3.3   Influence on Sustainability and Networks 170

3.4   Conclusions and Recommendations 172

SECTION E: 175

FUNDING SUSTAINABLE TOURISM IN THE EUROPEAN UNION 175

1.   **The Structural Funds** 177
       1.1   Objective 1, 2 and 3 Mainstream Programmes 177
               1.1.1   European Regional Development Fund (ERDF) 178
               1.1.2   European Social Fund (ESF) 179
               1.1.3   Financial Instruments for Fisheries Guidance (FIFG) 179
               1.1.4   European Agricultural Guidance and Guarantee Fund (EAGGF) 181
       1.2   Innovative Measures 181
       1.3   Community Initiatives 182
               1.3.1   INTERREG III: trans-European co-operation for balanced development 182
               1.3.2   URBAN II: Economic and Social Regeneration in Urban Areas 183
               1.3.3   LEADER+: Links between Actions for the Development of the Rural Economy 184
               1.3.4   EQUAL - Development of Human Resources 185

2.   **The Cohesion Fund** 187

3.   **Other Financial Instruments** 188
       3.1   Pre-accession Instruments: PHARE, ISPA, SAPARD 188
       3.2   CULTURE 2000 189
       3.3   LIFE III 189
       3.4   RTD Framework Programmes (FPs) 191
       3.5   Others 192

4.   **Public Private Partnerships: Merits, Challenges and Opportunities** 194
       4.1   The Concept and Critical Factors of PPP Success 194
       4.2   Areas and Role of PPPs in Europe 197
       4.3   Areas and Role of Local and Regional Authorities in Developing and Implementing PPP and
               PFI 199

5.   **Conclusions and Recommendations** 201
       5.1   Funding Instruments 201
       5.2   Public and Private Partnerships 202

RECOMMENDATIONS 205

ANNEXES 217

1.   **Bibliography** 219

2.   **Other Internet links and sources** 231

3.   **List of Presented Best Practices and Case Studies** 235

4.   **Metadata** 237

List of Acronyms

AEBR	Association of European Border Regions
BOO	Build-Operate-Own
BOT	Build-Operate-Transfer
CBD	Convention on Biological Diversity
COP	Conference of the Parties
CoR	Committee of the Regions
COTER	Commission for Territorial Cohesion Policy
CSD	Commission on Sustainable Development
CSR	Corporate Social Responsibility
CORDIS	Community Research & Development Information Service
DG	Directorate General
EAP	Environmental Action Programme
EC	European Commission
ECEAT	European Centre for Ecological and Agricultural Tourism
ECOSERT	European Co-operation for Sustainable Environmental Regional development through Tourism
EEA	European Environment Agency
EIA	Environmental Impact Assessment
EIB	European Investment Bank
EMAS	Eco-Management and Audit Scheme
EMS	Environmental Management Systems
ERDF	European Regional Development Fund
ERF	European Union Road Federation
ESDP	European Spatial Development Perspective
ESPON	European Spatial Planning Observation Network
EU	European Union (25 Member States)
EU 15	European Union (15 Member States, prior to 1 May 2004)
Eurostat	Statistical Office of the European Communities
FP	Framework Programme
GATS	General Agreement on Trade in Services
GDP	Gross Domestic Product
GIS	Geographical Information System
GMES	Global Monitoring for Environment and Security
GVA	Gross Value Added

ha	hectare
HACCP	Hazard Analysis and Critical Control Point
HELCOM	The Helsinki Commission
ICLEI	International Council for Local Environmental Initiatives
ICZM	Integrated Coastal Zone Management
ICT	Information and Communication Technology
INSPIRE	Infrastructure for Spatial Information in Europe
IPP	Integrated Products Policy
ISPA	Instrument for Structural policies for Pre-Accession
IUCN	International Union for Conservation of Nature
LA 21	Local Agenda 21
MAP	Mediterranean Action Plan
MCSD	Mediterranean Commission on Sustainable Development
NACE	Nomenclature of Economic Activities in the European Communities
NCST	Network of Cities for Sustainable Tourism
NTO	National Tourism Organisation
NUTS	Nomenclature of Territorial Units in the EU
OECD	Organisation for Economic Co-operation and Development
PFI	Privately Finance Initiative
PPP	Public Private Partnership
R&D	Research and Development
RES	Renewable Energy Sources
RST	Regional Strategy for Tourism
SAPARD	Special Accession Programme for Agriculture & Rural Development
SARS	Severe Acute Respiratory Syndrome
SDS	Sustainable Development Strategy
SDT	Sustainable Development of Tourism
SEA	Strategic Environmental Assessment
SGEI	Services of General Economic Interest
SIDA	Swedish Agency for International Development Cooperation
SMEs	Small and Medium Enterprises
ST-EP	Sustainable Tourism – Eliminating Poverty
SUT	Sustainable Urban Tourism
SUVOT	Sustainable and Vocational Tourism
TENs	Trans-European Networks

TEN-T	Trans European Networks-Transport
TEMPUS	Tourism towards the Information Society
UN	United Nations
UNCTAD	United Nations Conference on Trade and Development
UNECE	United Nations Economic Commission for Europe
UNEP	United Nations Environment Programme
WES	World Ecotourism Summit
WTO	World Tourism Organisation
WTTC	World Travel & Tourism Council

Executive Summary

Progress towards sustainable tourism has become imperative in the European Unio . The tourism industry has grown to massive proportions in the last decade and so ha. its environmental impact. Since tourism is above all an economic activity, a better management of tourism is not only necessary to mitigate its negative effects on the environment, but also to minimise the potential conflict with other economic activities such as agriculture, forestry and fisheries.

Tourism is a global phenomenon that is shaped locally. As such, tourism is primarily a matter of local and regional responsibility.

The tourism sector supports the development of local facilities (recreational infrastructure, shops, restaurants), creates jobs and income, and is considered a valuable driver of development goals in a broad sense. But tourism also promotes intercultural relations and mutual understanding and is widely recognized as a major opportunity for enhancing the territorial cohesion within Europe.

The enlargement of the European Union and the expected economic growth of the new Member States should result in an increase of tourism demand. Although this demand is likely to largely favour the domestic tourism of the new Member States, it will also significantly trigger more trips from these countries to the leading and well-known destinations of western European regions, in particular to the southern European coasts and main tourist cities. This expected trend further stresses the evidence that Europe needs to move along the path of sustainable development.

Section A provides a comprehensive, quantitative overview of the tourism industry at European level, highlighting the new challenges for the future development of tourism, its strengths and weaknesses.

Section B focuses on the definition, principles and objectives of sustainable tourism (chapter 1). The idea of sustainable tourism is not solely a concept but a vision that needs to be shared by all stakeholders. At policy level, some recent developments have boosted the move towards a sustainable management of the tourism sector. These developments are reviewed under Chapter 2 of this section. Some common, general principles and strategic objectives constitute the necessary baseline for actions plans, programme and strategy elaboration. A quantitative assessment of the sustainable development of tourism at national and regional levels is provided in Chapter 3. By defining homogeneous areas with similar features, problems and/or constraints related to tourism, three tourism types and three sub-types have been identified. The assessment also highlights the need to further develop indicators, monitoring and evaluation systems.

Section C is about the role of sustainable tourism in fostering territorial cohesion: a brief introduction to relevant Community policies is followed by an analysis of how tourism, with its structural and economic characteristics may contribute to regional cohesion (chapter 1 and 2). Chapter 3 provides a comparison between the tourism types outlined in section B and the economic and social indicators commonly used in cohesion analysis, namely GDP per capita and unemployment rates.

Sustainable tourism can support and drive the territorial cohesion towards a harmonious and balanced development of Europe, throughout the Union. It has a high potential to enhance cohesion among regions because it fosters the promotion of the identity of each region and the sharing of the diverse European natural and cultural heritages, traditions and languages. It increases knowledge regarding European values with respect to their regional peculiarities and boosts the feeling of belonging to the same territory. It is largely recognised that tourism has brought prosperity to impoverished areas and is an ideal vehicle for the exchange of cultural experience. Moreover, in order to be and remain a successful tourist destination, attention must be paid to the environment. For its several horizontal and vertical links with other activities, sustainable tourism is also able to produce a positive impact on other sectors such as transport, industry and agriculture. Finally, since tourism is mainly a locally based activity, the role of local and regional institutions is further emphasised, confirming that they are central to the mission of territorial cohesion policy at the European Union level.

Section D investigates the way tourism is governed in the European Union. Chapter 1 introduces the general principles of good governance, specifically in the tourism sector, and describes the tourism industry stakeholders. Chapter 2 attempts to suggest typologies and good governance methods for very diverse environments in the European regions. Finally, chapter 3 is dedicated to the role of Information and Communication Technologies (ICTs), being a major driver of change in the industry.

While significant changes are already observed, it is expected that the increasing diffusion of ICTs, both of already known but also of future services, will further affect the interaction between the various actors and lead to new forms of governance.

Section E provides an overview of the main sources of funding for tourism and sustainable tourism, as well as examples of funded initiatives (chapter 1 to 3). Chapter 4 suggests possibilities for establishing public private partnerships that will enable strategies for sustainable tourism to be implemented.

Introduction

This study on "Sustainable Tourism as a Factor of Cohesion among European Regions" is based on the following milestones:

- that regional and local authorities play a key role in the cohesion process fostered by the territorial policies of the European Union;
- that destinations are responsible for improving their level of sustainable development, in line with the subsidiarity principle;
- that the tourism industry is an important contributor to the social and economic development of regions, also influencing the land use planning process and representing a vital development opportunity for those territories having accessibility problems.

The study aims to: disseminate updated and useful information on sustainable tourism policies and best practices; provide an overview of available funding instruments to foster development of sustainable tourism; recommend on the role of sustainable tourism as a factor of cohesion among regions.

The study has been carried out by Progress Consulting S.r.l.[1] within the frame of a service contract awarded trough public tender procedure by the Committee of the Regions (CoR). It is based on the contributions provided by a multi-disciplinary team of experts led by Rossella Soldi – Project Coordinator – and including: Aurelie Pelletreau on Sustainable Tourism, Lena Tsipouri on Governance and ICT, and Giuliana Torta for GIS application.

The publication is based on the collection and analysis of existing information. It focuses on the role regional and local authorities play in fostering the sustainable development of the tourism sector and in promoting territorial cohesion among European regions. The main topics addressed in relation to sustainable tourism include: governance, i.e. rules, procedures and practices affecting how powers are exercised; and territorial cohesion, i.e. the drivers moving towards an harmonious and

---

[1] Progress Consulting S.r.l. - Projects, Research and Sustainable Development in Agriculture, Forestry and Environment - E-mail : info@progresscons.com Web site: www.progresscons.com

balanced development of Europe through the reduction of economic and social disparities, the prevention of imbalances and the making of sectoral policies having a spatial impact more coherent with regional policy.

The adopted methodology encompasses three main principles: integrated approach; qualitative analysis; quantitative analysis and clustering.

The integrated approach implies an analysis of the tourism sector in respect of governance and relevant Community policies. Emphasis has been given to the role territorial authorities may have in fostering the sustainability of this economic activity. The qualitative analysis is based on the presentation of best practices and case studies whose aim is to integrate, illustrate and support the understanding of specific topics as well as to promote the dissemination of good principles to other regions.

The Committee of the Regions considers that information is a key issue for the sustainable development of tourism and that tourism is often characterised by its severe lack and by the necessity of further transparency. To address this need for quantitative analysis and to avoid providing generic recommendations, several statistics from internationally acknowledged sources have been collected and compiled into datasets and indicators. The combination of these indicators has allowed the classification of the EU territory into clusters at regional level characterised by common features related to sustainable tourism, such as high/low density of tourism and high/low pressure on the territory. This clustering process has been visualised into easily understandable and "high impact" maps providing direct transfer of messages and comprehensive overviews at European level.

This publication is structured into: an introductory part; five main sections addressing the core themes of the study; a chapter summarising recommendations; annexes, including the bibliography, other relevant Internet links and sources, the list of presented best practices and case studies, and dataset metadata.

Each main section is divided into chapters. Maps are included to illustrate the results of the clustering process; boxes report on specific cases or relevant topics. Best practices and case studies are described using a one-page layout.

SECTION A:
TOURISM IN THE EUROPEAN UNION

1. Tourism in the European Union: an Assessment

1.1 The Key Issues

1.1.1 European Tourism in Figures

In the European Union (EU) tourism is an increasingly important activity contributing to both economic growth and social development. The impact of tourism development within regions and local communities may be measured in terms of economic development (GDP, GVA) and employment (demand for skilled jobs and seasonal workers). Tourism also contributes to smooth regional disparities (territorial cohesion) and, recently, it has boosted the adoption of information and communication technologies. However, tourism features and peculiarities also put pressure on the environment, jeopardising the availability of resources.

The following paragraphs provide an overview of the sector referring to the latest available data.

1.1.1.1 The industry's size

Tourism is the largest service industry in the European Union and the third economic sector worldwide, after the automotive and petrol.

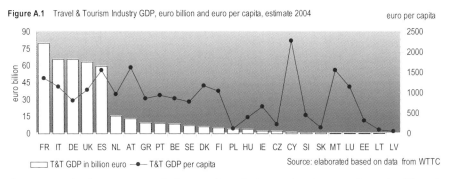

Figure A.1 Travel & Tourism Industry GDP, euro billion and euro per capita, estimate 2004

euro per capita

T&T GDP in billion euro —●— T&T GDP per capita

Source: elaborated based on data from WTTC

The economic importance of the tourism industry in the EU has significantly increased over the last five years both in terms of Gross Domestic Product (GDP) and employment. According to the Travel & Tourism Satellite Accounts[2], the direct impact of the travel & tourism industry in 1999 included about 8.7 million jobs and € 365.5 billion of GDP, while estimates for 2004 point towards 10.6 million jobs, equivalent to 5.3% of total employment, and € 428.2 billion of GDP, equivalent to 4.6% of total GDP. Also taking into account the indirect impact of the Travel & Tourism industry, it generates € 1158.98 billion of GDP and over 24.6 million jobs.

In 2004, the EU is estimated to reach a real growth of the Travel & Tourism demand of 3.1%, this value being higher than the average economic growth, thus making tourism one of the fastest growing industries. This rate is expected to increase to an annual real growth of 3.8% over the next ten years, with higher values expected for some of the new Member States such as Poland, Czech Republic and Hungary. The recent enlargement of the European Union is in fact considered to bring a further, unexploited potential for the economic growth of the sector[3]. Referring to the percentage variation of the tourism industry's GDP over the period 1999 – 2004, there are

Table A.1 Percentage variation of T&T GDP over the period 1999-2004

Source: elaborated based on data from WTTC

	%		%		%		%		%
SK	+116	EE	+ 44	FI	+ 26	IE	+ 16	SE	+ 8.7
SI	+ 70	LV	+ 32	PL	+ 22	NL	+ 12	MT	+ 5.2
CZ	+ 59	PT	+ 32	FR	+ 21	LT	+ 11	BE	+ 5.2
HU	+ 50	ES	+ 31	IT	+ 21	DK	+ 9.7	UK	+ 2.9
GR	+ 45	CY	+ 29	AT	+ 17	DE	+ 9.3	LU	- 15

seven new Member States in the first top ten countries showing the highest increase of GDP, with Slovak Republic, Slovenia, Czech Republic and Hungary having an increase of over 50%. Within the European Union, only Luxembourg showed a negative trend (- 15%). Tourism & Travel GDP per capita show the highest values in Cyprus (€2276), Austria (€1622) and Malta (€ 1556).

DEFINITIONS:

Travel & Tourism Industry refers to all products and services delivered to visitors. Services may include transport, accommodation, food and beverages, entertainment, recreation etc.

Travel & Tourism Industry Employment refers to jobs implying direct contact with visitors, such as airlines, hotels, restaurants etc.

Eurostat, the Statistical Office of the European Communities, provides information on the Gross Value Added (GVA) of the NACE branch "hotels and restaurants" at

---

[2] World Travel & Tourism Council, 2004 (a)
[3] World Travel & Tourism Council, 2004 (b)

regional level. The five leading regions in the ranking of GVA for hotels and restaurants in 2002 were Ile de France (FR), Cataluna (ES), Comunidad de Madrid (ES), Andalusia (ES) and Lombardia (IT)[4]. Among the 57 regions exceeding the average value of Mio € 1.154, fifteen are in the United Kingdom, eleven in Italy, ten in Spain, nine in France, three in Austria, two each in Greece and the Netherlands, and one region each in Ireland, Portugal and Sweden, as well as Denmark.

Table A.2 shows the ten highest and the ten lowest regions referring to per capita values of hotels and restaurants GVA. Among the ten lowest regions, eight are in Poland. In

Table A.2

Regional GVA per capita, NACE category "hotels and restaurants", 2002, in euro

Source: Eurostat

	The highest ten	€		The lowest ten	€
1	Islas Baleares (ES)	5150	1	Lubuskie (PL)	46
2	Notio Aigaio (GR)	3317	2	Vychodne (SK)	44
3	Tirol (AT)	3052	3	Latvia	44
4	Inner London (UK)	2372	4	Lodzkie (PL)	44
5	Salzburg (AT)	2243	5	Kujawsko-Pomorskie (PL)	41
6	Valle d'Aosta (IT)	2120	6	Podlaskie (PL)	38
7	La Rioja (ES)	2015	7	Sietokrzyskie (PL)	37
8	Ionia Nisia (GR)	2001	8	Opolskie (PL)	37
9	Cantabria (ES)	1628	9	Lubelskie (PL)	34
10	Comunidad de Madrid (ES)	1588	10	Podkarpackie (PL)	30

general, regions belonging to the new Member States show very low values of GVA per capita, with two major exceptions: Cyprus (€ 1.323/person) and Malta (€ 674/person), both being traditional tourism destinations.

Figure A.2 Travel and Tourism Employment, European Union

Travel & Tourism Employment ▬▬▬ T&T employment index (1999 = 100)

Source: elaborated based on data from WTTC

The tourism sector is largely dominated by small and medium-sized enterprises (SMEs) with around 2 million tourism businesses, out of which 94% have less than 10

---

[4] Data are not available for Germany and Finland

11

employees. They represent 7.4% of all SMEs, generating 6.5% of the total turnover of SMEs[5]. Within the "hotels and restaurants" category Eurostat reports over 1.4 million enterprises in 2001, 89% of which being located in the EU 15.

Figure A.3 Employment: Travel & Tourism Industry, million, estimate 2004

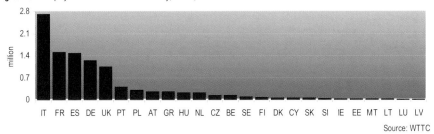

Source: WTTC

Tourism highly depends on short-term circumstances. Employment dynamics, although positive over the period 1999-2004, show only a slight increase of jobs since the year 2000. The limited growth in 2001 was due to a general depression of the economy but also to a series of dramatic events, the most relevant being the 11 of September 2001 attack, and the outbreak of the Severe Acute Respiratory Syndrome (SARS) in 2003. In 2001, the business volume is reported to have decreased by 10% globally, with some countries experiencing much higher falls up to 30%. Impacts

Table A.3 Percentage change in employment over the period 1996 – 2002, Slovak Republic

Source: elaborated based on data from Eurostat

Bratislavský	+53.3 %
Západné Slovensko	+124.2 %
Stredné Slovensko	+103.9 %
Východné Slovensko	+ 6.5 %

varied according to the type of tourism and region, with leisure tourism being less affected than business travel; changes in tourism demand and behaviour in terms of selected mode of transport, length of stay and destination also occurred[6].

DEFINITIONS:

Government expenditures to individual visitors, by agencies and departments providing visitor services such as cultural, recreational and immigration/custom.

Government expenditures collective, made by agencies and departments associated with Travel & Tourism, but generally made on behalf of the community at large, such as tourism promotion, aviation administration, security and sanitation.

Capital Investments by private and public Travel & Tourism providers for facilities, equipment and infrastructure to visitors.

---

[5] 1997 data for EU 15
[6] Belau D., 2003

Traditional Western Europe destinations such as Italy, France and Spain show the highest employment levels, in absolute values, for the "hotels and restaurants" segment of the tourism industry, confirming the relevant role of this sector with in their economy. However, similarly to the trend observed for GDP, it is likely that the highest growth rates in employment are recorded in the new Member States. Data for Slovak Republic, for example, show a national average increase of 54.7% over the period 1996-2002 (with a peak of + 124.2% for Západné Slovensko), against a national average increase for Italy of 37.3%, over the same period. Regional deviations are very diverse within each country; in Italy, the lowest increase is recorded in the North West regions (+ 29.8%) and the highest in the Southern regions (+ 48.2%) with a difference of about 18 points; while in the Slovak Republic this difference goes up to 118 points.

Table A.4 Key figures of the Travel & Tourism Industry in the EU Member States, 2002

Source: data extracted and elaborated from WTTC national reports

Country	Government expenditures to individual visitors (billion US$)	Government expenditure - collective (billion US$)	Capital investments (billion US$)	T&T Employment (% of national accounts - direct impact only)	T&T GDP (direct impact only) (billion euro)
AT	1.18	0.74	5.95	6.63	12.73
BE	0.96	0.81	3.17	3.55	8.42
CY	0.05233	0.12	0.40347	18.81	1.44
CZ	0.14	0.33	2.57	2.74	1.90
DE	5	3.49	23.95	3.3	64.27
DK	0.81	0.34	3.89	3.28	6.18
EE	0.03031	0.06953	0.49314	4.79	0.36
ES	4.56	3.36	29.46	8.68	53.94
FI	0.58	0.32	3.11	3.6	5.00
FR	6.79	4.39	21.86	6.1	74.45
GR	0.31	0.5	4.73	6.66	8.45
HU	0.12839	0.29963	1.1619	5.76	3.16
IE	0.37	0.22	4.27	1.82	2.36
IT	5.27	3.18	18.98	4.91	59.39
LT	0.02495	0.05723	0.39601	1.64	0.28
LU	0.05289	0.03792	0.3827	2.7	0.51
LV	0.01619	0.03713	0.2449	1.14	0.11
MT	0.02611	0.06006	0.26916	19.26	0.55
NL	1.27	1.07	7.49	3.37	14.82
PL	0.28	0.64	4.15	2	3.84
PT	0.9	0.6	3.68	7.91	8.71
SE	1.05	0.5	2.51	2.34	6.75
SI	0.05694	0.1306	0.52637	4.3	0.70
SK	0.0308	0.07061	0.7719	2.17	0.57
UK	5.54	3.44	23.89	3.52	62.61
EU 25	35.42891	24.81271	168.30955	130.98	401.50
Average	1.4171564	0.9925084	6.732382	5.2392	16.06

1.1.1.2   Visitor and tourist: a definition[7,8]

Tourism is primarily a demand-driven sector, i.e. oriented by those persons engaging in this activity. These persons are called visitors. The term 'visitor' describes '*any person travelling to a place other than that of his/her usual environment for less than twelve consecutive months and whose main purpose of travel is other than the exercise of an activity remunerated within the place visited*'. The term 'visitor' (domestic and international) comprises tourists and same-day visitors. An overnight visitor is a 'tourist'.

An *international tourist* is an international visitor staying at least one night in a collective or a private accommodation in the visited country.

A *domestic tourist* refers to a domestic visitor staying at least one night in a collective or a private accommodation in the place visited in her/his own country.

Therefore, a 'tourist' *is a person who travels to a place other than that of her/his usual environment (home, working and studying places) for a minimum of one night and a maximum of one year, and whose main purpose of travel is other than the exercise of a remunerated activity.*

1.1.1.3 Tourism in the European Union, a matter of EU citizens

The European region - from Iceland to Turkey - has long since been the world's favourite tourist destination with almost 58% of the world market share and about 399 million international arrivals in 2003. The three top European countries destinations were France, Spain and Italy, with 75, 52 and 39 million, respectively[9]. These three countries were also among the world top four, with United States ranking third before Italy. According to Eurostat, the 25 countries of the European Union totalled about 220 million of arrivals of non-residents in 2003.

European tourism is mainly driven by the demand of its citizens (almost 87%) while the remaining 13% is inbound tourism, i.e. tourists coming from outside Europe.

---

[7] Council of the European Union, 1995
[8] Task force on Methodologies linked to Tourism Statistics, 2002
[9] World Travel Organisation, 2004

National tourism is the dominant form of tourism with two out of three EU citizens travelling within their own country. As for the foreign tourism intra-EU 25, three out of four tourists remain within the EU area[10], the remaining quarter travelling to other parts of the world. The intra-Europe tourism flows are the most significant for the general growth of tourism demand.

In 2003, tourism revenues for the EU reached nearly 213 billion euro. Eurostat data on household expenditure on EU 15 countries show that one tenth of 2001 spending was for tourism-related consumption; this share is increasing, most probably due to an increase in transport use, the latter accounting for the largest part of tourism expenditure. However, these global figures hide the large disparities existing among European countries, and even more among regions, in terms of tourism volume.

France, Spain, Italy, Germany and the United Kingdom account for three-quarters of the total nights spent in hotels, while only 7% of the total refers to the new Member States. However, in line with the trend highlighted for the industry's GDP, the highest growths during 2004, according to Eurostat data, have been recorded for Estonia (+30%), Poland (+29%), Latvia (+16%) and the Czech Republic (+10%). This is a further demonstration of the rapid boom of the tourism industry in these countries, their attractiveness having increased during the enlargement process of the Union.

Figure A.4.   Tourism arrivals by country, 2003 or latest available year

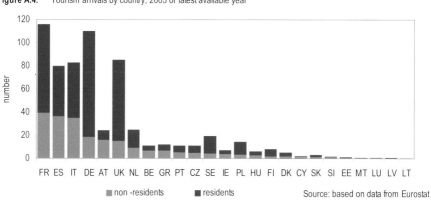

---

[10] Schmidt, H., 2005

15

The Mediterranean and the Alps are the most favourite destinations. In 2000, about 35% of international tourist trips by EU 15 citizens were to Mediterranean areas, mostly along the coasts, while 8% travelled to the Alps. Some small countries such as Cyprus, Luxembourg and Malta depend more on foreign tourists. In Cyprus and Malta, the international tourists arriving each year are three times higher than the number of local residents, while in France, Greece, Portugal and Spain they are almost equivalent. It is evident that tourism, in these cases, has a significant pressure on the territory[11]. Germany is the most oriented towards domestic tourism with a share of 86.5% of overnights spent by residents in hotels and similar establishments[12].

In 2003, the top 20 tourist European regions (NUTS1 level) accounted for more than half (57%) of the total nights spent in collective accommodations in the EU[13], the three top ranking regions being East of Spain, North East of Italy and Canary Islands. Taking into account only the nights spent in hotels, East of Spain and North East of Italy were still at the top, followed by Ile de France (Paris). Among the top 20 tourist regions, the Italian regions accounted for 15% of total nights, the Spanish for 14% and the French for 10%.

1.1.1.4 European Tourist behaviours and main tourism features

Tourists favour sea destinations but niche markets are growing

The main drivers of tourism demand are scenery and climate (beauty of landscapes, beaches and sun). According to a Eurobarometer survey held in 1997, Europeans mainly choose the sea as a destination site (63%), followed by mountains (25%), cities (25%) and countryside (23%)[14]. Recent surveys[15,16,17] show that tourists' interest in natural and cultural heritage sites is growing. Also, leisure activities are more and more oriented towards a direct contact with nature, as is the case for mountain biking, climbing or trekking. Ecotourism - encompassing all forms of tourism driven by the observation and appreciation of nature - although small in absolute terms with only

---

[11] Schmidt H., 2005
[12] Schmidt H., 2002 (a)
[13] Schmidt H., 2005
[14] European Commission, Directorate General for Enterprise, 1998
[15] World Tourism Organisation, 2000
[16] World Tourism Organisation, 2002
[17] English Tourism Council, 2002

7% of all international arrivals - is the fastest growing market segment in the European tourism industry, with an annual growth rate of 8% between 1998 and 1999[18]. Tourism in natural protected areas, such as national parks, is also becoming more popular as well as agro-tourism.

Tourists prefer the car but the share of flights is increasing

Tourist journeys continue to grow and are largely dominated by road and air transport, the most environmentally-damaging modes. Tourist trips are also highly concentrated in time, and the resulting seasonal saturation of road transport infrastructures often leads to the decision by national and regional authorities to supply more infrastructures and services [19].

Data from Eurostat indicate that in 2003, for all long holidays (4 plus nights) within their country and abroad, 66.4% of the Europeans[20] travelled by road, 23.3% by air, 6.6% by train, and 3.7% by sea. The preference for the car is due to its high degree of freedom and flexibility, and its capacity to provide a door-to-door service minimising the problem of baggage handling; if compared to public transport it has also become cheaper than it was twenty years ago, in particular for families. Thus, the choice of the car has a special attractiveness for holiday travel, much more than for business trips or commuting[21]. In France, 80% of domestic tourist travel is by private car. The plane would be assumed to be the favourite mode used for long-distance tourism travels, but even for distances over 1500 km, several tourists still continue to use their car[22]. This is the case for 58% of French tourists against only 6% of the German tourists. In the new Member States, most of the visitors arrive by road, although the train network and access are good.

Although most air travel remains relatively short-distance, long-haul travel is the most rapidly growing form of tourist transport, both in absolute and percentage terms. Since 1997, the air travel share has tripled, mostly at the expense of the railway. In addition, the average distance to travel to a destination has increased to about 900 km, while it

---

[18] World Tourism Organisation, 2002

[19] European Environment Agency, 2003

[20] Missing data for Cyprus, Hungary, Lithuania, Malta and Poland.

[21] European Environment Agency, 2003

[22] Rechatin C., Dubois G., Pelletreau A., 2000

was 850 km a few years ago[23]. This is partially due to the impact of the deregulation of the air transport system, liberalisation of pricing and market, with the consequent boom of low-cost airlines. The latter have encouraged the development of important inter-regional connections, often providing access to peripheral regions, and having a positive impact on territorial cohesion[24].

Figure A.5 Number of trips by mode of transport, holidays purpose, 2003 (or latest available year), in million

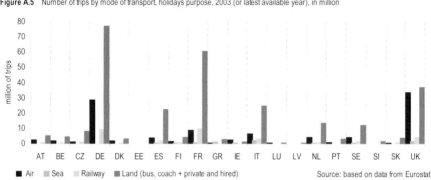

■ Air   ■ Sea   ■ Railway   ■ Land (bus, coach + private and hired)   Source: based on data from Eurostat

As a general observation reflecting world tourism patterns, Europeans are likely to take trips more frequently and further from home.

Most tourism trips still occur during summer

Tourism activity is characterised by its seasonality. Tourism remains highly concentrated over short periods of the year, 60% of all long holidays in the EU being undertaken during July, August and September, with a peak during August for most of the countries (Nordic countries prefer July).

Short holiday trips (from 1 to 3 consecutive nights) are more popular during the rest of the year. At the EU 15 level the number of short trips tends to equal the volume of long holiday trips. In 2001, business trips represented 10% of all tourism trips and 5% of all overnights spent, mostly concentrated over the January-March period. International tourism is less seasonal than domestic tourism. This trend may be explained by the offer of low cost travel packages during autumn and spring. These

---

[23] European Environment Agency, 2003
[24] Committee of the Regions, 2004 (b)

low season tourist products, mostly targeting the main European cities and the traditional destinations, are becoming popular and contribute to reducing the seasonal nature of the industry, although only in well-known destinations[25].

Figure A.6   Arrivals of residents and non-residents over the period July 2003 - Jun 2004

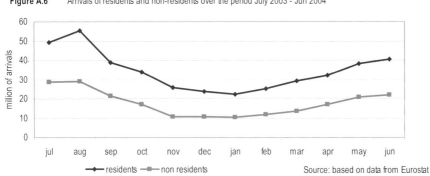

Hotels are still the most favourite accommodation form but agro-tourism is increasing

Tourists favour hotel and motel lodging during their trips in Europe. Out of the total nights spent by residents and non-residents tourists, 58% are spent in hotels. Less popular accommodations are collective facilities, accounting for less than one third of the total tourism overnights; camping and caravanning sites account for 18% of all overnight stays while furnished accommodations account for 12%. Stays in hotels and with family and friends have increased between 1994 and 2000, while the use of self-catering facilities has decreased.

Hotels are the accommodation type most used all during the year (41% of occupancy rate in average, i.e. 30 weeks), although there are differences among countries. According to Eurostat data, in 1999, in Greece, the hotel bed-places occupation rate reached 90% in July but it was only 32% in February. In Austria, where tourism facilities are popular all year around, the utilisation of bed places is equivalent during summer and winter.

However, the analysis is unlikely to be comprehensive because of the lack of data on private accommodations, leading in particular to underestimate the importance of

---

[25] In figure A.6 no data available for Greece, Ireland, Lithuania and Malta

second homes. In France, second homes represent 73% of the national tourism bed-places capacity; 18% of all nights spent by the French in 1999 were in second homes[26, 27], a trend apparently common to other western European countries.

Recently, less conventional accommodations than hotels are emerging. In Italy, for example, the major increase in construction refer to holiday dwellings and other accommodations types, such as agro-tourism infrastructures, with some new 84.000 establishments in 2000 versus 34.000 hotels. The European Centre for Ecological and Agricultural Tourism reports about 34.000 beds available in agro-tourism spread over 12 European countries. In 1996[28], Austrian farms were providing 109.000 guest rooms, about one sixth of total tourist bed capacity, and 7.5% of all farmers were offering tourist accommodations. In the west part of the United Kingdom, it was estimated that 23% of farms were involved in some type of farm tourism enterprise.

Tourism products are mostly booked through a travel agent or a tour operator

According to Eurostat data referred to six European countries (Denmark, Finland, Germany, Italy, Luxembourg and Spain) tourists book their holidays more and more frequently through a travel agent or a tour operator (for 90% of the tourism trips), thus relying less than before on direct reservation. This applies mainly to outbound tourism and partially to domestic tourism. In 2000, 16% of total overnights for domestic tourism and 52% of all tourism overnights for trips abroad were organised by a travel agent; the increase since 1997 was equivalent to 60% and 18%, respectively. Also, among the tourism products, the offer of 'holiday packages' has multiplied. Booking a holiday package with a travel agent is quite usual when travelling to a foreign country but data show that 59% of the products chosen for domestic tourism are also holiday packages.

Changes in tourism demand are diverse

EU citizens are asking for more quality at all levels, in their living conditions in general and specifically concerning the environment, products and services. With regard to tourism, the level of expectations are even greater than for other industries

---

[26] European Environment Agency, 2003
[27] Rechatin C., Dubois G., Pelletreau A., 2000
[28] European Partners for the Environment, 1996

because the holiday experience is expected to at least provide better conditions that those at home. Tourists want to enjoy nature in a beautiful frame with suitable accommodations and active leisure activities, while respecting high quality standards and a secure environment. Tourists are evolving; they are mature, hybrid, spontaneous and ask for new products that can respond more and more closely to their specific needs. These factors make the tourist demand extremely diverse.

Tourism is also affected by more general trends such as changes in demography and family structure. The ageing of the European population may imply that the elderly will represent a major tourist category in the near future. According to Eurostat data, people over 65 years accounted for 19.5% of all travellers in 2000, against the 16% of 1997. By adding to this share the 10% of tourists already recognised as handicapped and suffering from reduced mobility, tourism products and services will need to go through a substantial adaptation process[29].

1.1.2   Strengths and Weaknesses

1.1.2.1 The strengths of Europe as an attractive destination….

Europe offers the greatest diversity and density of tourism attractions in terms of landscapes, countryside and major historical cities. The rich heritage of Europe and its great natural beauty assets allow the development of various destination products such as cultural and historical, coastal or mountainous, sport or religious, thermal or gastronomic, business, and shopping tourism.

There is a large number of tourism services and facilities such as hotels, bars and restaurants, leisure parks, sports centres, and museums all over the territory. The tourism offer is very diversified in each thematic area, from a luxurious hotel to a mountain refuge or from Euro Disney in Paris to the Uffizi Gallery in Florence.

Europe also benefits from a good reputation in terms of the wealth level of its economy, quality of life and social living conditions; it has a recognised worldwide health system, a democracy respecting human rights, safe and relatively secure places with respect to criminality.

---

[29] Leidner R., 2003

In general terms, the transport system is dense and rather efficient when considering connections among main European cities, allowing for rapid transfers by road, railway or air. Together with improved communication infrastructures, the declining visa barriers (the Schengen Agreement gathering 13 countries out of the 25 of the European Union) and the progressive introduction of a single currency (the euro, being adopted by 12 countries out of 25) are making distances smaller and easier to be covered by both Europeans and foreigner travellers.

The combination of these factors creates a great environment for spending holidays, as demonstrated by the first top position ranked by Europe among the tourism destination regions of the world.

Figure A.7   Density of road and railway networks, 2000/2001

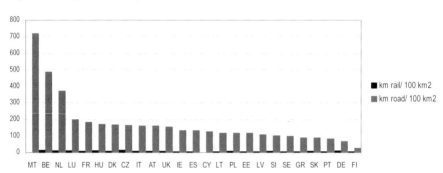

Source: elaborated based on data from UNECE and ERF

1.1.2.2 ....and its weaknesses

On the other hand, European tourism is a highly fragmented industry (travel agencies, tour operators, carriers, hoteliers, restaurateurs) characterised by several vertical, horizontal and transversal integrations, more frequent than in other economic sectors.

The industry is composed of a large number of tourism enterprises, mostly of small and medium size, vertically integrated. Horizontally, tourism affects, and is affected by, diverse businesses with their representatives, destinations with their different activities, and public and private interests and priorities. Tourism also interacts transversally with other main policies such as transport, environment, spatial planning, sports and leisure, industry and trade, and consumer protection. The complexity of these interrelationships makes the identification of a clear identity of the industry difficult, a circumstance that may explain why tourism has maintained until recently a very low profile at political level when compared to its economic and social importance.

Access to destinations is also a precondition for engagement in the tourism industry, but many regions within Europe still lack sufficient transport networking or have low or scattered options of transport modes, representing a real constraint on the development of these areas.

Tourism is a very seasonal phenomenon. It is thus difficult to exclusively rely on this economic activity to tackle regional development. Moreover, visitor peaks imply great periodic pressures on the territory and the need to invest in all necessary infrastructures. In terms of human resources, the seasonal workers employed by the industry often lack the necessary skills, do not enjoy fair working conditions, salaries and career opportunity, and often, since several activities occur within the black market, there is a lack of social protection.

1.1.3   Risks

There are several risks faced by the European tourism industry, some driven by global events and on which control is limited or absent; these include the occurrence of dramatic events (oil slicks along the coasts, natural disasters, SARS, wars and terrorist violence), economic depressions, climate change side effects on the environment, or competition by cheap overseas destinations as is currently the case of south east Asian countries.

At the European level, other risks may include the significant increase of environmental pollution and the consequent degradation of the natural environment, the physiological decline of some most popular mass destinations, the concentration of tourism businesses under the control of few, large operators, and the European Union integration process.

The growth in tourism demand may generate more environmental pollution

There is no tourist activity that does not rely on environmental resources in some way. Tourism unavoidably affects the state of the environment and the growth in tourism demand may consequently lead to significant environmental impacts. The most relevant pressures come from transport, the use of water and land, the use of energy by tourism buildings and facilities, the generation of waste, the erosion of soils and the loss of biodiversity. Moreover, when on holiday, it is recognised that people tend to consume more resources than they usually do at home[30].

Since tourism is a seasonal activity, the pressures on the environment exerted during the peak seasons may become unsustainable, leading to a decline of the resources in the long term or to a degradation of the environment at destinations. Being a spatial activity, tourism is also often concentrated in the most environmentally sensitive areas (coastal and mountains zones, small islands) where the terrestrial and aquatic environment, including living and non-living components, are most fragile.

The potential decline of mass tourism destinations

Tourism development can produce negative socio-cultural impacts on local communities, especially in the mass tourism regions. These risks include standardization, the loss of authenticity to respond to the conventional tourism demand, cultural clashes and crime generation. Some mass tourism destinations are already experiencing a decline. Failing to invest and adapt to the structural change which occurred in holiday trends, may cause a degenerated infrastructure, higher unemployment, low average earnings and increased levels of crime. Well established destinations along the Costa Brava in Spain would be an example of this phenomenon.

The possible assimilation of small industries within bigger ones

The European tourism industry is largely dominated by SMEs, with a total of about 2 million tourism businesses. These enterprises play a vital role within the regions for job creation, but recently they have experienced a growing pressure by bigger entities. In fact, there is a growing trend of concentration of activities into few, large companies with high economic importance. Within the segment of tours operators and travel agencies, for example, the five largest EU travel organisers (TUI at the top) represent a market share of 70% of the total turnover in 2002. Since 1997, this share has doubled, showing the growing concentration of this activity[31]. This trend is also

---

[30] European Environment Agency, 2003
[31] Leidner R., 2003

facilitated by the low level of public intervention and support in the sector and the rise of the global market-driven economy.

Unbalances within the European Union integration processes

Wealthy countries are often more capable of profiting from tourism than less economically developed countries. Among the reasons are the large-scale transfer of tourism revenues out of the host country and the exclusion of local businesses and products. This is a specific risk the new Member States may face in developing their tourism industry.

European regions that depend primarily on the tourism activity for their economy and employment also face some risks. In places where tourism is not managed by balancing the diverse interests, the economic benefits obtainable from the industry may compromise the social conditions, the cultural and natural assets of the receiving regions, as well as the quality of the environment.

1.2   The European Tourism Facing New Challenges

The main challenges regarding the development of tourism in Europe, including tourism industries and destinations, are the following: achievement of oriented-quality competitiveness, better management of the tourism demand growth with respect to its impacts on the environment, and an integrated planning by destination.

The continued growth in the tourism demand volume may create negative impacts on the environment as well as in society. **If managed improperly, this growth may jeopardize the tourism industry's future, making sustainability for European tourism not an option but a necessary action.**

Global competitiveness

Supply and demand in the tourism sector are evolving and adapting faster than in any other domain. The tourism demand for more varied and quality products and services requires new types of tourism to be developed and poses a challenge to both the industry and regions of destination.

Within the industry, the main challenges arise for the SMEs that will have to rely on their corporate associations as they cannot control the whole value chain. Potential solutions will lay in the networking of all concerned players and in the set up of private/public partnerships[32]. The increased adoption of new information and communication technologies will help to facilitate the exchange of information and in create useful networks, although, according to a study commissioned by DG Enterprise in 2002, only half of the tourism SMEs have incorporated Internet in their daily activities[33].

Competitiveness of the regions will be judged by their economic growth and the level of satisfaction of the visitors, the latter being highly linked to the quality of services provided, also by public infrastructure, and to the skills of the labour force employed. Employment represents a big challenge for the sector. Working conditions (salaries, career opportunity, social security, skill enhancement) are expected to be improved in order to secure the future of the industry.

Transport and infrastructure growth

Hosting a large number of tourists over a short period of the year implies the existence of all the necessary logistics within the holiday place, including accommodations, leisure, food, trade, transport infrastructures, sanitary equipment to provide drinking water, and cleansing for waste processing. These logistics – besides the considerable cost - may have a rather significant impact in terms of size, especially on the less populated communities, and related effects may easily extend over a much wider region. Cooperation with local and regional authorities is therefore essential.

The access to tourism destinations represents an important challenge for the sector. Although progress has been made in setting up some local and public means of transport within destinations, these are not sufficient to shift the dominant use of the car by tourists. Currently, there is no incentive to use less-environmentally damaging modes of transport, and innovations in tourism transport system to reach destinations are only slowly developing. The transport issue needs to be managed on a more global scale, in cooperation with national governments, and at a trans-European level, instead of being left only at the destination level.

---

[32] Leidner R., 2003
[33] European Commission, 2002

Preservation of the environment and of natural resources

Tourism activity is strongly based on the natural resources of destinations; most of the generated pollution directly affects the destinations environment, giving the local industry and the regional authorities the primary responsibility of managing preservation and pollution problems.

The environmental management of the tourism sector is a crucial issue: the quality of the environment affects tourist choices and behaviours while congestion and pollution generate extra costs. The environmental management challenge is even greater in those destinations where natural resources (water, energy, land) are scarce.

Integrated sustainable management at destinations

As governance becomes more decentralized throughout Europe, tourism policies may play a major role in the process of implementing sustainable development in the tourism destination regions. As many destinations are public sector managed, the development of public private sector partnerships for tourism constitute an essential tool that will be further analysed under Section D of this study.

SECTION B:
CONCEPTS AND PRINCIPLES OF SUSTAINABLE TOURISM

1. Sustainable Tourism: Definition, Principles and Objectives

1.1 What is Sustainable Tourism?

The 'Sustainable Tourism' concept derives from the concept of 'sustainable development' applied to the tourism sector.

Sustainable development is a political concept for the balanced development of societies on the basis of available natural and human resources. The concept has been proposed for the first time in the "Our Common Future" report, prepared in 1987 by the World Commission on Environment and Development, and often referred to as the "Brundtland Report" from the name of the then Prime Minister of Norway chairing the Commission. In this report sustainable development is '*a development that meets the needs of present generations without compromising the ability of future generations to meet their own needs*'[34].

Sustainable development, thus, implies a balanced relationship among human beings, economic development and environment. It means to integrate the economic, social and environmental dimensions at the same level of consideration. The implementation of this concept implies thinking about the future of humankind; it is about creating a vision.

Sustainable development for Europe has been defined in the EU Strategy for Sustainable Development[35] in response to the global Agenda 21: '*Sustainable development offers the European Union a positive long-term vision of a society that is more prosperous and more just, and which promises a cleaner, safer, healthier environment – a society which delivers a better quality of life for us, for our children, and for our grandchildren. Achieving this in practice requires that economic growth supports social progress and respects the environment, that social policy underpins economic performance, and that environmental policy is cost-effective*'.

---

[34] Brundtland, G. (ed.), 1987

[35] European Commission, 2001 (a)

1.1.1 The Sustainable Tourism Definition

The most quoted definition of 'sustainable tourism' is given by the World Travel and Tourism Council (WTTC), World Tourism Organisation (WTO) and Earth Council in the 1996 Agenda 21 for the Travel and Tourism Sector. *'Sustainable tourism development meets the needs of the present tourists and host regions while protecting and enhancing the opportunity for the future. It is envisaged as leading to management of all resources in such a way that economic, social and aesthetic needs can be fulfilled, while maintaining cultural integrity, essential ecological processes, biological diversity and life support systems'.*

The United Nations Environment Programme (UNEP) endorses the definition putting emphasis on the full integration of all resources and needs, equal sharing of the economic benefits, environmentally-sensitive areas, good social working conditions and active participation of all actors, especially the population of tourism destinations[36].

The Council of Europe defines sustainable tourism as *'any form of tourism development or activity which respects the environment, ensures long-term conservation of natural and cultural resources, is socially and economically acceptable and equitable'*[37].

The European Commission provides a concise definition of sustainability in tourism in its 2003 Communication on basic orientations for the sustainability of European tourism[38]: *'Tourism that is economically and socially viable without detracting from the environment and local culture'.*

In general, the key point is that the limits of the natural, economic, social and cultural base resources define the sustainability of tourism. All types of tourism must be sustainable, whether they are in natural areas or not. The sustainable development of tourism involves social responsibility, a strong commitment to nature and to the integration of local communities in any tourist operation or development, and in particular an equal sharing of the economic benefits. This also means that it

---

[36] United Nations Environment Programme, 1995

[37] Council of Europe, 1995

[38] European Commission, 2003 (a)

encompasses broader dimensions such as spatial planning, territorial cohesion and transport, where the latter is used for tourism purposes.

Several different terminologies are used when referring to the concept of sustainab e development of tourism, often leading to some confusion. *'Sustainable development of tourism' (SDT) or 'sustainability of tourism' indicates the full integration of all aspects of development, including related transport.*

Other terms such as 'sustainable tourism', 'responsible tourism', 'soft tourism', 'minimum impact tourism' and 'alternative tourism' are used by destinations managers or tourism operators as an argument for selling products and attracting visitors but are not SDT concepts.

The tourism policy must be redefined to take into account the need for sustainability. Tourism must contribute to growth and environmental protection and further social progress.

The overall goal to achieve tourism sustainability in the European regions becomes:

- to sustain a sound environment, to safeguard the recreational quality of natural and man-made landscape and to integrate natural, cultural and human environments;
- to promote and sustain the competitive quality and efficiency of the tourism business;
- to create satisfactory social conditions for tourists and the local population.

1.2   Respecting General Principles

Several attempts have been developed to define general principles, goals and objectives to support the process for implementing the sustainability of tourism, general views converging towards the same direction.

General key principles to support the sustainability of the European tourism include[39, 40, 41, 42, 43].

---

[39] UNEP, MAP, MCSD-BLUE PLAN, 1999
[40] Merchadou C., et al., 2001

- make sustainable development the overall aim of tourism policy;
- integrate identified measures into the other economic, environmental and social policies affecting tourism development;
- respect the subsidiarity and the 'bottom-up' approaches;
- converge objectives with adapted implementation tools;
- promote cooperation and pro-active participation of all actors engaged in tourism, in particular by recognizing the key role of the local and regional authorities and the peculiarities of the SMEs and micro-enterprises that characterise the industry;
- favour voluntary instruments and partnerships with private and civil society groups;
- support funding for sustainable tourism development, and in particular devote additional resources to the new Members States.

1.3   Matching Strategic Objectives

Strategic objectives support the concrete implementation of the sustainability of tourism. Such objectives will remain common throughout Europe, while the implementation tools for their achievement will be controlled by national, regional and local authorities as well as by the private sphere of the economy. Specific objectives related to the management of the growth in tourism demand will need to be considered at a broad European scale; avoiding congestion on the transport network and at destinations, for example, will require specific recommendations such as the review of the European calendar for festivities and the improvement of the trans-European transport system that supports the use of environment-friendly modes like the train.

There are several strategic objectives for implementing the sustainability of the European tourism. How these objectives are organized into sustainable development strategies for tourism, promoting economic growth without jeopardizing the rich natural and cultural heritage attracting tourists, is a common challenge faced by all European regions. Usually, the development of a Strategy and Action Plan for

---

[41] Council of the European Union, 2002

[42] European Commission, 2003 (a)

[43] Sustainable European Regions Network, 2004

sustainable tourism guarantees efficient and coordinated action; the action plan is supposed to be based on the understanding of the issues, the design of an implementation plan tackling operational responses, and the set up of a monitoring system to follow up progress.

Main strategic objectives belong to three broad dimensions, environmental (objective 1 and 2), economic (objective 3), social and ethical (objective 4)[44]:

- objective 1: prevent and reduce territorial and environmental impacts of tourism development in regions of destination;
- objective 2: manage the growth of transport related to tourism and its negative effects on the environment;
- objective 3: encourage a tourism favouring local sustainable development managed by the tourism's actors;
- objective 4: promote a responsible tourism factor of social equity.

Key objectives include[45]:

Governance, regulation and policy integration

- Integration of sustainable tourism development into overall strategies.
- Integrated sector policies and coherence across all levels.

Encouragement of stakeholder synergies and cooperation

- Cooperation of local and regional authorities and national governments, in particular for improving the inter-modality of the European (passenger) transport system, to shift to the use of less polluting and energy consuming modes of transport for tourists.
- Cooperation of local and regional authorities with the local industry, to regularly apply the Environmental Impact Assessment (EIA) to tourism infrastructures.
- Citizen participation both as consumers and workers.
- Networks development facilitating building-capacity.

---

[44] Merchadou C., et al., 2001
[45] European Commission, 2003 (a)

Sustainable entrepreneurship, business practice and employment (including new technologies) through the promotion of:

- Sustainable patterns of tourism consumption and production.
- Low-season tourism products.
- Corporate Social Responsibility (CSR) for large companies.
- Employment, job creation and quality employment conditions.
- ICTs to better exchange information and best practices, especially for SMEs, remote areas and new Members States.

Sustainable destination planning (including value enhancement of the heritage sites)

- Intelligent use, management and promotion of the natural and cultural heritage.
- Implementation of Local Agenda 21 for tourism destinations, including the regional level.
- Strengthening of regional management plans, and set up of some Strategic Environmental Assessments for tourism projects.
- Promotion of the Community Integrated Coastal Zone Management (ICZM) strategy for Member States to develop national strategies, including generalization of Integrated Quality Management of Tourism Destinations tool.

High-quality information, management tools, observation and measurement

- Consumer-oriented awareness raising.
- Monitoring and indicator systems for the overall tourism activity chain and destinations.

Financial support for sustainable tourism development

- Development of legal and fiscal frameworks for sustainable tourism, including incentive tools for environmental and local population compensation.
- Intelligent and improved use of the EU funding systems.

Tourism development constitutes an opportunity for the sustainable development of Europe. In 2001, the European Working Group D on *The promotion of the environmental protection and sustainable development for the tourism sector: Towards a European Agenda 21 for Tourism* highlighted a series of key statements on tourism:

- tourism may have a positive impact on the major policy areas of the European Union such as sustainable development, economic growth, employment, economic and social cohesion, spatial planning and territorial cohesion, democracy and peace;
- tourism can play a major role in the process of implementing sustainable development at all levels, locally and internationally;
- tourism, whose offer is mostly managed through SMEs, has a great potential to support the economy of the European regions and can help maintaining local jobs threatened by the employment crisis of other sectors;
- tourism may represent an opportunity for the conservation of a clean and unspoilt environment, contributing to the value enhancement and preservation of the cultural, historical and natural assets of the European regions;
- tourism can create a more balanced territorial and spatial development, reducing disparities between regions and allowing for a better sharing of the economic benefits, a circumstance that is particularly important for the new Members States;
- tourism enhances the mobility of European citizens, is a vehicle for increasing tolerance, and reinforces the building up of a European citizenship identity.

Given the great potentials and risks of European tourism, it is evident that tourism development policies deserve greater political attention at both European, national and local level.

2. Sustainable Tourism: Policies and Strategies at International and European Union Level

2.1 Recent Developments of Sustainable Tourism Policies

There is no coherent overall strategy for tourism in the European Union, yet. Encompassing a wide range of activities horizontally linked to several other sectors, tourism is currently regulated by a number of Community policies and programmes that either include a tourism dimension or have a significant impact on tourism related activities. Specific reference is made to Community policies regulating transport and energy, environment, spatial planning, competition, internal market, education and culture, consumer protection, regional development and structural instruments, trade and international relations, and enlargement.

Taking into account only those policies most directly linked to the sustainable development of the tourism sector, the recent progresses at international and European Union level are presented hereafter.

2.1.1 General Framework: Sustainable Development, Environment and Sectoral Integration

At the international level, the topic of sustainable development of tourism is addressed by the United Nations Commission on Sustainable Development (CSD). In 1999, the CSD adopted Decision 7/3[46] requesting the development and implementation of policies, national strategies or master plans for sustainable tourism based on Agenda 21.

The Earth Summit held in Johannesburg in 2002 (Rio+10) and its Plan of Implementation - focusing on changing unsustainable patterns of production and consumption - also targets tourism as a priority policy area to achieve sustainable development. Furthermore, the designation of 2002 as the International Year of Ecotourism and the World Ecotourism Summit (WES) held in Quebec in May 2002, reinforced the effort to put the sustainable development of tourism on the international scene.

---

[46] United Nations Commission on Sustainable Development, 1999

BOX B.1	Main Documents and Set Priorities

The main policy documents from UN organizations and the European Commission related to the sustainable development of tourism include:
- UN Commission on Sustainable Development (CSD), Report on the 7th session
- UN Convention on Biological Diversity (CBD), COP 5 (Decision V/25)
- EU Sustainable Development Strategy (SDS)
- EU Fifth Environmental Action Programme (5EAP)
- EU Sixth Environmental Action Programme (6EAP)
- EC EIA Directive 85/337/EEC, Amended by 97/11/EC

Main priorities set in each of these policy documents, particularly relevant to tourism and environment are:

CSD	• Develop and implement policies and national strategies or master plans for sustainable tourism based on Agenda 21. • Develop eco-efficiency for tourism facilities and managements systems to minimize all forms of waste, conserve energy and freshwater resources and control emissions to environmental media. • Use low impacts designs, materials and technologies for new infrastructures. • Encourage more responsible behaviours among tourists by increasing public awareness.
CBD	Encourage environmental management systems (EMS), environmental impact assessments (EIA) for tourism facilities, strategic environmental assessments (SEA), standards, industry performance-recognition programmes, eco-labelling, code of good practices, economic instruments, voluntary initiatives and agreements, indicators and benchmarking.
SDS	• Limit climate change and increasing the use of clean energy. • Address threats to public health. • Manage natural resources more responsibly. • Improve the transport system and land use.
5EAP	• Better dispersion of tourism in time and space. • Promotion of environment friendly forms of tourism. • Reduction of private car use in favour of public transport. • Better management of mass tourism • Awareness raising of tourists.
6EAP	Promote the integration of conservation and restoration of the landscape values into other policies including tourism, taking account of relevant international instruments.
EIA	Establish environmental impact assessments EIA for tourism projects especially in skiing areas, marine, holiday villages, camping areas, and all potentially damaging tourism projects to be covered in future.

Recently, the importance of the role of tourism in the sustainable use of biological resources and the potential impacts of tourism on biodiversity have also been re-affirmed by the Convention on Biological Diversity (CBD), COP Decision VII/14 on "Biological diversity and tourism"[47]. The Decision also adopted some international guidelines for sustainable tourism.

Within the European Union, the European Council of Cardiff asked in June 1998 for the outlining of strategies aimed at the integration of environmental issues into

---

[47] Conference of the Parties, 2004

specific sectoral policies, among which tourism. This request was drawn from EU policy documents such as the Fifth Environmental Action Programme (5EAP) that defines transport and tourism as the main sectors having an impact on the environment.

The EU Sustainable Development Strategy[48] - that is the European level response to the global Agenda 21 - in 2001, and the Sixth Environmental Action Programme (6EAP) in 2002, highlighted the question of natural areas' carrying capacity with regard to tourism development. Again in 2001, at the European Council of Gothenburg, a political commitment was reached, recognising that in long term economic growth, social cohesion and environmental protection are to proceed hand in hand. Since then, those calling for a more sustainable development have asked for this main goal to become a pre-requisite of any political decision, plan and programme. This constitutes a major step towards the establishment of a positive long-term vision for the future of the European Union.

Several Directives related to the environment are relevant to tourism, among which Natura 2000, the Water Framework Directive, and the EU Integrated Coastal Management Zones Strategy. More specifically, the European Commission, in making its proposal to amend the Environmental Impact Assessment Directive (85/337/EEC, Annex II), included a wider range of projects potentially damaging tourism. The Amendment was adopted in March 1997 and was ratified by EU Member States in March 1999. It recalled the need to establish EIA for tourism projects especially in skiing areas, marine, holiday villages and camping areas.

Among the most relevant policy documents affecting tourism are: the 2001 White Paper on 'European transport policy for 2010: time to decide'[49], outlining how to achieve tourism transport that is more efficient, sustainable and of higher quality; the European Spatial Development Perspective[50] (ESDP); the EU White paper on the Corporate Social Responsibility[51] (CSR); and the EU Integrated Products Policy[52] (IPP) that already comprises aspects related to tourism and environment integration.

---

[48] European Commission, 2001 (a)
[49] European Commission, 2001 (b)
[50] European Commission, 1999
[51] European Commission, 2001 (c)
[52] European Commission, 2001 (f)

In 1995, the Council of Europe, in its Recommendation R(95)10 related to a policy for the development of sustainable tourism in natural protected areas, recommended to allocate part of the tax on overnight stays to the financing of environmental infrastructures and the preservation of the environment. The Council of Europe *European Landscape Convention* is also of relevance for tourism in natural areas. The tourism sector is further expected to comply with the guidelines given by the EU White Paper on governance.

2.1.2 The European Union Tourism Policy

Article 3(1) of the Treaty of Maastricht established the principle of subsidiarity for the tourism policy. Although the EU does not have specific competence in the area of tourism policy, the Treaty acknowledges that Community actions should include measures in the field of tourism in order to contribute to the achievement of other Community objectives, for example employment and economic development.

The European Commission has put tourism on the policy agenda only recently, tourism development being considered primarily a matter of private company management. However, national, regional and local authorities were already implementing significant forms of control and support on tourism in areas such as tax policy, transport and telecommunications infrastructures, regional development, protection of the environment, training of personnel and promotion of tourism attractions and businesses.

The Commission involvement – along with the Council, the European Parliament, the Economic and Social Committee and the Committee of the Regions -, has been increasing since the mid-nineties as a recognition of the important role tourism plays in the economy.

Since the 1997 and 1999 European Council's conclusions on 'Employment potential of European Tourism', the policy direction has been broadening up towards the sustainability of European Tourism. In 1999, the European (Internal Market) Council recognised the significant economic role of the European Tourism Industry as well as the need to improve its competitiveness on the basis of balanced and sustainable development and environmental protection. The following European Council of Helsinki recalled the need to adopt a strategic approach for tourism in relation to other common policies. In addition, the opportunity to include tourism in the economy-environment integration process (initiated by the Cardiff Council in 1998) decided by the European Council in 2000 was raised.

In 2000, the European Commission set up five EU Working Groups on central topics: information, training, quality, sustainability, and new technologies. These groups reached concrete conclusions after a one year process, among which the decision of formulating a Community Agenda 21 for Tourism as proposed by the Working Group D. The conclusions of the five groups have been partly endorsed by the Commission in its Communication entitled '*Working together for the future of European tourism*'[53] that announced ten measures for action, in particular to promote sustainable development for tourism by further implementing the Agenda 21 guidelines. This issue received strong support from the European Parliament, the Council, the European Economic and Social Committee and the Committee of the Regions.

Complementary events included the ministerial conferences in Vilamoura (Portugal), Lille (France) and Bruges (Belgium), held by the Member State holding the EU presidency and open to all the stakeholders involved in European tourism. These have given steady support and encouragement to the co-operation process. The Vilamoura conference, on 11 May 2000, called for improving the coordination of national policies and political recognition of the role of tourism. In Lille on 22 November 2000, the Presidency focused on setting up a network of pilot regions to promote sustainable tourism, facilitating exchange of information, improving the knowledge of the tourism sector and providing training. The 'Tourism for all' conference in Bruges, on 2 July 2001, called for the need to make tourism activities accessible to sensitive targets groups such as young and elderly people, those living on the threshold of poverty, the unemployed and the disabled.

In 2001, the important developments on the EU scene – namely, the Gothenburg European Council and the EU Sustainable Development Strategy, the EU White Paper on Transport Policy, the EU White Paper on Corporate and Social Responsibility - called upon for an effective knowledge based-approach to sustainable tourism policies. The process culminated with the Resolution adopted by the European

---

[53] European Commission, 2001 (d)

Council on 21 May 2002 on the future of European tourism[54] and the subsequent Parliament Decision, for the first time specifically dedicated to tourism.

The Resolution devotes a large section to information needs (statistics, satellite accounts, indicators, best practices). Specifically, the Council calls upon the '*definition of sustainable development indicators in the field of tourism*' and requests the Commission and Member States '*to provide the necessary legal and statistical information as well as harmonized tourism indicators to enable an integrated evaluation of tourism activity throughout the European Union.*' The European Parliament states '*to closely follow the work carried out with regard to the definition of sustainable development indicators in the field of tourism in view of the preparation of an Agenda 21 for the European tourism*'. The Council calls upon a better coordination of policies affecting tourism. The Commission and Member States are therefore invited to agree on a framework of coordination between Community policies related to the tourism sector and to adopt the appropriate measures.

The Tourism Unit of the European Commission's Directorate General for Enterprise coordinates tourism-related initiatives across the different services of the European Commission, in order to ensure that the interests of tourism are fully taken into account in the preparation of legislation and in the operation of programmes and policies not established in the context of tourism objectives. DG Enterprise worked on the definition of the so-called **European Agenda 21 for Tourism**: the process started in 2001, following the suggestion and contribution of a group of experts nominated by the Member States; it continued along 2002 and 2003 with the setting up of a Steering Committee including high representatives of the tourism stakeholders. The Steering Committee was given the responsibility to decide on the form of the Agenda 21 for European Tourism as well as on the required consultation process. The Agenda 21 for Tourism programme included an integrated evaluation of tourism activity throughout the EU, the development of an integration strategy for the sector, and the elaboration of harmonised indicators of sustainable development for tourism. The conclusions of the Steering Committee were reported in the Commission Communication of November 2003 '*Basic orientations for the sustainability of European tourism*'[55]. This document deals with the policy issues related to tourism and constitutes a key step in the preparation process of the Agenda 21 for European Tourism. The importance of

---

[54] Council of the European Union, 2002
[55] European Commission, 2003 (a)

establishing guidelines to implement the sustainability of the tourism sector is recognised for the first time, the primary condition being to build the Agenda 21 on the basis of the involvement, the co-operation and the pro-active participation of all concerned stakeholders at all levels. The Communication specifies that the preparation of a final document will be finalised by 2007, at the latest. To tackle the preparation of this document the Commission launched a *Tourism Sustainability Group* in February 2005. The group includes representatives from various stakeholder categories involved in tourism and sustainable development, local, regional and national authorities, tourism companies, trade unions and civil society organisations. This group will have the responsibility of drafting a detailed framework for action, including specific activities for the stakeholders with an agreed timetable for implementation. The intention is clearly to stimulate multi-stakeholder efforts in the tourism field, across all territorial and administrative levels, and to outline how the Community and other stakeholders can further contribute.

The Commission has also taken the formal decision to set up an Annual European Tourism Forum gathering the main tourism stakeholders' representatives. The first forum was held on 10 December 2002 in Brussels. This initiative aims to contribute to the tourism policy-making and to better governance within the framework of European Union common policies.

Policy developments related to tourism clearly indicate that the tourism sector is fully subject to the *Lisbon and Cardiff process*. Tourism must take the path of a sustainable development because it has become a policy objective of the European Union as well as of the European tourist destinations. Some European regions have initiated their own actions to promote sustainable tourism.

Tourism is covered in the Mediterranean area by the Barcelona Convention and the Mediterranean Action Plan (MAP) and supported by the MEDA programme. The Mediterranean Commission on Sustainable Development (MCSD) has adopted some recommendations and proposals for action on tourism and sustainable development. Tourism in the Alps is covered by the Additional Protocol on Tourism and Recreation to the Alpine Convention and in the Baltic countries by the Agenda 21 for the Baltic Sea region[56].

---

[56] Baltic 21 Tourism Group, 1998

Besides these policy developments, the European Environment Agency (EEA) has worked on the set up of a reporting mechanism on environmental and tourism issues at pan- European level. In close collaboration with the Tourism Unit of DG Enterprise of the European Commission and of Eurostat, the EEA has developed a core set of sustainable tourism indicators[57] that are supposed to be further elaborated and implemented by the individual Member States. More details on the use and constraints of these indicators are provided under chapter 4.

Main milestones in the development of the future Agenda 21 for European Tourism are summarised below[58]:

Strategic Approach	• Define advantages brought in by the subsidiarity principle and the bottom-up approach.
	• Examine individual components, sub-sectors, areas and aspects, and their specific problems, rather than treating tourism and its sustainability as a individual issue.
	• Obtain consumer information to ensure market forces are exerted to promote sustainable consumption and production patterns.
	• Recognise the peculiarities of the small and medium enterprises and of the micro-enterprises of the industry.
	• Ensure the social and economic viability, as well as the environmental sustainability, of rural and coastal communities.
EU policy option	• Promote effective implementation of existing initiatives and reinforced efforts of stakeholders.
	• Through Community initiatives, (a) optimise the effect of the Community policies and measures on the sustainability of European tourism and (b) define and implement complementary tourism specific measures to promote sustainability.
General concept for future action	The European Community will undertake complementary activities and encourages stakeholders to put policy measures into practices.

---

[57] EEA web page on tourism indicators: http://themes.eea.eu.int/Sectors_and_activities/tourism/indicators
[58] European Commission, 2003 (a)

What the Commission plans to do	• Ensure suitable working arrangements enhancing the contribution of Community policies to the sustainability of European tourism. • Encourage stakeholder synergies and co-operation. • Promote sustainable patterns of tourism consumption and production, better transfer of approaches, initiatives, instruments and good practice to involved stakeholders.
What the European tourist destinations and local and regional authorities can do	• Lead, promote and facilitate Local Agenda 21 process. • Apply good governance principles: openness and transparency, participation, accountability, effectiveness and coherence, interdisciplinary and integrated approaches. • Ensure public management to balance economic development with social cohesion and environmental protection, triple-bottom-line reporting. • Apply interdisciplinary land-use management, impact assessment procedures, monitoring and indicator systems. • Promote active partnerships with private business and civil society groups. • Pay particular attention to quality and carrying capacity. • Develop practical instruments making those who generate social and environmental costs pay for them. • Create policies for a diversified local economy. • Implement suitable training and education schemes for sector practitioners, sustainable knowledge and skills enhancement of tourism destination managers and public bodies.

2.1.3   The Committee of the Regions and Tourism

The COTER Commission of the Committee of the Regions is responsible for following European Commission initiatives and preparing opinions on official Communications in the areas of social policy, public health, consumer protection, research and tourism.

In its Opinion[59] dated April 21, 2004 on the Commission Communication *'Basic orientations for the sustainability of European tourism'*, the CoR notably *'considers that, although there are other equally useful standpoints on sustainability, such as the European Spatial Development Perspective (ESDP), the main value of this Communication resides in the fact that it outlines actions that need to be taken, in particular by regions and destinations, if sustainable tourism is to move from theory to practice'*. It also *'points out that the Commission is offering local and regional authorities new opportunities to base sustainable tourism policy on the three pillars of sustainability, and that working together and good governance are key methodologies which will promote progress in the industry and remedy the lack of consistency between the many existing practices'*.

"Tourism must contribute to growth and environmental protection and further social progress". The CoR believes that *"tourist products that do not offer local benefits on the economic, social and cultural and environmental levels will lack legitimacy.*

The CoR particularly recalls for *'a more holistic approach that should be adopted'….* *'Such approach will allow for more comprehensive assessments of sustainability from the point of view of tourism consumption patterns'*.

The CoR submitted a series of considerations to the European Commission regarding all the contents of the Communication. Considering the challenges and objectives of sustainable tourism, the CoR points out that it is not only tourism in the Mediterranean and the Alps that faces great challenges to move towards sustainability but also other areas notably the island destinations, the outermost regions and developing countries. It also highlights that the difficulties in mass tourism destinations may be exacerbated in areas that are too economically dependent on tourism activity and could be even greater in the fragile and remote islands, upland areas and territories that are isolated.

The CoR emphasises the major role to be played by the local and regional authorities, while recognising the key role of the tourism industry and SMEs, to challenge the sustainability of tourism. In line with a bottom-up approach, local and regional authorities have a special responsibility in tourism planning and management. Tourism is an activity that mainly occurs locally (except from the trips to destinations and returns) and has an impact on the local communities. This process should help

---

[59] Committee of the Regions, 2004 (a)

them to establish the necessary synergies with other sectoral policies and to implement good governance practices to achieve the objectives. The CoR also calls for the support of the tourism initiatives through a close cooperation with national governments and European institutions. As it is believed that the demand for sustainable tourism products is far from being negligible, the challenge for destinations and companies is to offer such products and to promote them.

Regarding the general concept for future actions designed by the Commission, the CoR shares the Commission's recommendation on the need for all stakeholders to formulate their own Agenda 21 at sectoral level. This implies the re-defining of local and regional tourism policy on the basis of *'sustainability criteria'*. This will also help free up the Agenda 21 processes – which *"are currently on the administrative, political, business and social backburner in many European regions and tourist destinations"*- towards locally adapted objectives, actions and techniques, which would better suit the peculiarities of the regions. Also, it is important to define sustainable tourism indicators, which contribute to establishing such a sustainability process in a concerted manner. The proposed actions related to training are also considered essential to build up the capacity of the tourism destination managers and local and regional governments for making them more familiar with the challenges.

The CoR calls on national governments and European institutions to support the tourism sustainability process by further granting the local and regional initiatives that are developed and by planning substantial and specific financial allocations dedicated to tourism. In particular, the European institutions should establish and support networks of destinations that are capable of producing and exchanging information and good practices.

Moreover, the CoR especially recommends, as a first effective action, the inclusion of the reference to the European Charter of the Rights and Duties of Tourists, for European tourists to be properly informed.

Finally, the CoR considers *'that information is also a key issue for the sustainable development of tourism. Tourism is characterised by a severe lack of transparency and information. Industries and destinations will only be able to adopt sustainability strategies properly if they are given vital information relating to their activity'.*

2.2 Initiatives to Support the Development of Sustainable Tourism

Although much has been done to support the sustainability of tourism, these efforts remain relatively small in size, sparse, not coordinated and not fully integrated to respond to the sustainability requirements. As a consequence, no real change can be noted in the unsustainable pattern of tourism consumption and production.

In 1995, with the World Charter on Sustainable Tourism - also referred to as the Declaration of Lanzarote -, the key concepts of sustainable tourism were defined. Again in 1995, the UNEP initiated the first Environmental Code of Conduct for Tourism followed by some Draft Principles for the Implementation of Sustainable Tourism in 1998. The most recent developments in 2002 ended up with the launching of the Tour-Operators Initiative and the coordination of the Global Reporting Initiative (focusing on large enterprises), aiming to support tourism companies and tour-operators to implement concrete actions, develop indicators and monitoring systems to tackle the sustainability goals.

In 1999, the WTO developed the Global Code of Ethics for Tourism, today internationally recognized as a major reference. The recent working agreement with the UNCTAD has led to the creation of the Sustainable Tourism – Eliminating Poverty (ST EP) Initiative, this initiative focuses on supporting the implementation of small size tourism projects in developing countries with the aim to create economic resources that are effectively distributed to the host population by enhancing, or without disturbing, the natural and cultural heritages.

The necessary information and incentive to undertake proper initiatives at the local and regional level are still lacking. High level policy formulations are often too complex and unclear and the burden of their implications seems *a priori* too heavy for local and regional managers to move in such a direction, paralysing any further possible action. Finally, some local initiatives suffer from their low profile due to the lack of promotion instruments, remaining confined to a very restricted and local market.

The tourism industry itself recognises the need to maintain its main assets, among which the attractiveness of destinations. The WTTC has finalised various documents to this regard, such as the 1996 Agenda 21 for the tourism and travel industry in collaboration with the WTO and the Earth Council, and the 2002 publication on Corporate Social Leadership. Although the concept of a successful industry is now linked to ecological and social management, more efforts are needed to move towards a broader, integrated and effective approach. Hence, the practice remains far from theory.

The old EU Member States have several examples of sustainable initiatives in the tourism sector, mainly because these countries have been experiencing tourism and its pressures for a long time. France, Spain and the United Kingdom are well ahead in developing environmental or sustainable development indicators for tourism at national level. Denmark, the Flanders region, France, the Netherlands and Switzerland have a chapter dedicated to Tourism in their State of the Environment report. At local and regional level, some tourist destinations are also developing environmental indicators for tourism such as Spain (Balearics and Murcia), Italy (Province of Rimini and town of Ravenna), France (ten pilot sites under a project supported by the Ministry of Tourism), and also Austria, Denmark, Finland, Germany and Sweden (10 pilot destinations under the LIFE VISIT project).

Among the new Member States there are valuable initiatives, mainly related to tourism in natural protected areas, as is the case of Czech Republic (Sumava Biosphere Reserve), Hungary (Aggtelek National Park), Poland (Babia Góra National Park Biosphere Reserve) and Slovakia (Pol'ana Biosphere Reserve). The PAN (Protected Area Network) Parks initiative developed by WWF aims to gather European natural parks into a certification scheme ensuring sustainable tourism practices.

The European Charter for Sustainable Tourism in the Natural Protected Areas is a good example of collaboration between the public and the private sector, drawn from the experience of the *Charter for sustainable tourism in the protected areas*, initiated by the Federation of the Natural Regional Parks (France) and supported by the EUROPARC Federation. It is a trans-national trial gathering 13 natural parks belonging to 6 European countries committed to the criteria of the Charter. Some Eastern and Central countries have also participated in the working group established on "sustainable tourism in protected areas" in Europe. The European Community aims at applying this charter to protected areas, especially in the Natura 2000 proposed sites, with a scope for tourism. The Charter consists of five sections outlining ten principles of sustainable tourism in protected areas and describing the objectives for authorities, businesses, tour-operators and transport companies.

The Mediterranean countries are implementing some tourism policies within spati. l planning regulations, Spain playing the leading role. France is currently developing a National Strategy for Sustainable Tourism that takes into account the governance of the tourism administrations. Sweden has already developed an Agenda 21 for Tourism mainly focusing on the industry. Usually, the Northern and Central European countries are more oriented towards market-based strategies addressed to the tourism industry and promoting voluntary agreements such as Environmental Management Systems (EMAS and ISO 14001) and eco-labels. However, the latter can be found almost everywhere throughout Europe, in Austria, Denmark, Estonia, Germany, Italy and Latvia, while France and Sweden are also combining their strategies with eco-labels.

Eco-labelling has indeed shown some potential to encourage an ecologically sensitive tourist industry, contributing to increase public awareness and a more responsible behaviour not limited to tourism activities. Nevertheless, its application as a quality tool is limited and so is its dissemination. In 2000, 46 tourism products were awarded eco-labels, most being related to hotels and campsites. In 2004, there were 253 tourism products in the EU 25 area, indicating an impressive growth in eco-labelling. However, the numerous eco-labels with their own criteria for evaluation do not help the consumers to clearly distinguish among all products. As a consequence their use remains limited and the impact is still difficult to assess. For instance, the Austrian Eco-label for Tourism, which is the most developed scheme, reached a penetration rate of only 0.12% in the total of accommodation establishments by June 2000[60].

In February 2003, the creation of an EU Eco-Label Award Scheme for tourism was launched[61] with the aim of improving the credibility of the labelled products and services. This will also facilitate the evaluation of the penetration rate and the effects of tourism eco-labels in the future.

---

[60] European Environment Agency, 2001
[61] DG Environment web site on eco-label
http://europa.eu.int/comm/environment/ecolabel/whats_eco/index_en.htm

The Blue Flag initiative is a good example of profitable investment by the destinations in the labelling campaigns. The popularity of the Blue Flag has in fact been increasing rapidly among tourists, creating a positive competition among the 'water' destinations towards quality tourism. This is part of an important process leading to increased sustainability in the industry: the label communicates a clear message to the tourists and destination managers recognize the advantage of the label and foster its adoption. *The Blue Flag Campaign*, developed by the Foundation for Environmental Education in Europe, implies compliance with the bathing water quality criteria set by the EEC Bathing Water Directive of 1976. The criteria for beaches and marinas to be awarded a blue flag cover four areas: water quality; environmental management; safety, services and facilities; environmental education and information. For beaches, additional criteria are added dealing with wastewater treatment, Local Agenda 21 activities, and facilities for disabled people in particular. For marinas, the possibility of introducing an eco-management system is under consideration. In 2004, 2925 Blue Flags were attributed to beaches and marinas in Europe, with seventeen countries within the European Union taking part in the campaign. The top country is Greece with 752 Blue Flags followed by Spain with 429 (see table B.1). The region of Ellada in Greece is the most awarded with 385 Blue Flags, followed by Denmark with 286.

Table B.1
Blue Flags awarded, 2004

Country	Number of Blue Flags
GR	752
ES	429
FR	292
DK	286
IT	250
DE	137
PT	132
UK	129
SE	109
IE	77
NL	75
CY	41
SI	9
EE	8
FI	8
LV	6
LT	3

Tourism indeed has an impact and the mitigation of this impact has a cost. Although this cost is often of a complex nature, depending on the characteristics of tourism in each type of destination, usually it has a financial dimension. Some authorities have experienced specific instruments aimed at recovering this financial cost. Examples include the UK visitor payback scheme, the tax on boat-passengers travelling to small islands in France, and the taxes on sports that can potentially damage the natural environment in the natural reserve of Medes Islands (Spain). In the latter case, these taxes levied about € 130.000 in 1996 corresponding to almost 70% of the budget of the reserve[62].

To implement sustainable tourism with concrete actions, it is crucial to support local authorities with efficient exchange of information - including best practices – tools.

---

[62] Agence Française de l'Ingénierie Touristique, 2000

Among these tools are the networking initiatives. There are several examples of networking initiatives in the tourism sector. Some are entirely developed by the private sector, while others are supported by local authorities, or by Community and international bodies. The new information technologies enable initiatives today, often at a very low cost, that were not possible in the past.

Those developed by private operators and by local authorities usually aim at defining niche markets offering the tourist demand specific products or at emphasising tourism features of the territory. Their ultimate scope is marketing and advertising, although they usually also provide additional services to members or users[63].

As there is an increasing tourism demand for experimenting nature, the development of measures to mitigate the impact of tourism on the most beautiful and sensitive natural areas of destinations may be guaranteed by the presence of protected areas, such as those established in accordance to the IUCN (International Union for Conservation of Nature) categories I-IV. Combining the number of blue flags and the percentage coverage of protected areas within each country, an understanding of progress achieved by regions towards a better management of tourism in their territory and their natural areas is obtained.

The map shows that the most awarded regions are the most visited by tourists. At the EU 25 level, about 16.5% of the terrestrial and sea areas are covered by

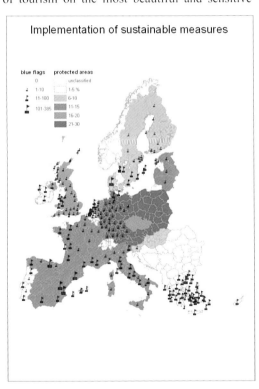

Implementation of sustainable measures

---

[63] The 'yourGreece' and its network of great small hotels is an example of private initiative addressing sustainability while providing its members a centralised booking services: www.yourgreece.gr

protected areas. The development of protected areas is particularly significant in Central and Eastern Europe. This indicates that those countries with large and precious natural resources are well ahead on reinforcing their natural heritage protection mechanisms and that the sustainable management of tourism demand for visiting such areas is feasible. The German regions have the highest percentage (30%) of natural protected areas in the territory, followed by Austrian, Polish, Slovakian and English regions.

2.2.1 The Local Agenda 21

Together with the lack of a coherent tourism policy at the European Union level, the heterogeneity of these measures can be explained by the variety of institutional organisations dealing with tourism in each Member State, from regional boards to Ministries.

Most of the measures implemented so far are at destination level through Local Agenda 21 (LA 21), although national campaigns need to sustain this process. Policy developments are supported by the International Council for Local Environmental Initiatives (ICLEI). According to a survey carried out in 1997[64], up to 35% of the European municipalities (of which 96% are in EU 15 countries) that have committed to the process of Local Agenda 21 or sustainable development plans have considered tourism as a priority; up to 28% of them indicated tourism as the first activity underlying the overall strategy. The Agenda 21 of Calvià in Balearic Islands (ES) is the most advanced in this domain.

Unfortunately, municipalities often implement Local Agenda 21 when tourism development has already strongly compromised the quality of life and environment of their territory, thus using this tool as a remediation measure rather than a preventive one.

---

[64] International Council for Local Environmental Initiatives web site: http://www.iclei.org

National Tourism Strategy and Monitoring System: the British case

CS_1

In 1999, the British government published 'Tomorrow's Tourism', identifying sustainable tourism as a priority and giving the English Tourism Council (ETC) the leading responsibility for developing policy in the domestic market. ETC was then the only UK National Tourist Board (NTB) with a dedicated sustainable tourism strategy and without a marketing function, the others being VisitScotland and the Wales Tourist Board. In 2001, 'Time for Action – a strategy for sustainable tourism in England' was published. The three main objectives were: protect and enhance the built environment; support local communities and their culture; benefit the economy of tourism destinations. These objectives were turned into 16 recommendations for action, each to be implemented by either the ETC, the local authorities or destination management groups.

In conjunction with the national strategy, ETC further designed a set of 20 national sustainable tourism indicators to monitor and assess England's progress towards making tourism more sustainable. Both the strategy and the indicators are reported in the publication "The Sustainable Growth of Tourism to Britain". In 2002, the 'Measuring Sustainable Tourism at the Local Level' was published. However, in 2003, the English Tourism Council merged with the British Tourist Authority to form VisitBritain, the national lead tourism marketing organisation supported by the UK

Key issues:

⇨ Shared vision and common goals to reach sustainable tourism at national level.

⇨ Originally, strategy and objectives to be progressively monitored against a set of 20 indicators related to sustainable tourism.

⇨ More recently, inter regional benchmarking of tourism performance and more coordinated action with the EU for the development of sustainable tourism indicators.

Department for Culture, Media and Sport (DCMS). This merge was part of an overall reform programme of the institutions involved in the support of tourism. In July 2004 the Government published 'Tomorrow's Tourism Today' and the 'Review of Tourism Statistics" providing, respectively, the outline of the new national strategy for tourism and a quality review of the tourism data collection and analysis systems. The latter recommended *"Maintaining contact with work on inter regional benchmarking of tourism performance, and the developments of the EU's QUALITEST and of sustainable tourism indicators to ensure that they take full account of measurement practicalities and production of any necessary data is planned"*.

Links & references:

Department for Culture, Media and Sport, 1999.Tomorrow's Tourism – a growth industry for the new Millennium.

The Sustainable Growth of Tourism to Britain, 2001.
http://www3.visitbritain.com/corporate/Sustainable_Growth_of_Tourism_to_GB_Report.pdf

UK Department for Culture, Media and Sport , 2002. Measuring Sustainable Tourism at the Local Level - An Introduction and Background.
http://www.culture.gov.uk/global/publications/archive_2002/sutainable_tourism.htm?properties=archive%5F2002%2C%2Ftourism%2FQuickLinks%2Fpublications%2Fdefault%2C&month=

Department for Culture, Media and Sport , 2004. Tomorrow's Tourism Today
http://www.culture.gov.uk/NR/rdonlyres/73FDC3ED-BCA6-4323-A683-63C6FCF5F79B/0/TomorrowsTourismToday.pdf

Department for Culture, Media and Sport , 2004. The National Statistics Review of Tourism Statistics.
http://www.culture.gov.uk/global/publications/archive_2004/Review_Tourism_Statistics.htm?properties=archive%5F2004%2C%2Ftourism%2FQuickLinks%2Fpublications%2Fdefault%2C&month=

The members of the Tour Operators Initiative (TOI) are committed to introducing sustainable development practices in their tourism business. The initiative - supported by the United Nations Environment Programme (UNEP), the United Nations Educational, Scientific and Cultural Organization (UNESCO) and the World Tourism Organization (WTO) – was launched on March 2000 by 15 tour operators. In 2002, the initiative counted 23 tour operating companies accounting for a total of 30 million international tourists each year.

Membership is open to all tour operators. All members have signed a 'Statement of Commitment' to implement the principles of sustainable tourism through a corporate policy. Each member pays an annual membership fee, proportionate to its turnover, to support joint activities.

The three main objectives of the initiative include: the adoption of best practices; the broadening of the cooperation with other tourism sector stakeholders; and the broadening of the membership to reach a critical number of committed tour operators.

A Sector Supplement to the Sustainability Reporting Guidelines produced by the Global Reporting Initiative was approved

Key issues:

⇨ Example of corporate engagement to foster sustainable tourism, although on a voluntary basis.

⇨ Effort to develop tools and approaches (indicators, reporting mechanisms) to measure performance in economic, social and environmental terms.

in 2002; it presents 47 indicators developed to measure the tour operators' performance in terms of environmental, economic and social impacts of their business. Indicators refer to five main areas: product management and development, internal management, supply chain management, customer relations, and cooperation with destination. In 2003, a pilot phase on the implementation of the reporting initiative started; it is expected to disseminate the know how on reporting principles and practices as well as to provide further information, based on experience, for the review of indicators.

The TOI activities encompass research and information exchange, technical support and capacity building. It organises workshops and collect case studies of good practice. Four thematic working groups focus on sustainability reporting, cooperation with destinations, supply chain management and communication.

Links & references:

Tour Operator Initiative: http://www.toinitiative.org/

Storstrøm County is located in the south of the greater Copenhagen area; it covers 8% of Denmark and 5% of the country population. It is characterised by saltmarsh, shallow water, small fishing harbours, sailing ports, abundant wildlife, environmental tourism and organic agriculture. LA 21 Action Plan was adopted in 1997 but similar initiatives were launched since 1991 ("Green Region project"); despite not being a major driving force in the County's economy, tourism was targeted as a priority area in the Action Plan. Tourism is concentrated in summer months and focuses on family groups. Domestic tourism prevails. In the low season, it compensates for declining employment in fishing, agriculture, industry and - to some extent - shipping. Activities are recently being diversified with sport (golf, sailing, fishing), business and cultural tourism, bathing and relaxation.

Since 1991, i.e. before the Rio Conference, the County has encouraged a number of demonstration and awareness-raising activities with innovative regional and local approaches aiming at sustainable and rational use of resources. The target of an integrated sustainable development is to be

Key issues:
- ⇨ Foresighted adoption of LA21 on tourism activities.
- ⇨ Tourism set as a priority in master plan, not driven by stringent environmental pressure.
- ⇨ Target of sustainable development within a composite industrial and agricultural territory.

reached in a territory characterised by a mixed industrial (metal, electronics, food and beverages) and agricultural (grain and sugar beet) economy.

Successful tourism activities involving the public as well as the private sector have been developed within the frame of LA 21 Action Plan: the ETE (Environmentally-friendly tourism enterprises) project to reduce consumption and load on the environment; the eco-labelling of holiday houses in the Island of Møn foreseeing a 9-criteria labelling system; an 85-criteria national labelling scheme for hotels; a 21-goals and indicators label for tourism areas following the principles of sustainable development. The County has an international dimension with over 40 projects undertaken with partners from other countries; participation in international networks; achievements of major national and international awards.

Links & references:

United Nations Environment Programme & International Council for Local Environmental Initiatives, 2003. Tourism and Local Agenda 21 – The Role of Local Authorities in Sustainable Tourism. United Nations Publication.
http://www.stam.dk/www.uneptie.org/pc/tourism/documents/Tourism%20and%20LA21/la21_part4.pdf

http://www.sustainable-euroregions.net/documentbank/Profil%2CSustai.Dev.Network%2CFinal.doc

The sustainable development programme of Varese Ligure, Italy
CS_2

Varese Ligure (La Spezia) is a small rural municipality in the Liguria region. With a population of only 2500 inhabitants spread over 20 hamlets and 14,000 ha, it is one of the broadest Italian municipalities. The territory is located between the Po valley and the coastal area with 95% of the land area devoted to agriculture and forests. There are no industries and mainly wood handicraft and agricultural activities. Between 1961 and 1998 the resident population dropped of one third; today, about 50% of the overall population is aged over 60. Given this structural situation and the deteriorating economic conditions, a development strategy focused on renovation of the urban centre, promotion of organic farming and tourism was targeted by the local administration. This led to the first ISO 14001 certified Italian municipality (October 1999) and the first European EMAS-registered municipality (November 1999).

The ambitious target of Varese Ligure is to reach 100% of renewable energy and 100% organic agricultural and livestock production through a comprehensive programme of sustainable development. One important aspect is the focus on renewable energy sources (wind, solar and biomass) and on energy saving; at the same time, the ISO 14001 and EMAS certifications have been instrumental in raising people's environmental awareness and promoting a sustainable approach in the use of resources outside the municipal boundaries, involving tourists as well.
In 2003, it gained the award from the European campaign "Renewable energy for Europe" as "100% Renewable Energy Communities – Rural".

Key issues:

⇨ First EMAS-registered municipality in Europe.

⇨ Target to become 100% renewable and 100% organic.

⇨ Environmental and cultural tourism as main employment source and economic driving force.

The positive employment trend in the tertiary sector is due to tourism activities attracted by the natural environment and the picturesque historical centres. In the past 5 years, visitors increased by 200% with provenience mainly from Germany and the UK. Besides seasonal (summer) tourism, mainly accommodated in second homes and - to a lesser extent - in hotels or resorts, peaks of presence are reached during weekends and week holidays. During summer time, emigrants return to the place of origin and contribute to the re-boost of social and economic activities. In the past few years, local organic agriculture and other typical products have consolidated their niche market besides a steady increase of agro-tourism and horse riding. 95% of all organic livestock and agricultural enterprises achieved environmental certification and the valley was re-named as the "Organic Valley" of Varese Ligure. Environmental awareness raising campaigns and promotion of local culture and traditions target local population and tourists at the same time, with the latter being considered as an integral part of the territory and not as a mere source of seasonal revenues.

Links & references:

Verdesca D. and Falorni S., 2003 La certificazione ambientale degli enti pubblici e del territorio. Il Sole 24 ore.
http://europa.eu.int/comm/energy/en/renewable/idae_site/deploy/prj083/prj083_1.html

Varese Ligure web site: http://www.comune.vareseligure.sp.it/index.asp

3. Characterization of European Regions with respect to Sustainable Tourism

The European regions present similarities and disparities, and so do their tourist destinations. Although each region has to develop its own diagnostic policy according to its features and targets, a common framework would support the implementation of coherent sustainable tourism strategies. In this context, the definition of suitable indicators provides a better understanding of the issues, as well as the tools to assess and monitor developments.

To further extend the analysis of sustainable tourism within this study, the European Union territory has been categorised into homogeneous zones or clusters having common features related to sustainable tourism. The clustering process is based on statistical data compiled from Eurostat New Cronos database.

3.1 Tourism Environmental Indicators

3.1.1 The Development of Indicators

Tourism indicators have been developed by the European Environment Agency since 2000 as the tourism sector started being fully integrated in the overall work of the European Commission on sustainable development indicators. EEA tourism indicators focused on the environmental impacts of the tourism sector and on other key tourism development issues such as transport at pan-European level (51 countries).

The methodological approach of indicators' development is policy driven, thus it starts from the analysis of policy information needs and is not constrained by the real availability of statistical information. Moreover, the approach takes into account the major issues commonly shared by diverse European regions and is not intended *a priori* to respond to specific issues of individual countries. Key steps of the process include to:

- identify what the main policy questions are; these should address the tourism sector's shape and development, the environmental problems it engenders, the policy responses developed by the sector;

- identify a set of indicators that can help to provide answers to such questions;
- map existing statistics against the indicator list, identifying data gaps and improving the data system accordingly (in a multi-year perspective);
- develop indicator assessment by the gradual development of detailed indicator fact sheets and by regular indicator-based reporting, starting on the basis of existing statistics and gradually improving as data and methods develop.

Five key policy questions provide the structural framework for the tourism and environment indicator monitoring system:

1. What are the environmental impacts of tourism?
2. Are we getting better at matching the tourism demand to the need to preserve resources?
3. What characterises and drives the demand for tourism?
4. Are we moving towards a more environmentally market-based management of the tourism sector?
5. How effective are environmental management and monitoring tools towards a more integrated tourism strategy?

The list of the EEA tourism indicators is reported in Box B.2. Such a list was developed in liaison with various Commission services, national experts, other international organisations and researchers in order to comply with the statistical provision and the policy issues addressed by the EU Agenda 21 for European Tourism. However, tourism is not considered as a priority in the process for the sustainable development integration into the sectoral policies, yet, and it has not been integrated in the EEA core set of indicator publications[65]. The possibility to establish a methodology for developing sustainable tourism indicators within Eurostat is under discussion. This methodology would constitute the common reference document for all Members States to develop their statistical system in accordance to data needs. Table B.2 provides the reference to other sets of sustainable tourism indicators developed at international, regional and national levels.

---

[65] European Environment Agency, 2005

BOX B.2/1	EEA core set of tourism indicators*	
		*key indicators are in bold
Generic question	**Policy Issue**	**Indicator title**
What are the environmental impacts of tourism?	Air pollution relating to transport	**Tourism's contribution to gas emissions and energy consumption from transport**
	Resources consumption (energy, water, land)	Energy use by tourism
		Water use by tourism
		Land take by tourism
	Biodiversity and land use (fauna, landscapes)	Potential disturbance to biodiversity from tourism
	Protection of resources (positive effects)	Bathing water quality (in tourism regions)
	Environmental risks	Risks caused by ski activity (avalanche occurrence)
	Impacts to territories (waste and soils)	Waste generated by tourism (facilities)
		Quality of wastewater services of tourism accommodations (or in tourism regions)
		Tourism density (bed-places per km2 NUTS 3 level)
Are we better managing the tourism demand to the need to preserve environment?	Management of tourism infrastructures	**Tourism intensity (bed-places per 100 inhabitant NUTS 3 level)**
		Land use for tourism activities (tourism destinations versus land cover)
		Construction of tourism facilities: accommodations (including second homes) and tourist attractions (golf courses, yacht marinas, amusement parks) versus number of tourists
		Plans of prevention of natural risks in tourism zones
	Management of tourism frequentation	Number of visitors to protected areas and cultural heritage sites
	Management of tourism mobility and access to destinations	Traffic density of tourism transport (congestion)
		Modes of transport used by tourists (international and domestic tourism)
		Access to mass tourism destinations by public transport
		Development of less environmental damaging transport system for tourism travels (services)

BOX B.2/2	EEA core set of tourism indicators*	*key indicators are in bold
Generic question	**Policy Issue**	**Indicator title**
What characterises and drives the demand for tourism?	Characteristics of the tourist demand	**Tourism arrivals in Europe versus residents and non-residents breakdown**
		Overnights spent in tourism accommodations, by mode and related bed occupancy
		Seasonality of tourism and duration of trips
		Growth in travel distance for tourism
	Characteristics of the tourism offer	Economic value of tourism industry (GVA) as in % total GDP
		Household expenditure versus tourism prices
		Market share of type of holidays (tourism packages and ecotourism products)
		Share of local employment in tourism, as % of total employment of the sector and % of tourism employment versus total employment at regional level
		Use of Internet by tourism SMEs versus total tourism businesses and versus total SMEs, including a breakdown between urban and rural areas
Are we moving towards a better internalisation of the external costs in the tourism sector?	Internalisation of external costs	**Tourist tax revenue versus Public expenditure for conservation of heritage sites**
How effective are environmental management and monitoring tools towards a more integrated tourism strategy?	Tools of industry	Uptake of environmental management systems by tourism companies (EMAS, EIA)
		Implementation of eco-labels for tourism facilities
	Measures of local stakeholders (at destinations)	**Progress in initiatives implemented by local stakeholders (Integrated Quality Management, local Agenda 21, SEA, ICZM; in tourism destinations)**
	Sustainable tourism strategies of national authorities	Progress in integration of tourism and environment into national strategies and monitoring systems
	Tools and measures of the EC transversal policies	European Union's support to sustainable tourism projects

Table B.2 Other sets of sustainable tourism indicators

OECD (countries comparisons)	Organisation for Economic Co-operation and Development, 2002. Working group on Environmental information and outlooks: Indicators for the integration of environmental concerns into tourism policies: ENV/EPOC/SE(2001)3/REV1
WTO (destinations managers)	World Tourism Organisation, 2004. Indicators of sustainable development for tourism destinations, A guidebook. Compilation of initiatives at local, regional, national and international levels: http://www.world-tourism.org/frameset/frame_sustainable.html
UNEP (tours-operators)	Tour Operator initiative (UNEP) and Global Reporting Initiative (GRI): Tour Operators' sector supplement, Sustainability reporting guidelines: http://www.toinitiative.org/reporting/documents/TourOperatorsSupplementNovember2002.pdf
Baltic Sea region	Institute for tourism and recreational research in Northern Europe (NIT). Indicators for the development of sustainable tourism in the Baltic Sea region, Federal Environment Agency, Berlin, December 2001: http://www.nit-kiel.de
United-Kingdom – national	English Tourism Council. National Sustainable Tourism Indicators, Monitoring progress towards sustainable tourism in England, English Tourism Board, 2001. http://www.visitbritain.com/ukindustry/
France – national	French Institute for the Environment (IFEN), 2000. Tourisme, environnement, territoires : les indicateurs', Edition 2000; http://www.ifen.fr/ Outline in English Indicators for an environmental diagnosis of tourism in France.
Balearic Islands (Spain) – local	CITTIB (Centre for Tourism Research and Technologies of the Balearic Islands) Indicadores de sostenibilidad del turismo en las Islas Baleares.
Rimini province (Italy) - regional	Strategies and tools toward sustainable tourism in Mediterranean coastal areas. LIFE project MED-COASTS S-T: http://www.life.sustainable-tourism.org
10 pilot destinations in the EU – local and regional	European Indicators for sustainable tourism development in destinations. LIFE project VISIT: http://www.yourvisit.info/initiative/cont_org_b_.html# and the International Friends of Nature: http://www.nfi.at

3.1.2 Problems and Constraints in Developing Sustainable Tourism Indicators

The lack of data is an important concern when dealing with tourism statistics. In the economic field, data on domestic tourism (including tourism transport system) and private accommodations, such as second homes, are crucially lacking. Only a few countries such as France, Spain and the UK carry out national surveys including these information. With regard to the impact of tourism on the environment, very few data exist and most of them are on a destination level; examples of natural resources consumption by tourism facilities are provided within the tourism industry reporting mechanisms (mostly hotels). Thus, the majority of tourism and environment related data are based on the international arrivals compiled within the WTO database, and the collective tourism accommodations within the Eurostat New Cronos. Study cases and surveys are necessary to illustrate the contribution of the tourism sector to environmental pollution.

In general, statistics on tourism are weak in many countries, although some are implementing their own Tourism Satellite Accounts. When data are collected, definitions are in most cases not harmonised, making comparison difficult. The undefined vision of the tourism identity has indeed contributed to this situation. In 1998, Eurostat developed a Community methodology on tourism statistics, mostly focussed on economic data. The launch of a study on the proposition of a methodology to elaborate sustainable development indicators for tourism is currently under discussion. This process should provide solutions in the short to medium term; while significant steps are taken, many challenges still remain for the creation of harmonized data and its effective use to support policy issues.

The trend of an indicator is usually compared to the agreed policy targets, in order to understand whether the development is implemented in the right direction. The current lack of a consolidated European tourism policy constitutes in this sense a significant methodological problem.

Moreover, as widely discussed in the previous paragraphs, tourism encompasses a wide range of stakeholders belonging to diverse sectors and having diverse objectives and priorities. It is unlikely that indicators will respond to such a wide range of technical and administrative demand; as a direct consequence, indicators for tourism will likely be less reliable than those used for other sectors. Main concerns include:

- the very large scope of tourism activities;
- a highly fragmented industry;

- the geographical coverage or spatial scale: from the local (tourism facilities, tourism resorts, natural protected areas, coastal and mountains regions) to global (climate change, international transport);
- seasonal nature vs. high and low tourist season;
- wide range of stakeholders: public (national and regional governments, municipalities) and private (big and small enterprises such as hoteliers, tourism and travel agencies, leisure activities managers), transport services, syndicates, associations of consumers, environmental NGOs, engineering, researchers and consultants;
- frequent absence of policy on tourism and lack of established benchmarks.

3.2   The Clustering Process

3.2.1   Assessment of Sustainable Tourism Development in the European Regions

As tourism destination regions are mainly characterized by the concentration of tourism establishments for accommodation, the density and intensity of tourism in a given region provide a reasonable understanding of the pressure exerted by this industry. Tourism flows in the region will influence economic choices and may create social pressures.

Traditional regions of mass tourism - mainly seaside and small island destinations - should develop specific responses to the challenge of sustainability of tourism development. These responses may differ greatly from those of the regions that are still under low tourism development, such as new destinations or remote areas, and that wish to further engage into tourism as an economic sector for development. Rural areas and urban areas face different challenges, too.

Maps were created using the NUTS-99 shape file version and ARCVIEW GIS (vers. 8.3). Class thresholds were manually rounded based on the *natural breaks* classification. Metadata of datasets are reported in Annex 4.

DEFINITIONS:

Natural Breaks: the default classification method in ArcView. It identifies breakpoints between classes using a statistical formula (Jenk's optimization). This method is rather complex, but basically it minimizes the sum of the variance within each of the classes groupings and patterns inherent to the data.

(As defined in the ArcView 3.1 Manual)

Indicator 1: Tourism intensity

This indicator is defined by *the number of tourism bed places per inhabitant*. It provides an understanding of where tourism is a major activity for the receiving local communities and shows the spatial distribution of the potential socio-economic pressures.

Assessment

The IND_1 map shows the level of importance of tourism within the economy of the regions, i.e. it is a measure of tourism development.

At the national level, the countries with the highest tourism intensity are Luxembourg (15.3 bed-places/100 inhabitants), Cyprus (13.5) and Austria (11.3). Luxembourg is well-known for its tourism business vocation, mainly due to the presence of several Community institutions; Cyprus has an economy largely based on tourism, the main source of foreign incomes. The least developed tourism economies are in Latvia, Lithuania and Poland.

At the regional level, the top 20 European regions with the highest tourism intensity are: Balearics (52.53 bed-places/100 inhabitants), Notio Aigaio – Cycladics (49.03), Ionia Nisia and Kriti for Greece, Valle d'Aosta (44.18), Trentino-Alto Adige and Marche for Italy, Corse (42.31), Languedoc-Roussillon and Aquitaine for France, Tirol (38.36), Salzburg, Kaernten and Vorarlberg for Austria, Algarve (33.28) for Portugal, Province of Luxembourg in Belgium (32.28), Zeeland (30.06) and Drenthe for the Netherlands, Aaland (28.97) in Finland, and Luxembourg (15.29). All these regions are famous tourist destinations, either for international or regional tourism. Luxembourg is still a unique case, due to the low ratio of residents in comparison to the large (non-residents) tourism for business purposes.

Tourism is a key industry in many alpine areas, but it is also embedded in a wider socio-economic structure having strong links with agriculture and others sectors. Fifteen regions among the top 20 are seaside areas, accounting for 7% of the total European coastline; some 25000 km out of the 47000 km of the Mediterranean coast have already been developed. In France, municipalities along the coasts and in high mountains (representing 4.5% of all the municipalities of France) provide 48% of the accommodation capacity[66]. In the Balearics, the number of bed-places (excluding second homes) is ten times higher than the average in the whole of Spain. The lowest tourism intensity values are found in Poland, with seven Polish regions under the last ten European ones.

Table B.3   Regional values of tourism intensity(bed places/ 100 inhabitants), 2003

Source: Eurostat

	The highest ten			The lowest ten	
1	ISLAS BALEARES (ES)	52.5	1	PODLASKIE (PL)	1.1
2	NOTIO AIGAIO (GR)	49.0	2	LUBELSKIE (PL)	1.0
3	VALLE D'AOSTA (IT)	44.2	3	OUTER LONDON (UK)	0.9
4	CORSE (FR)	42.3	4	PODKARPACKIE (PL)	0.9
5	TRENTINO-ALTO ADIGE (IT)	39.6	5	LIETUVA	0.8
6	TIROL (AT)	38.4	6	LATVIJA	0.8
7	IONIA NISIA (GR)	34.6	7	SLASKIE (PL)	0.7
8	ALGARVE (PT)	33.3	8	MAZOWIECKIE (PL)	0.7
9	LUXEMBOURG (BE)	32.3	9	SWIETOKRZYSKIE (PL)	0.6
10	ZEELAND (NL)	30.1	10	LODZKIE (PL)	0.6

According to tourism flows (demand side), figures provided for overnight stays per 100 inhabitants do not differ much from those calculated as bed-places every 100 inhabitants (tourism supply intensity) for the top destination regions. Eurostat data for 2000[67], in this sense, show significant differences only for Ireland and Italy[68]. In Ireland, the Border, Midlands and Western regions recorded the minimum tourism demand intensity (overnight stays) while the Southern and Eastern regions recorded the maximum values; this figure was reverse for the tourism supply intensity (bed-places). In Italy, the Trentino-Alto Adige region showed maximum value in tourism demand intensity while it was Valle d'Aosta recording the highest tourism supply intensity.

On the other hand, when considering the regions with low tourism intensity values, results vary largely, depending on whether the demand side or supply side indicator is used.

The bed-place indicator focuses on the capacity of the tourism establishments to invest in the tourism economy. The construction of buildings and facilities are important for their impact on the environment and the creation on potential conflicts with other

---

[66] Rechatin C., Dubois G., Pelletreau A., 2000

[67] data refer only to EU 15 countries

[68] Schmidt, H., 2002 (b)

sectors. The overnight stay indicator highlights the tourism flows to destinations and thus is more focused on the potential socio-cultural pressures within the local communities. The difference between these two population indexes may also reflect the disparities in economic performance to manage the destinations efficiently. The ratio of bed-places per number of overnight stays indicates the net use of bed-places in tourism accommodations. For example, a region like Sicilia in Italy with a low intensity of bed-places per 100 inhabitants shows the minimum tourism development, while Piemonte has the minimum Italian rate of overnight stays per inhabitant, indicating that this region is under visited compared to its capacity.

The tourism intensity indicator (IND_1) represents the first criteria for our classification of the European regions with regard to tourism development, following the choice to focus more on the economic side of tourism and thus on the supply side.

Indicator 2: Tourism density

This indicator is defined by *the number of tourism bed places per km^2*. It provides an understanding of the spatial distribution of the tourism development (supply side), highlighting those regions that may potentially suffer from environmental pressures.

Assessment

The first and more evident information that may be gathered from IND_2 is that tourism is not an activity homogeneously distributed over Europe. In particular, Scandinavia, the Spanish inlands and Eastern countries are less tourism intensive than other regions, mostly because of climate and accessibility. Secondly, tourism accommodations are principally concentrated in the main European cities, as well as on coasts, small islands and mountains zones, the last three being the most environmentally-sensitive areas.

At the national level, the countries showing the highest tourism density values are Malta (126.5 bed-places/km²), The Netherlands (33.9) and Luxembourg (26.3), these values being a combination of their relative small country land area and of the high number of infrastructures.

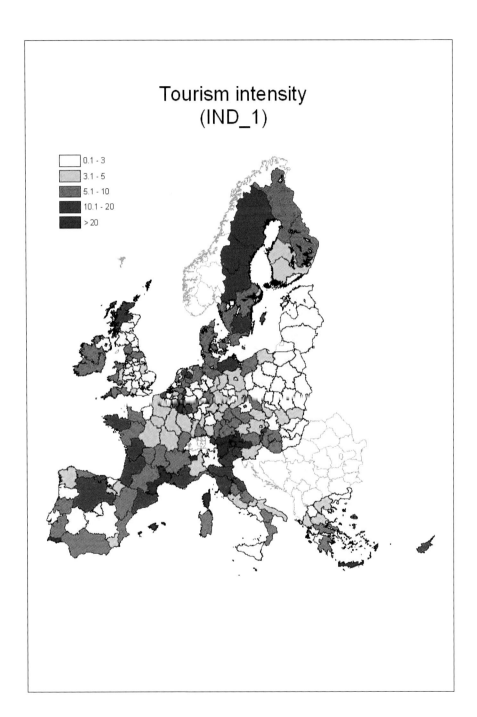

Tourism intensity
(IND_1)

0.1 - 3
3.1 - 5
5.1 - 10
10.1 - 20
> 20

Table B.4 Regional values of tourism density(bed places/km^2), 2003

Source: Eurostat

	The highest ten			The lowest ten	
1	INNER LONDON (UK)	415.8	1	EXTREMADURA (ES)	0.7
2	REG.BRUXELLES-CAP (BE)	200.7	2	PODLASKIE (PL)	0.6
3	PRAHA (cz)	141.1	3	CASTILLA-LA MANCHA (ES)	0.6
4	MALTA	126.5	4	EESTI	0.6
5	WIEN (AT)	105.0	5	ITA-SUOMI (FI)	0.6
6	ISLAS BALEARES (ES)	85.8	6	OEVRE NORRLAND (SE)	0.5
7	BERLIN (DE)	80.4	7	LIETUVA	0.4
8	ZEELAND (NL)	62.8	8	DYTIKI MAKEDONIA (GR)	0.4
9	NOORD-HOLLAND (NL)	60.0	9	POHJOIS-SUOMI (FI)	0.3
10	GREATER MANCHESTER (UK)	59.0	10	LATVIJA	0.3

Among the countries with the lowest tourism density values are Estonia (0.6) and Finland (0.7). While for Estonia the indicator highlights a real low spatial distribution of the tourism development, for Finland it is undoubtedly biased by its extended uninhabited areas. This indicator provides particularly meaningful information by comparing countries having a similar size, as it is the case of Denmark and Slovakia, showing a density of 9 and 3.3 bed-places/km^2, respectively.

The top five tourism density regions are urban areas with London in first place (415.83 bed-places/km^2), followed by Brussels (200.71), Prague (141.13), Malta (126.55) and Vienna (105). Hotels in urban areas must generally comply with very strict specifications and have the advantage of integrating well into the urban environment. Unfortunately, this may not be the case for outside urban areas.

Among the seaside destinations, the highest tourism density regions are the Balearic Islands (85.83 bed-places/km^2), Zeeland in The Netherlands and Algarve in Portugal. The Greek Notio Aigaio (Cycladics) and the Italian Trentino-Alto Adige, favourite seaside and mountain destinations, respectively, show also high density values.

In the case of small islands, that are particularly environmentally sensitive areas, some re-known tourism destinations such as Mykonos (Cycladics), Porquerolles and Ré (France), and Capri (Italy) have reached the upper limit of their tourism carrying capacity. The coastal strip (500 m from the shore) of Mallorca (Balearics), one of the most popular destinations of Spain, had 27 % of its territory urbanised in 1995[69]. In Italy, 17% of the coast of Rimini, a mass sea destination, was occupied by man-made infrastructure, with a rate four times higher than the inland and equivalent to an

---

[69] European Environment Agency, 2003

increase of 500% since 1950. In the Emilia-Romagna region, the highest tourism density is found in Cattolica with 95 tourists per hectare[70].

Mountain destinations are not part of the top 20 regions with regard to tourism density. However, some of the most popular mountain regions such as Valle d'Aosta (27.17 bed-places/km²), Rhone-Alpes (14.48) and Tyrol (8.66) start experiencing some changes due to tourism development. These include an altered landscape due to more frequent buildings and facilities and increasing disturbance to the fauna (noise and skiing, for instance). Additionally, many outdoor sports affect areas that were previously undisturbed and nearly inaccessible areas such as gorges and rock faces.

Rural areas, in general, are not suffering from tourism. Tourism usually concentrates close to special sites with a natural (national parks) or cultural (historic, gastronomic, etc.) value. There is indeed a substantial potential for tourism development in the least wealthy European regions. The regions under the lowest tourism density values (less than 0.65 bed-places/km²) are mainly located in Finland and Sweden but also in Latvia, Lithuania, Estonia, Poland (Podlaskie), Spain (Castilla La Mancha and Extremadura) and Greece (Dytiki Makedonia).

This indicator (IND_2) may be considered the second criteria for the sustainability of tourism where:

- urban areas have High Tourism Density;
- seaside and small islands have Medium to High Tourism Density;
- mountain areas have Low to Medium Tourism Density; and
- rural areas have Low Tourism Density.

---

[70] Ambiente Italia, 2001

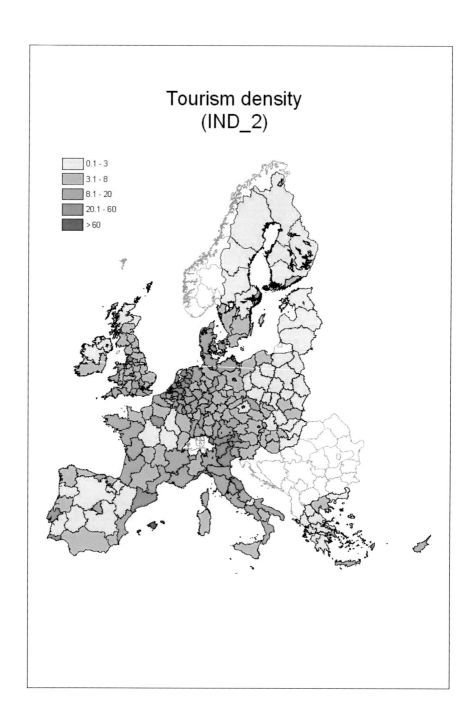

Tourism density
(IND_2)

0.1 - 3
3.1 - 8
8.1 - 20
20.1 - 60
> 60

Indicator 3: Land take by tourism

This indicator is defined by *the number of tourism establishments every 100 km²*. It provides an understanding of the impact of the tourism activity over the territory and the ecosystems, as well as the potential competition for land resources with other economic sectors.

The tourism sector requires some land space, directly for infrastructures such as tourism facilities (marinas, parking places, etc.) and accommodations (resorts, hotels, etc.), and indirectly for leisure activities (golf courses, ski slopes, trails). As a result, high value ecosystems may be modified to host tourism activities and needed land may be drawn from agricultural, forest and other natural landscapes, creating potential conflicts and competition with other economic sectors. Another impact of tourism buildings is to increase the urban sprawl in the main European cities.

Assessment

Although highly variable, the average land consumption 'footprint' of one tourist hotel bed is estimated by the Blue Plan at 30 m² in 1995; this value goes up to 100 m² per room (or two bed-places), when all surfaces are included, to 50 m² for a rented flat and for a camping site, and to 100 m² for a second home[71]. It is reasonable to estimate the land take by a tourist staying in a second home to be 250 m² when garden is included. A second home takes up 40 times the land area required for a flat, since it is occupied only a few weeks per year.

The land area required for an average 80-bed places hotel is 3000 m², corresponding to one eightieth of that required by a second home (combining occupancy rates of each type over a year). The size of the hotels varies according to the regions. The EU average is of 60.5 bed-places per establishment, with an average of 52.5 beds for hotels and similar establishments and of 69.5 beds for the other collective accommodations. Preliminary estimates indicate that to host 150 million tourists on the Mediterranean coast, the land taken would be ranging between 7.500 km² (all tourists staying in 60 bed-places hotels) and 37.500 km² (all tourists residing in second

---

[71] Lanquar R. et al., 1995

homes)[72]. For comparative purposes, the land surface of the Netherlands is of 33.873 km².

The EU has an average of 20 establishments for collective accommodation every 100 km². According to the same land take estimates, the land area taken by European tourism would total, on average, 6% of the European territory, which is comparable to the industry land take. Those European regions with a number of tourism establishments above the average (with values ranging between 23.1 and 72 establishments every 100 km²) would total a land take of about 14% of the territory. The highest values with more than 72 tourism establishments per 100 km², indicate that more than 21.6% of the territory would be dedicated to tourism. This extreme situation is found in London (267.7 tourism establishments per 100 km²), Veneto (234.58), Cornwall and the Islands of Scilly (137.25), Friuli-Venezia Giulia (121.7), Prague (121.19) and Brussels (112.14). Among the top 20 regions with the highest land taken by tourism, 11 are from the United Kingdom, mainly along the western coasts. Malta and Tyrol are also included within these top 20.

Furthermore, there are an estimated 5.6 million golfers and about 5000 golf courses in Europe (EU 15). At an average of 50 hectares per 18-hole course, there is a total estimate of 200000 hectares dedicated to golf courses. The largest number is in England where golf courses cover an estimated 0.6% of the land surface[73]. Theme parks also develop over large spaces, from a few ten to hundred hectares. For example, Alton Towers in the UK covers 300 ha and Euro Disney close to Paris covers 600 ha when including the associated accommodation park.

The fact that main cities are expected to offer the largest bed-place capacities together with seaside resorts is worth noting. The Scandinavian countries, in particular, show some great sized tourism establishments[74]. In these areas, the land take indicator will be overestimated.

The IND_3 will thus be considered the third criteria to characterise tourism regions, keeping in mind that it may attribute too much importance to the main European cities.

---

[72] Pils M., Eltschka-Schiller G., 1999
[73] European Golf Association Ecology Unit, 1995
[74] Schmidt, H., 2002 (a)

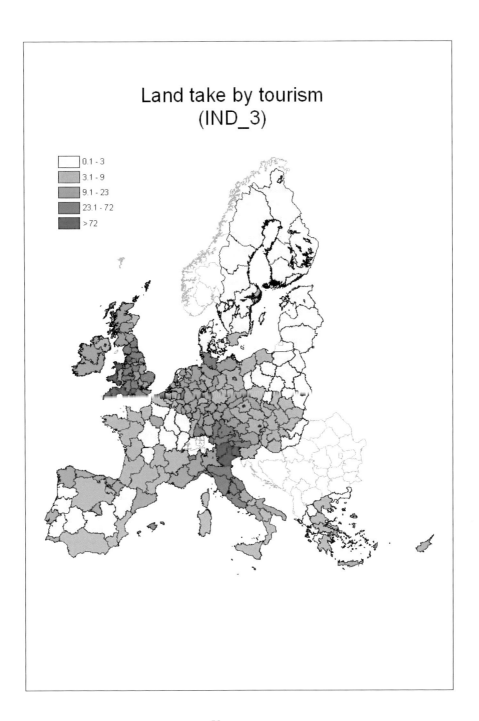

Land take by tourism
(IND_3)

0.1 - 3
3.1 - 9
9.1 - 23
23.1 - 72
>72

3.2.2   Identified Tourism Typologies

In 2002[75] Eurostat proposed a classification mostly based on topographical features
and distinguishing tourism into: seaside, island, urban, rural, and mountainous (Box
B.3). Within this classification limitations exist: lack of reference to the administrative
boundaries of regions, use of different terminologies, apparent difficulty in
distinguishing between seaside and urban tourism and between mountain and rural
tourism.

BOX B.3	Main features of the European regional tourism according to Eurostat
Seaside tourism	• Strong concentration of relatively small sized establishments. • Predominantly domestic tourism. • Average length of stay of 3 days (higher than urban tourism, lower than for islands). • Existence of competition within the sector (with other seaside areas) and with other sectors. • Wide spatial planning.
Urban tourism	• Business tourism, with a wide range of attractions. • Large sized hotels spread around the major European cities. • Predominantly nights spent in hotel. • Low level of domestic tourism, with a few exceptions. • The lowest average in terms of length of stay.
Island tourism	• High concentration of large establishments (comparable in size to those of urban tourism). • Predominantly non-resident tourism (foreign or national). • High length of stay (the highest for foreign tourists, within the average for national tourists).
Rural tourism	• Nature or rural locations are the main attraction. • Length of stay within national average. • Predominantly domestic tourism, notably nearby clienteles.
Mountain tourism	• Highly seasonal. • Majority of overnight stays during winter. • In general, low hotel bed-places capacity; it becomes high in mass destinations. • In general, low length of stay; it becomes high in mass destinations. • Predominantly domestic tourism, with the exception of the Alps.

In order to facilitate the analysis that will be carried out in the following chapters, the
European Union has been divided into homogeneous areas showing similar features.
The classification is based on the indicators presented in the previous paragraph. In
particular, it is based on the combination of the three indicators each ranging from low
to medium and high values.

This categorization of the European tourism development into types also sets the basis
for the development of the following sections of this study where governance and
territorial cohesion aspects are analysed.

---

[75] Schmidt, H., 2002 (a)

Type 1: Most visited regions

Most visited tourism destinations are constantly expanding, in some cases reaching a point of saturation or even losing importance. Those regions are under high tourism development pressures: Low to High Tourism Intensity (IND_1), High Tourism Density (IND_2), Low to High Tourism Land Take (IND_3). Low values of Tourism Intensity characterise the densely populated regions, among which the urban tourism destinations. Very high values of the three indicators define the mass destinations.

Focus is on well developed destinations, main cities, small islands and coastal areas. Within type 1, two sub-types are distinguished: densely populated regions (including urban areas) and mass tourism destinations.

In the densely populated regions, the development of tourism does not cause environmental and social pressures. Tourism accommodations are generally spread around the major European cities and are of large size. Most of the densely populated areas in Europe are also the most visited regions. Main cities predominantly receive international tourists (with the exception of Madrid). They attract visitors for business purpose stays and because of the presence of a wide range of attractions (historical and cultural buildings and shops).

Island tourism and seaside tourism fall within the mass tourism destination sub-type. Island tourism is characterised by a high concentration of establishments and long journeys, usually by non-residents (national or foreign). Seaside tourism is characterised by a strong concentration of establishments and predominance of domestic tourism. Usually, tourism establishments are of relatively small size (less than 100 bed-places). The average length of stay is 3 days (more than for urban tourism and less than for islands). Competition exists within the sector (with other seaside areas) and between sectors (with other industrial activities). There is a wider spatial planning than for the seaside resorts.

Type 2: Traditional and new tourism destinations

Traditional and new tourism destinations, especially those located in far or formerly less accessible areas, grew to a point to attract a large number of tourists. These regions are under average tourism development pressures: Low to Medium Tourism

Intensity (IND_1), Low to Medium Tourism Density (IND_2), Low to Medium Tourism Land Take (IND_3).

Focus is on coastal and mountains areas, natural protected areas and rural areas. Mountain tourism is a highly seasonal activity, with the majority of overnight stays occurring during the winter season. Overall, it is characterised by low bed-places capacity of hotels. Overnight stays are relatively low. There is a dominance of domestic tourism, with the exception of the Alpine regions

Within this type, one sub-type 2.1 is distinguished: new destinations, found throughout the European Union. These regions with potential for further tourism development have Medium to High values of Tourism Intensity. Rural tourism destinations belong to this sub-type. Getting back to nature, development of alternative accommodations, nature or rural locations are the main attractions. This tourism form is characterised by average length of stay with predominance of domestic tourism notably nearby clienteles.

Type 3: Less visited regions

Less visited regions are characterised by Low Tourism Intensity (IND_1), Low Tourism Density (IND_2) and Low Tourism Land Take (IND_3). Focus is on less economically developed regions (rural areas, industrial converted regions and new Members States).

Table B.5 Summary of tourism types main features

	IND_1 Tourism Intensity	IND_2 Tourism Density	IND_3 Tourism Land Take
	Degree of importance of tourism	Degree of potential environmental pressures	Degree of potential conflicts with other activities
Type 1: Most visited regions	> 0 If IND_1 < 7, densely populated regions (sub type 1.2)	> 10 If IND_2 > 18 and IND_3 > 25, mass tourism destinations (sub type 1.1)	> 3 If IND_3 > 25 and IND_2 > 18, mass tourism destinations (sub type 1.1)
Type 2: Traditional and new tourism destinations	< 20 If IND_1 > 5, potential for further development of tourism (type 2.1)	< 10	< 72
Type 3: Less visited regions	< 5	< 5	< 9

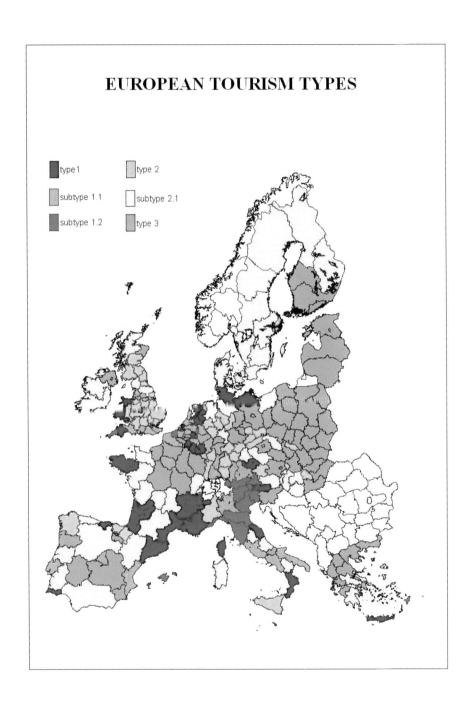

EUROPEAN TOURISM TYPES

type 1
type 2
subtype 1.1
subtype 2.1
subtype 1.2
type 3

4. Recommendations

1. A Community methodology on indicators and monitoring system for sustainable tourism based on low cost and reliable time series data should be developed, recognizing the need to balance the three dimensions of sustainable development: environment, economic, and social. A specific study on this issue should be carried out, to be coordinated and monitored by the existing group on tourism statistics within Eurostat.

2. The European Commission should reinforce its support to the diffusion and exchange of best practices on sustainable tourism development for tourism destination managers and businesses (in particular SMEs). Guidelines, indicators and tools, and useful methodological examples are needed to foster the concrete and operational implementation of sustainable tourism in the regions of destination. Attention should be paid to the creation of a network of pilot territories that are leaders in implementing a specific domain of sustainable tourism.

3. The cooperation between, on one hand, local and regional public authorities and, on the other hand, all the tourism stakeholders, including industry and representatives of the consumers, should be promoted further. Stronger collaboration is essential especially for spatial and territorial planning, strategic environmental assessment and environmental impact assessment. A discussion platform could be set up, chaired by the Committee of the Regions, or within the Sustainable European Regions Network.

4. Communication on the preparation of the Agenda 21 for European Tourism should be improved, internally, within the concerned Directorates General, and externally, with federations representing the various stakeholders of the tourism sector. Local public and private tourism managers and tourism small-sized suppliers shall be sufficiently represented within the EC Sustainable Tourism Group.

5. To ensure the follow-up and monitoring of the implementation of the Agenda 21 at local, regional and national levels, it is suggested to establish a "*Committee 21*" for European Sustainable Tourism. Its long-term activity

would maintain the consultation process among the representatives, allowing for further improvements and adaptations along the development of sustainability.

6.   Indicators and good practice exchanges are crucially lacking: a European Observatory on Sustainable Tourism, acting as a technical body of the *"Committee 21"*, could be in charge of collating and disseminating the necessary information. This observatory could also be part of a Network of Regions of Tourism Destinations.

Recommendations related to the tourism types identified under chapter 3 are reported under section C.

SECTION C:
SUSTAINABLE TOURISM AND TERRITORIAL COHESION

1.　Sustainable Tourism and Territorial Cohesion Policies

1.1　Concept and Rationale of Territorial Cohesion

The European Union is characterised by the spatial concentration of poles of economic development. It is widely recognised that capitalism and economic growth are concentrated on the 'most productive forces' of certain regions, creating unevenly distributed growth and regional economic disparities. Thus, the ambition to achieve economic convergence between the European regions and long term welfare, needs to be complemented by social cohesion policies, capable of addressing these imbalances among individuals, with a territorial dimension able to tackle the spatial disparities.

This political acknowledgment led to the introduction of the principle of 'Economic and Social Cohesion' in the Single European Act, where special emphasis is given to *'reducing disparities between the levels of development of the various regions and the backwardness of the least favoured regions or islands, including rural areas'*[76]. The Treaty establishing the Constitution for Europe goes one step beyond in the introduction of the territorial dimension as a third pillar of the cohesion concept to achieve the 'harmonious development'[77] of the Union as a whole.

Economic cohesion refers to the reduction of disparities between the levels of development of the regions. In order to assess economic convergence reference is made to GDP per capita.

Social cohesion targets unemployment, levels of education and demographic trends in the Union. In this respect, cohesion policies aim to reduce inequalities among Member States and regions in achieving economic cohesion, as well as inequalities among individuals in tackling social cohesion[78].

Territorial cohesion aims to contribute to the harmonious and balanced development of the EU by reducing economic and social disparities, by preventing territorial imbalances from emerging, and by making sectoral policies with a spatial impact more coherent with regional policy. Territorial cohesion also aims to improve

---

[76] Treaty establishing the European Community, 1957, art. 158
[77] Treaty establishing a Constitution for Europe, 2004
[78] Committee of the Regions, 2002 (b)

territorial integration and encourages co-operation between regions[79,80]. In practice, territorial cohesion implies that people should not be disadvantaged by virtue of where they happen to live or work.

The territorial dimension is an essential complement to the cohesion policies. The process of recognising this dimension as a policy objective has been addressed in the European Spatial Development Perspective (ESDP), whose definitive text was adopted in Postdam in 1999 by the informal Council of Ministers for spatial planning and regional policy. The European Commission's proposals for the Structural Funds 2007-2013 notably emphasises the convergence and integration of the lagging behind regions with the aim of contributing significantly to the promotion of territorial cohesion. This dimension has also been recognised in the European Constitution, where Article III-220 reads: '*In order to promote its overall harmonious development, the Union shall develop and pursue its action leading to the strengthening of its economic, social and territorial cohesion'. [...] 'Among the regions concerned, particular attention shall be paid to rural areas, areas affected by industrial transition, and areas which suffer from severe and permanent natural or demographical handicaps such as the northernmost regions with very low populated density, and island, cross-border and mountain areas'*.

The 3rd Cohesion Report highlights that in this territorial perspective all sectoral policies should join in a single strategy. New forms of mutual consultation and flexible co-ordination are to be introduced to facilitate the integration of policies. Regional policy cannot be an independent policy domain. Regional programmes need to be supported by relevant policy sectors, among which tourism, characterised by a strong territorial dimension. Despite the fact that this necessity is well acknowledged by policy-makers, various sectoral policies of the EU may still be working against the objective of territorial cohesion.

Coherence between regional policy and sectoral policies with a substantial territorial impact is also necessary for the territorial cohesion objective to be effective. Priority for coordination is in the areas of innovation (R&D, enterprise, information society), networking (transport, communication), training and competition. Competitiveness policies have a particular relevance in this context (reference is to paragraph 2.3 of

---

[79] Ireland's Presidency of the European Union, 2004
[80] European Commission, Directorate General for Regional Policy, 2004 (c)

this section). In the 3rd Cohesion Report, the Commission acknowledges that consistency between cohesion and competition policies is a key issue; contributors to the Third Cohesion Forum made the case that regions emerging from Objective 1 and facing a significant withdrawal of Structural Funds need to retain the capacity to promote investment. Adding the European Union sustainable development goal, an unduly restrictive state aid regime could exacerbate the problems of these regions. Negative economic, social and environmental consequences resulting from sectoral policies would then require enhanced regional policy response.

Notwithstanding these recent developments, the territorial dimension is still to become a top priority within the Community regional policy. The main instrument of the EU regional policy, the ERDF (European Regional Development Fund), for example, continues to follow an economic convergence logic that does not necessarily translate into a balanced distribution of economic activities[81].

The sustainable development of the tourism sector is fully in line with the cohesion objectives of a balanced development of the Union's territory. Tourism has the potential to allow for a more even distribution of economic activities and of employment opportunities over the Union's territory. The sustainable development goals applied to tourism activity will ensure its good management under fair economic and social conditions while contributing to environmental protection, including the preservation of the natural EU heritages.

This service sector is a peculiar one in the sense that it is not always driven by the 'most productive forces'. The tourism sector is usually considered as based on secondary educational skills and it generally requires relatively low investment costs. Moreover, it is not a centralized industry but a locally-based activity spread over the territory. As a consequence, the most varied people and regions can benefit from it, including the sparsely populated areas and regions with access difficulties. Regions with geographical handicaps (outermost regions and border regions) may have assets of biological importance or attractiveness that can lead to new opportunities or forms of development among which tourism.

---

[81] Committee of the Regions, 2002 (b)

1.2 The Dimension of Sustainable Tourism within Cohesion Policies

Tourism development, and especially sustainable tourism, is unique because it does not follow the same patterns of other economic activities. Firstly, since the tourism economy is largely a small business based industry, it allows a greater dissemination of the benefits through the economy and society, thus contributing to the convergence objective. Secondly, it creates a capillary request of labour force, both skilled and unskilled. Thirdly, it usually concentrates outside the major economic poles of development. The spatial and seasonal concentration of tourism activity requires special attention while developing Community policies. Thus, besides the three pillars of the cohesion policy, there are other dimensions of regional policy that are to be considered, in particular the ESDP, the principle of equal access to Services of General Economic Interest enshrined in the European Constitution, and the TENs programme.

1.2.1 Cohesion Policies and the European Spatial Development Perspective

The ESPD was adopted by the informal Council of Ministers for spatial planning and regional policy in Potsdam in 1999. Its formulation was based on the territorial cohesion and sustainable development concepts. The Ireland Presidency in its Discussion Paper on Territorial Cohesion of May 2004 stresses that: '*The ESDP aims to combat territorial disparities and achieve a more spatially balanced pattern of development by promoting polycentric urban development, a new relationship between urban and rural areas, equal access for all regions to infrastructure and know-how, and prudent management of natural and cultural heritage*'.

The ESDP is designed as a means for guiding and shaping territorial policies in support of economic growth, employment creation and sustainable development across the Union. The synthesis report of the ESDP transnational seminars, mentions that attention must be paid to the need for a polycentric and decentralised development path, enabling all regions to realise their economic potential while safeguarding their national and cultural heritage[82]. Sectoral industries and authorities,

---

[82] European Consultative Forum on Environment and Sustainable Development Secretariat, 1999

including tourism, shall be involved and bear clear responsibilities in territorial planning.

The ESDP provides the first comprehensive analysis of the EU from a territorial perspective, the use of a spatial framework for co-ordinating a wide spectrum of policies, and a trans-sectoral proactive approach to planning. Identified areas for improvement include social and cultural concerns, such as potential conflicts[83] and inequalities[84], and environmental concerns such as transport, Strategic Environmental Assessment and relevant indicators[85].

Sustainable tourism development may be supportive of improvements in spatial planning (importance of zoning at destinations level) and in transport development systems (friendly transport modes, better connecting infrastructures).

On the other hand, the sustainability of tourism may greatly benefit from an integrated planning. Uncontrolled tourism growth has already led to the damage of the environment of some mass destinations. Integrated spatial planning based on lessons learnt may:

- support the most visited regions and the traditional tourism regions in planning the development of main destination surroundings,
- provide new destinations and less visited regions willing to engage in tourism activities, with the tools for a fully integrated plan, in order to comply with economic, environmental and social expectations.

Early spatial planning should consider the territorial implications of tourism development in areas that have potentials for development, areas that would require protection or areas that would be, or remain, dedicated to other socio-economic objectives. In the latter case, conflicts could be avoided or overcome. Integrated

---

[83] Conflicts may arise on the use of the natural resources by other sectors than tourism, i.e. agriculture and domestic consumption for land and water; conflicts may also arise between local residents and tourists on improper behaviours, such as noise caused by specific attraction places (bars, discos), or delinquency.

[84] For instance, related to access to employment opportunities at destinations between foreigners and local residents, or inequalities arising from the increase of the basic prices of local products (food) and facilities, as well as houses and land so as they are no longer affordable to the local population.

[85] European Consultative Forum on Environment and Sustainable Development Secretariat, 1999

spatial planning would allow the prevention of non-sustainable patterns, as well as the occurrence of irreversible strategies, if promptly applied.

Spatial planning is a collective decision process that must encompass the stakeholders, representatives of various interests, especially within the local population. Such a planning process is the only way to avoid future conflicts and complaints. A strong ownership dimension in the planning of tourism activities is also a pre-requisite for the acceptance of tourism projects, and a guarantee that the local population will benefit from created tourism opportunities[86].

1.2.2 Sustainable Tourism and the Services of General Economic Interests

Equality of access to basic facilities, essential services and knowledge for everyone, wherever they live, is recognised as a key condition of territorial cohesion. The 'Services of General Economic Interest'[87] include water, electricity, postal, telecommunications and transport services. The Constitutional Treaty, which incorporates the Charter of Fundamental Rights of the Union, recognises this principle of equality of access. Article II-36 (Access to Services of General Economic Interest) states that *'The Union recognises and respects access to services of general economic interest .... in order to promote the social and territorial cohesion of the Union.' The Union and the Member States, each within their respective powers, are required to take care that such services operate on the basis of principles and conditions, in particular economic and financial, which enable them to fulfil their missions* [88].

Tourism creates economic and social benefits but also puts pressures on environmental resources, especially on water and sewage disposal facilities. These pressures are particularly relevant in islands or coastal resorts, in cities and during drought periods. The seasonal characteristic of tourism leads to a population concentration in a time that occurs mainly during summer. Coastal areas, small islands and mountainous areas, as well as sparsely populated areas are more affected, while the impact is not so significant on main cities and major tourism destinations where supply and water treatment systems are properly dimensioned. It is indeed evident that

---

[86] Sustainable European Regions Network, 2004
[87] European Commission, 2003 (b)
[88] Treaty establishing a Constitution for Europe, 2004

some situations may be exacerbated in those regions where the tourism sector is an important contributor to the regional economy, where tourism is highly seasonal and where natural resources are scarce. Another factor that may negatively influence collective access to these services is the liberalization of some services and the transfer of their management from public to private bodies.

The local increase of demand due to tourism is spatially related with recreational uses (swimming pools, golf courses, aquatic parks), introducing a competitive factor among different land uses, especially agriculture. Alternative options such as desalinisation and reuse of water are increasingly being developed in some coastal areas to guarantee a constant supply.

BOX C.1 Examples of pressure on water resources caused by tourism activities

- In Greece, water use for tourism activities, which averages 450 litres per day per tourist in deluxe hotels, is several times higher than average water use by residents, placing a strain on water resources. The popularity of golf courses and swimming pools is a major factor causing high water intensity of the tourism sector. Tourism's heavy water demand may lead to over pumping of groundwater and salt intrusion into underground water lenses on islands. Wastewater from hotels and other tourist establishments creates a large treatment burden; when treatment capacity is insufficient, wastewater is discharged untreated, degrading coastal water quality. In the 1980s Greece fell far behind in providing sanitary infrastructure to serve its tourism establishments. This problem has to a large extent been addressed during the 1990s with the support of EU funding and the construction of water treatment plants and sanitary landfills.
- Different measures to cope with peak water demand are in place in the Mediterranean area, from carrying water by tankers (as in the Aegean Islands) to the use of non-conventional resources as desalination plants, the re-use of treated wastewater for irrigation purposes, especially for golf fields (Spain, Malta and Cyprus), and the development of sanitation infrastructure supporting tourism facilities (Portugal, Spain). The introduction of water saving campaigns to raise tourist awareness, the promotion of 'alternative' tourism in order to spread demand in space and time, and the application of economic instruments are part of the measures taken by different Mediterranean countries to reduce pressure.
- In Portugal, bathing waters are mostly in good condition, but in groundwater aquifers both quality and quantity have decreased as tourism development has increased, especially in the Algarve. Golf courses, which have been embraced as a way of spreading tourism demand away from the peak months, affect water supply. So do hotels, which consume proportionally much more water than households. A national programme encourages use of recycled water for golf course irrigation.
- In Hungary, the growth of mass tourism, along with an inadequate infrastructure, has contributed to several environmental problems including poor water quality at Lake Balaton, the degradation of some important tourist regions (e.g. Lake Velence, Bükk Mountains), deterioration of landscapes with fragmentation of ecosystems and biodiversity loss.

Source: Organisation for Economic Cooperation and Development, Environmental Performance Reviews for Greece (2000), Hungary (2000), Portugal (2001).

The indicator of international tourist arrivals as a percentage increase over the total resident population indicates the potential increase in water use due to tourism. Tourism arrivals may double the population in some of the continental mainland countries, but in island destinations, where water resources from conventional sources may be limited or seasonal, the influx of visitors increases the local population by 200 to 300%. This increase is likely to produce a similar increase in total water demand, although peak demands will be much greater during the main tourist season, i.e. from May to September. Some examples of pressure on water resources caused by tourism activities are reported in Box C.1.

Among the most sensitive services, that may be negatively affected by the tourism industry, is water distribution. Besides competition in accessing the resource, some difficulties may be created in the management of the resource and in the costs for dimensioning the necessary infrastructure while maintaining a high quality level. Private operators may, in fact, not be willing to afford these extra-costs induced by the tourism activity in the regions of destination, especially where the difference between the low and high tourism seasons is very important. This statement also applies to the waste and wastewater treatment services.

The tourism sector is energy-intensive especially with regard to the energy consumption of sport and leisure infrastructures, hotels and restaurants. The seasonal character of the activity and its spatial concentration may cause serious levels of competition in terms of energy demand with other economic activities or with domestic consumption. However, the tourism industry has many opportunities to introduce more efficient energy systems and to rely on renewable energy sources (RES), such as solar thermal. There are several examples of initiatives aiming at promoting the use of renewable sources for energy production in the tourism sector or a more efficient use of energy, such as the Biosphere Hotels[89], the Renewable Energy and Sustainable Tourism project[90], the White Paper for Cyprus project[91], just to mention a few.

With regard to transport, local and regional transport service needs for tourists and residents differ widely, in terms of density, intensity and schedule. According to the type of destinations, conflicts among tourists and residents may arise (for example, in terms of traffic congestion and parking availability in the mass tourism destinations), but residents may also benefit from the presence of tourists in their territory, through,

---

[89] Biosphere Hotel web site:
http://europa.eu.int/comm/energy/en/renewable/idae_site/deploy/prj045/prj045_1.html
[90] REST web site: http://www.energie-cites.org/rest/
[91] White Paper for Cyprus web site: http://www.erec-renewables.org/projects/proj_Cyprus.htm

for example, more frequent connections during the tourist season. The private sector plays an important role in responding to the highly flexible transport demand generated by tourism; however, the public sector and the local authorities have the opportunity to develop specific transport systems for tourists targeting sustainable behaviours such as the use of electric cars or buses, and bicycles.

As for the new ICTs, their use and access constitute a crucial issue as they play a major role in the commercialisation of tourism products. Electronic communication forms offer significant opportunities for less developed regions to build up their tourism sector but also for SMEs to enter a market which is mainly controlled by few major operators. In this context, tourism will be sustainable if access is facilitated. Policy measures to enhance e-business development should be primarily addressed towards SMEs, to improve necessary skills, and to create tailored ICT solutions.[92]

1.2.3   The Trans-European Networks

'The development of the TEN for transport, telecommunications and energy is part of the Community's general strategy for cohesion, aimed at harmonious planning and development across the Union. The objective of the trans-European networks (TENs) is to connect national infrastructures in a coherent manner and to ensure continuity of services between island, landlocked and peripheral regions and central regions, with aid in particular from the Cohesion Fund. The TENs programmes, including that for transport, aim to restructure and integrate the European space, transforming a patchwork of national networks into a pan-European system by developing links, nodes and corridors of European significance[93].'

Overall, the TENs are expected to efficiently connect the main economic centres and enhance European competitiveness. However, the 2nd Cohesion Report points out that the trans-European networks may not reduce but widen the differences in accessibility, and consequently also in economic opportunity, between central and peripheral regions of Europe. Planning shall follow the principles of sustainable development and take into account the dimension of regional transport.

The implementation of the TEN-Transport may have a significant impact on

---

[92] E-business W@tch, 2005
[93] Ireland's Presidency of the European Union, 2004

biodiversity, with the fragmentation of natural habitats by main transport roads, and on cultural heritage. It is therefore important to mitigate these effects and ensure the maintenance and the restoration of regional landscapes for environmental purposes, as well as for sustainable tourism development opportunities. Tourism cannot develop along the main EU roads unless natural and cultural heritages are preserved. Co-ordination of actions by local authorities and projects arising from the implementation of programmes such as LEADER +, INTERREG and LIFE is of crucial importance.

Low-cost carriers are fully in line with the EC policy for regional development. They contribute significantly to the development of the network of inter-regional air traffic with point to point connections. Besides reducing the transit via airport hubs, they contribute increasing inter-modality, reducing air congestion, improving air safety and limiting air pollution around capitals. Traditional national aviation operators and low-costs carriers generally differ in destinations as well as in passenger profiles. They may also contribute to a better distribution of tourism in Europe, and, in turn, to the reduction of mass tourism in specific areas, as well as to the mitigation of isolation of peripheral regions[94,95].

The development of tourism highly depends on accessibility and mobility within the concerned region. As the sustainability of a destination is critically linked to the preservation of its environment, spatial planning of transport is central to any sustainable tourism strategy. Although tourism travel is often considered an exclusive competence of the regions of destination, in fact, it encompasses a broader dimension affecting the whole transport system. Thus, effective transport planning has to acknowledge this comprehensiveness of tourism travel by fostering interaction and cooperation between national, regional and inter-regional levels.

The shift from an extensive use of private cars for tourism purposes to public transport modes should be made more attractive by means of increased quality and competitive prices. Private and public partnerships are of importance in this area. A higher level of cooperation between the tourism industry, transport service providers and responsible public authorities in the regions of destination is also required[96]. For this purpose, the principles of the European Charter of regional and local authorities for a progressive

[94] Assembly of European Regions, 2003
[95] Assembly of European Regions, 2004
[96] Committee of the Regions, 2001

and sustainable transport policy[97], adopted by the CoR, should be endorsed and implemented by the EU institutions and Member States.

1.2.3.1   The impact of tourism on transport

Because <u>there is no tourism without transport</u>, tourism heavily impacts on the environment through transport systems. Tourism is driving the growing demand for passenger transport and consequently contributes to air pollution and climate change, in addition to congestion and to the fragmentation of natural habitats through construction of transport infrastructures. Moreover, tourists use the most polluting transport modes (i.e. car and airplane) for travelling to and from destinations that are often, by their nature, of high environmental value. Since the number of tourist journeys per person and per year is increasing in several countries, the polluting effect from tourism transport is likely to grow exponentially. This trend is reinforced by the global concentration of tourism activities around major destination poles that augments the intensity of tourism traffic.

Such a negative impact threatens local and regional environmental sustainability and cultural heritage, and often reduces the quality of life of both visitors and residents. For the most visited regions, and in particular for those economically less developed, this impact may in the long term undermine their economic viability and vitality. All these developments inevitably work against sustainable growth.

The *seasonal saturation of transport infrastructures* often leads to the decision of supplying more infrastructures and services, enlarging roads, or building new motorways and airports. Some sub-regional rails of the British rail network are already running at 90 % of their capacity and most routes out of London will reach the same level by 2011[98]. There are similar developments in many European countries and in relation to all transport systems. Routes of strategic importance for tourism need to be re-assessed if the growth of tourism is expected to continue in the next 10-20 years[99].

---

[97] Committee of the Regions, 1998
[98] English Tourism Council, 2001
[99] European Environment Agency, 2003

At destination, transport problems are also highly evident. Noise, exhaust fumes, and poor traffic safety impair the environment quality of many tourist destinations. The transport system for tourism is often inadequate, as is the case of the Alps. Some mass tourism destinations have already reached their carrying capacity.

The current transport system access to mass tourism destinations does not encourage the use of less-environmentally damaging modes (Figure C.1). Innovations in tourism transport systems to reach destinations follow a slow development. Some provisions are made to set up local and public means of transport within destinations, but these are not sufficient to shift the dominant use of car by tourists.

Figure C.1 Mode of transport by trip, domestic and international tourism

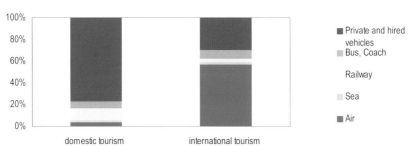

Declaring Countries: DE, DK, ES, FI, FR, IT, LU, PT, UK. Reference year: 2000   Source: based on data from Eurostat

It is necessary to develop public transport in general and rail transport in particular, and to promote tourism based on these transport modes. More tourists would travel by train if attractive offers were available[100]. Balancing the transport modal split in the tourism sector, would make a real difference for carbon dioxide emissions, road congestion, habitats loss from road and airports construction, and other transport-driven environmental impacts. Implementing inter-modality (direct connections, in particular between airports and train stations) for regional transport is crucial for the sustainable development of tourism.

Not concentrating holidays over specific periods would help reduce traffic congestion and related environmental problems. Economic instruments such as price differentiation, on the basis of transport mode used and period of use, may be

---

[100] United Nations Environment Programme, 2001

supportive. In France, for example, the Government has decided to test and implement a differentiation price system for the tollgate payment of the main roads. The system aims to discourage travels during rush hours and peak periods (from Friday evenings until Sunday evenings and during days of major departures and returns from school holidays) in order to reduce congestion.

Finally, there is a need to promote soft mobility tourism travel. Developing new tourism-transport alternatives to the use of the car at destination (that encourages the construction of car parks and increase traffic-jams), setting up efficient baggage handling systems, improving train capacity and security to stock luggage, allowing personal car transport over the train, providing sufficient taxi or public connections at the train stations, developing soft mobility roads such as green cycling roads, are all actions to be tackled to promote a sustainable development pattern. An example is reported in BP_3: sustainable mobility in Austria. To set up these alternatives it is necessary to gain a better knowledge of tourists' needs, and establish an effective cooperation between private and public transport operators and collaborative marketing strategies along the whole chain of tourism transport.

BOX C.2	Estimates on pollution from tourism transport

Energy use for holiday transport in EU 15 is estimated at 11% of the overall energy consumption of transport (including freight) and at 50% of the total passenger transport.

In Sweden, in 1994 energy use by holiday transport represented around 14-18% of all energy use for personal transport; holiday travelling accounted for approximately 15% of overall mobility in 1994 (excluding visits to second homes, visits to family and friends), while air transport accounted for 64% of both energy use and CO2 emissions from Swedish holiday travels[101]. In France, it is estimated that tourism transport is responsible for 5-7% of all greenhouse gas emissions. A journey from Paris to Nice, considered as a main 'holiday road', by a family travelling by plane will contribute 5 times more to global warming than by diesel train, and 2 to 4 times more than by car. When only one person is travelling, the plane seems to be better than the car, while train remains the least polluting mode in all cases[102].

---

[101] Organisation for Economic Co-operation and Development, 2000
[102] Rechatin C., Dubois G., Pelletreau A., 2000

The "Soft mobility – Car Free Tourism" is a 5 year project started in 1998. The project was initiated by the municipalities of Bad Hofgastein and Werfenweng, Austria, with the support of the Federal and Provincial Authorities (Government of Salzburg) and of the European Union. With 8.000 bed places and approximately 1 million of overnights per year, Bad Hofgastein, located in the Gasteiner Valley 850 m a.s.l., is among Austria's ten most tourism-intensive destinations.

The project aims at the multi-sectoral implementation of policy objectives outlined in several national (Austrian National Environmental Plan, Austrian Transport Concept, Transport Plan of Salzburg), and trans-national programmes (Community Action Programmes, Alpine Convention). Its objectives include:

- city centres free of motorised traffic, limited access to border zones, consideration of these goals in the city spatial planning (pedestrian and cyclists friendly areas, motorized traffic restricted, restructuring of parking space, car-sharing), adaptation of legal framework;
- car free journey to tourist resorts by train and bus and user-friendly logistics for luggage and shuttle services by bus and taxi;
- establishment of a mobility service center (car-sharing, rent-a-zero-emission vehicle, public transport information, tourist and travel information, travel demand management);
- promotion through incentives of the replacement of combustion-engine driven vehicles by zero-emission vehicles (or ultra-low-emission vehicles) and substitution of the diesel city-buses by zero-emission or ultra-low-emission buses;

Key issues:

⇨ Sustainable and environmentally friendly mobility in tourism.

⇨ Multi-sectoral implementation of policy objectives in the field of environment, transport, tourism and technology aiming at the improvement of living and environmental quality standards for residents and tourists.

⇨ Encouragement of public-private partnerships with transport and vehicle industry, public transport operators, tourism and travel agencies and logistics providers.

- optimization and integration of travel-information and traffic management systems for cars and lorries, linking public transport information, tourist information and booking systems.

The number of visitors of Werfenweng arriving during winter by train increased from 16% (1997/98) to 25% (2000/01). In the same period tourists arriving by car declined from 78% to 66%, with an overall reduction of 375 tons of carbon dioxide per year. The replacement of about 100 vehicles with internal combustion engines by electric vehicles led to a general reduction in pollution and noise. Werfenweng was awarded the NETS AWARD for Innovative holiday trips by train 2004/2005.

Links & references:

UNEP Industry and Environment, 2001. Tourism Focus N°13, January – June 2001
http://www.uneptie.org/pc/tourism/documents/newsletters/tourism13.pdf

SMILE project – Local experiences database:
http://www.smile-europe.org/locxpdb/front/show.php?lang=en&lxp_id=120

First Aid Convention in Europe 2004, http://www.face2004.org/transport.htm

The number of green routes in France is increasing. A national scheme for *'véloroutes'* and *'voies vertes'* has been developed as an inter-ministerial project aiming at facilitating travels with non polluting transport modes. The *véloroutes* (cycling roads) are itineraries for cyclists on roads of particular interest, linking regions and allowing safe crossing of urban agglomerations. The *voies vertes* (green tracks) are specific infrastructures developed in natural sites, and exclusively dedicated to non-motorised transport users such as walkers, cyclists, rollers and riders. Cycling roads imply smaller investments (service areas and road signs) than green tracks (land acquisition, services areas, road signs, security and landscapes planning) and return from investment is faster. The Green Avenue in Seine-Maritime, for example had a cost of 10.5 m€ for 70 km. It attracts around 100 000 tourist overnights per year, with a daily average expense per tourist of 60€, generating a turnover of 6 m€.

The success of a green route depends on how stakeholders are organised, as well as on their share of responsibilities in coordinating, building and commercializing the tourism products. Key

Key issues:

⇨ Coordinated strategy at national level to support regional development and economic value through sustainable tourism.

⇨ Partnership between private and public entities.

⇨ Specific target to develop a high quality soft mobility in natural environments, with the aim to promote regional territories and natural/cultural heritages.

steps include (i) strategy definition, (ii) realisation of a complete product (iii) quality of the offer.

New expectations for nature-based sports and leisure activities create opportunities for the development of local economies, the improvement of living conditions and the promotion of heritage. Local authorities and other tourism stakeholders seek to develop appropriate services to satisfy both residents and tourists. Another example, usually commercialised by the tour-operators, is the *'Loire à vélo'*, a sustainable tourism initiative based on the historic patrimony of the middle-age castles along the Loire river.

Links & references:

Association française pour le développement des véloroutes et voies vertes (AF3V) web site: http://www.af3v.org

Brochure *'Véloroutes et voies vertes'* : http://www.ecologie.gouv.fr

Communication from Sébastien Baholet, Direction of Tourism: sebastien.baholet@tourisme.gouv.fr

2.   Sustainable Tourism as a factor of Territorial Cohesion

Sustainable tourism has great potential to support or even drive the convergence process among regions, through competitiveness and territorial co-operation. Tourism can contribute to the creation of a Europe of Citizens, a Europe in which people learn to know each other and to understand and respect their diversity, in line with the philosophy *'se connaître pour se comprendre'*. The most acknowledged important goal for Europe is not to bring states together but to bring people together[103]. And tourism, travelling either within countries or outside national borders in the EU, is indeed a powerful way to get closer.

Among the economic activities, tourism is probably the only one that can reinforce the feeling of belonging to the same, while diverse European culture, and thus European citizenship.

Sustainability goals for tourism mean[104]:

- promote the protection of the environment and of sustainable development in general;
- re-think the place of tourism in the regional economy through devising specific strategic objectives and implementation means;
- improve the co-operation between regions and Member States on a territorial basis, by contributing to increase the convergence and cohesion of the regions within the Union;
- improve collaboration between the various actors involved in tourism at all governance levels, notably through the dissemination of partnerships among public authorities and between public and private actors, allowing a greater social responsibility and raising producers and consumers awareness on sustainability (Section D);
- support the initiatives that act towards an operational implementation of sustainable tourism through adequate funding, including the contribution of

---

[103] Committee of the Regions, 2002 (a)

[104] These views were supported by the EU Working Group D on the protection of the environment and sustainable development for tourism, in its final report of June 2001. This report outlines issues, principles, strategic objectives and recommendation for actions at all levels of governance.

tourism to finance the protection of natural and cultural European heritages (Section E).

It is essential to develop the basis to create a model European 'ecoregion' in terms of tourism development. The tourism supply has to be better organised and more oriented on quality services and products that respect both people (employees, local population and tourists) and the environment. Because tourism is a sector driven mainly by the demand, motivations and behaviours of citizens play a major role. Consumer awareness regarding sustainability in tourism must be raised, to orient visitor flows to prevent concentration in time and in space, and to reinforce the power of attraction of Europe through promoting the image of a global sustainable destination. Indeed, the tourism industry contributes positively to overall regional economic development. It increases the demand for environmental infrastructures and leads to greater awareness of the rich heritage of various civilisations.

For the tourism industry the preservation of the environment is a necessity because this means protecting its main assets, i.e. the attractiveness of destinations. In a context where European citizens ask for high quality products and services more frequently, and for a clean environment, the tourism sector has to prevent environmental damage by learning lessons from past experiences.

But tourism may also benefit greatly from the improved territorial cohesion of the regions. The saturation of certain destinations may, for example, be reduced by the spreading of tourism activity.

The mass destination regions (sub-type 1.2) are in coastal, island and mountain zones; they are the most prone to reaching their carrying capacity because of the fragile nature of their ecosystems. As the rhythm of tourism growth is globally increasing, on average by 3.8% a year in the EU, the trend towards degradation is likely to continue unless appropriate measures are taken. The other feature of tourism is its seasonality, causing high concentrations along relatively short periods of time and creating some important pressures on the environment, the natural resources and the population (competition for services, for example water availability, between residents and tourists) as well as congestion of the main roads and increase in traffic and pollution.

A better distribution of tourism activity in Europe, between the most and the less-visited regions, would help mitigate these pressures and provide significant benefits to the economies of some less-developed regions. The new beneficiaries could be either the inland of the mass destination regions or the outermost regions. Obviously, in the first case, the existence of the necessary infrastructures, as well as specific regional tourism marketing strategies aimed at promoting border regions or territories, would be a pre-condition. For the outermost regions with natural assets, the main preconditions would be reasonable access through improved transport systems and the capacity to offer quality tourism. For instance, tourists could be encouraged to go skiing to the northern mountains of Romania, where costs are lower and thus more attractive, rather than to the Alps. This would make certain areas of Romania, destinations with potential development. However, it is recognised that this type of shifting of pressure from mass destinations to new growing destinations (sub-type 2.1) requires the creation of adequate infrastructure and human resources.

Most of the less-visited regions also have structural problems; they are mostly included under Objectives 1 and 2 regions to facilitate their social and economic cohesion. Tourism may become a mean for the development of some of these regions, probably excluding those under Objective 2 undergoing an industrial conversion. Tourism can reinvigorate rural areas, creating employment and supplementary revenues through the development of nature-based activities and increased value of traditional products through a polycentric development addressing revitalisation and/or diversification measures. Regarding the peripheral regions, the development of new tourism destinations could support a more balanced distribution of economic activities. This is particularly true in several regions of the new Member States which have great potential for tourism development in terms of environmental resource. In this sense, exchanges of best practices and lessons from the past (bad practices) become the most urgent actions to develop.

All these opportunities, however, need a political acceptance of the major potential of tourism sustainability. Moreover, the engaged process towards new governance forms in the enlarged European Union, and in accordance with the subsidiarity principle, makes public authorities become more dependent on strategic interactions with other local and regional authorities, notably for creating the necessary synergies required to implement sustainable tourism strategies. As tourism is primarily a locally based activity, local authorities become an essential part of the European 'multi-level governance model' and need to strengthen their territorial co-operation. The traditional model of regional development (previously state-driven) is now being increasingly replaced by region-specific economic development strategies, designed and implemented by regional and local institutions to suit local conditions. Policies are grounded in the particular strengths and weaknesses of individual regions and built around target sectors, among which tourism or industrial clusters. The Study Group for European Policies (SEP/GEPE) has recommended in its 2002 report on Territorial Cohesion that sectoral policies should be adapted to the regions[105].

2.1   Co-operation with Border Regions and Sustainable Tourism

Cross-border, inter-territorial and trans-national co-operation strives to achieve integration and to limit the economic and social fragmentation brought about by national frontiers. The Commission states that *cross-border, inter-territorial and trans-national co-operation occur ...when all the parties involved stand to gain advantages in the administrative, social, economic, cultural, infrastructural or technological fields. Lasting co-operation therefore has a chance of success only if it has a popular basis and if co-operation takes place between all the parties involved*.[106]

Sustainable tourism development fully matches these principles. Tourism and travelling are mainly determined by the natural geographical features of the territory; tourism within the EU is facilitated by the freedom of movement of people, goods and services. However, as long as country borders remain, politically and administratively, outside the gradual growing Schengen area, the cross-border co-operation is of strategic importance for both sustainable development and tourism.

Since 1990, the Association of European Border Regions (AEBR) and the European Commission have worked together within the LACE (Linkage, Assistance and Co-operation for the European Border Regions) project. The new 2000-2006 cross-border cooperation programme financed under INTERREG IIIA contains specific targets among which tourism and leisure. The principles of the programme are in line with the principles of sustainable development and foster vertical and horizontal

---

[105] Committee of the Regions, 2002 (b)
[106] Committee of the Regions, 2002 (a)

partnerships and subsidiarity (involving the regional and local levels and delegating effective responsibility to them)[107].

Cross-border cooperation between the former EU border regions can help the less advanced regions to benefit from good practices and facilitate the development of sustainable tourism regional strategies. Trans-border networks can support such a process. European regions that are sparsely populated and suffer from the lack of economies of scale can also benefit from trans-national co-operation.

The Third Cohesion report has recommended that co-operation would need to focus on strategic priorities with a trans-national character such as R&D, information society, tourism, culture, employment, business and the environment. Since institutional structures to facilitate co-operation between states already exist, regional authorities should pursue the reinforcement of their collaboration with them.

There are several good examples of regional co-operation, among which the one developed in the Baltic region. The Baltic region is characterised by contrasting economic and social landscapes. There is a great biodiversity that must be protected, as well as economic and social imbalances that cause specific problems in under-populated areas. The INTERREG IIIB programme supports trans-national co-operation projects in thirteen identified zones belonging to eleven countries. Its aim is to promote concerted approaches to spatial planning and sustainable development focusing on specific areas such as coastal, islands and rivers[108]. The co-ordination between different sectors is also fostered. Trans-national commercial networks have been developed between small and medium-sized towns within the regions, involving SMEs or tourist centres. An important achievement is the Agenda 21 for the Baltic Sea Region, elaborated in 1998 within the framework of the Council of the Baltic Sea States, including the European Union. The Agenda 21 for the Baltic Sea region – 'Baltic 21' – focuses, among other policy areas, on tourism. It targets to enforce the legislation regarding sustainable tourism development, e.g. coastal codes and HELCOM recommendations, spatial planning and land use, as well as to promote the adoption by tourism industry of EMS and monitoring tools.

---

[107] Association of European Border Regions, 2000
[108] European Commission, Directorate General for Regional Policy, 2002

Another example of regional co-operation is found in the Alpine regions, institutionalised within the Alpine Convention, adopted in 1991 and signed by the concerned states (France, Italy and Switzerland) and the European Union. Among others goals, this treaty aims to bring tourism and recreational activities in the Alps in line with ecological and social requirements in particular by setting up zones of restricted activities. Later, it has been added a specific Protocol on Tourism and Recreational Activities specifically supporting tourism sustainability.

2.2   Outermost Regions and Regions with Natural Handicaps

The 3rd Cohesion Report defines the outermost regions as regions that are characterised by the permanence and combination of a series of handicaps; these regions share severe social and economic problems that are difficult to tackle because of the areas' remoteness, isolation, topological features, climate, small size of market and dependence on a small number of products, as recognised in Article 299(2) of the EC Treaty.

Regions with natural handicaps are those suffering from geographical constraints and developing regions such as rural regions or regions under industrial decline. It is recognised that there are insufficient external economies in all peripheral regions, either border regions or outermost regions.

The seven outermost regions – the Azores, Madeira, the Canary Islands and the four French overseas departments[109]– are full members of the European Union but are in a unique and special situation, quite different to that of other regions within the Community. These regions are among the poorest of the EU.

The priorities acknowledged by the European Commission for these regions include the Common Transport Policy, the Trans-European Transport Networks and the Trans-European Energy Networks, as well as the information society and technological innovations[110]. However, there is still no suitable framework for the outermost regions and no overall and coherent policy for their sustainable development, although requested by the Seville European Council of June 2002.

---

[109] Guadeloupe, Martinique, French Guyana, and Réunion
[110] European Commission, 2004 (b)

The Committee of the Regions has specified that '*many of the opportunities for growth, diversification and increased productivity available to the outermost regions centre on a few traditional sectors which present real comparative advantages, on tourism, and on seeking other alternative forms of production. It therefore believes that an effective strategy for modernisation, innovation and development in the outermost regions must take account of these activities*'[111].

For all these regions (with the exception of the Azores and French Guyana), the tourism sector is a major source of revenues. Apart from the primary sector, tourism seems to be the only economic activity that can boost their development. Sustainable tourism can foster economic growth, employment (rates of unemployment are among the highest in the EU), and preservation of the natural assets. Specific, required actions include:

- modernisation and 'greening' of tourism infrastructures, accommodations and leisure activity facilities;
- improvement in quality of tourism services and products delivered;
- training and skill enhancement in the tourism sector.

Specific to these regions is the Terra programme, a Community Initiative targeting those areas of the EU whose territorial features make them fragile but with the opportunity to develop an integrated strategy for the territory. The Terra programme encourages local and regional authorities to view the problems affecting their regions in a more European context enabling knowledge to be pooled and exchanged and common solutions to be found through co-operation. The Terra programme includes transport and tourism related measures.

Potentials for tourism development include rural tourism, agro-tourism, eco-tourism, cultural tourism, and tourism activities based on nature (sports and leisure). However, there are two main types of risks for these regions: economic dependency and threats to the environment.

Economic dependency makes a region having an unbalanced economy without other sectors able to properly sustain economic growth more vulnerable. Nature, as one of the main tourism attraction, may represent a concrete richness for peripheral regions

---

[111] Committee of the Regions, 2004 (d)

and their economy, but its uncontrolled use may easily cause several threats, including the loss of biodiversity. Specific codes of conduct as well as comprehensive monitoring systems are necessary, especially in the context of sustainable tourism planning.

National Parks are also increasingly affected by tourist activities; specific projects to protect these sensitive areas need to be established to prevent potential threats to the environment from tourism development. Several examples of ongoing initiatives are available to this regard, some of which have been highlighted in Box C.3.

BOX C.3 Examples of tourism potentials and impacts in protected and natural areas	
German Initiatives Towards Sustainable Tourism. Germany.	http://www.biodiv.org/doc/case-studies/tour/cs-tour-de-sustour.pdf
National Programme for Tourism in Nature; Wetlands in Portugal.	http://www.biodiv.org/doc/case-studies/tour/cs-tour-pt-coop.pdf
Tourism potentials and impacts in protected mountain areas: Pol'ana protected landscape area –Biosphere Reserve, Slovakia.	http://www.biodiv.org/doc/case-studies/tour/cs-tour-polana-sk-en.pdf
Tourism potentials and impacts in protected mountain areas, Sumava Biosphere Reserve, Czech Republic.	http://www.biodiv.org/doc/case-studies/tour/cs-tour-sumava-cz-en.pdf
Tourism potentials and impacts in protected mountain areas, Aggtelek National Park, Hungary.	http://www.biodiv.org/doc/case-studies/tour/cs-tour-agtellek-hu-en.pdf
Tourism and its impact on biodiversity: case study of Babia Góra National ParkPark/Biosphere Reserve, Poland.	http://www.biodiv.org/doc/case-studies/tour/cs-tour-babia-gora-pl.pdf

2.3   Sustainable Tourism and the Lisbon Strategy

The Lisbon Strategy sets the EU intention to move towards making Europe the world's most competitive knowledge-based economy. The Commission believes that the thematic priorities for the Lisbon objective that are Regional Competitiveness and Employment, address important determinants of territorial cohesion. It is expected that Member States and regions will have more flexibility to address territorial priorities.

The environmental dimension of the sustainable territorial development and the potential contribution of environmental factors to the competitiveness of territories are of great importance for tourism and its future development along the path of sustainability. This makes sustainable tourism of strategic importance to match the Union objectives.

Cultural routes and sustainable tourism in Europe

CS_3

The Cultural Routes programme was launched in 1987 by the Council of Europe. Resolution 98(4) was adopted in 1998 by 48 countries: development of initiatives and innovative projects in the field of cultural tourism and sustainable cultural development is a priority action.

The programme intended to demonstrate how the heritage of the different countries of Europe represented a shared cultural value. The Cultural Routes also provides a demonstration of the fundamental principles of the Council, namely: human rights, cultural democracy, European cultural diversity and identity, dialogue, mutual exchange and enrichment across boundaries and centuries. Specific aims of the programme are:

- awareness raising of a European cultural identity and citizenship;
- promotion of intercultural and inter-religious dialogue through a better understanding of European history;
- safeguard and enhancement of the cultural and natural heritage as a means for improving the quality of life and as a source of social, economic and cultural development;
- promotion of cultural tourism, with a view to sustainable development.

Key issues:

⇨ Cultural tourism as a factor of cohesion among European regions.

⇨ International framework for the development of initiatives and projects in the field of cultural tourism and sustainable cultural development.

Among the thematic routes of the programme are: the Pilgrim Pathways; Rural Habitat - Architecture without borders; Silk and Textile Routes; the Baroque Routes; the Monastic Influence Routes; the Celts Routes; Mozart Route; Schickhardt itineraries; Vikings and Normands; the Northern Lights route.

Recognising the importance of tourism in the economies of most European countries but also the potential damage it may bring to the most valuable sites, a conference on « Cultural Tourism - The Challenge of European Integration » was held in Luxembourg in April 2005. The workshop focused on how to encourage a responsible but viable tourism industry, more specifically on tools allowing for better management and governance of cultural tourism, quality assurance criteria and the influence of new technologies on the sector.

Links & references:

http://www.culture-routes.lu/: European Institute of Cultural Routes, Luxembourg

http://www.coe.int/T/E/Cultural_Co-operation/Culture/Action/Tourism/: the Europe of cultural cooperation, Council of Europe

http://eur-heritage.org/Evenements/05042202.htm: Cultural Tourism - The Challenge of European Integration, Conference, 21-22 April 2005, Luxembourg

The primary objective to promote competitiveness of European industry, within a knowledge-based economy, has to take into account important issues, such as:

- incentives for R&D, innovation and business creation;
- access to fair competition, use of new ICTs and CSR, within the economic policy dimension;
- special needs of SMEs;
- employment and high quality of education and training, within the social policy dimension;
- the environmental dimension, including the 6th EAP, the White Paper on Transport, biodiversity conservation, efficient use of resources, and the Integrated Product Policy (IPP).

Apart from the political intention, globalisation and the concentration of the tourism industry under the control of a few dominant suppliers, create anti-competitive behaviours. In this context, it can be difficult for the smaller operators to benefit from the potential of tourism development at regional level. Competition issues and anti-competitive behaviours are at the core of the problems regarding efficiency, viability and sustainability of tourism.

In this context, it is essential to: enhance the capacity of tourism destinations by intensifying the production of goods and services in accordance to sustainable tourism principles; provide incentives to reinvest tourism profits; increase the participation of domestic investors in the tourism industry; and enforce the domestic competition policy against the anti-competitive practices of the tour-operators.

The following actions are necessary to make European tourism more sustainable, more responsible, aware of the triple bottom line imperatives - social, economical and environmental -, and, finally, more competitive:

- development of market-based and voluntary approaches, including eco-taxation/differentiation;
- take up of a catalyst role by policy makers at all levels, to foster the dialogue with the industry and other stakeholders;

- balanced inclusion, in designed policies, of the three dimensions of sustainable development, to be achieved through dialogue and cooperation among the representatives of each policy dimension and an integrated approach;
- development of specialist information networks for sustainable tourism and provision of technical capacity and technological means to manage and operate such networks efficiently;
- promotion and coordination of exchange of experiences and know-how, especially among regions with similar features;
- ICTs support to micro and SMEs.

In this context, special attention should be paid to the current World Trade Organisation GATS negotiations that work for a further liberalisation of tourism services, particularly with regard to market access issues and fair business practices.

2.4 General Measures for Harmonisation to foster Sustainable Tourism Development and Regional Cohesion

The European Community must have a genuine European strategy for the sustainable development of tourism. It is time to make a real political commitment in recognising the importance of tourism not only as a service sector but also as a contributor to sustainable economic growth, without underestimating all possible positive and negative impacts. There is the need for the Agenda 21 for Tourism in Europe to be available soon.

It is also important to ensure the integration of sustainable development goals in all Community measures that impact on tourism, as well as the participation of tourism to all those programmes that strengthen the cohesion of the Union within the regions.

Indicators and monitoring systems should be developed, in line with existing sets of indicators at Community level, namely the EEA core-set of indicators for the environmental dimension and the structural indicators for the economic and social dimensions. Tourism indicators have also been developed within WTO and OECD; they can serve as a basis with which to develop a consistent set of sustainable indicators adapted to the European objectives. The indicators development and the associated monitoring system should be linked to ESPON and the INSPIRE

(Infrastructure for spatial information in Europe) framework, in relation with the GMES (Global monitoring of environment and security).

Local authorities should assess the financial and administrative costs occurring because of tourism in the preservation of the European heritages, in order to make sure that tourists share the burden of this cost. This is particularly important in mass tourism destinations and new tourism destinations.

Economic instruments such as environmental taxation are important tools in the field of tourism. In broad terms, visitors pay direct and indirect taxes, notably through the Value Added Tax system on tourism products and services. In general, the revenues are not channelled back to environmental actions such as restoration of walking paths or cleaning of beaches that are left to local municipalities or non-profit associations.

Popular tourism destinations can receive a special subvention from the central governments to manage infrastructures for tourism development but not for sustainability, as it is the case in France. The regional government of the Balearic Islands in Spain established an eco-tax on hotel stay in May 2002, the first of its kind specifically addressed to tourism; however, such tax was cancelled shortly after (September 2003). In France, there is a tax for passenger transport to small islands.

Several surveys confirmed the potential economic benefits from sustainable tourism management as a gain of market-share for the industry. In a 2002 UK survey, over 80% of the UK residents said that they would choose an attraction or accommodation provided that it was part of a green accreditation scheme[112]. For most people (83%), the quality is an important feature compared to the price (74%). The majority of consumers would be willing to pay higher prices to tourism businesses that had been awarded, showing the substantial desire of consumers for businesses to adopt sustainable tourism practices. 45% of consumers would be willing to pay an extra 5%, and 25% to pay an extra 10% or more to stay in such accommodation. Two-thirds of those interviewed would even be willing to make a contribution for the up-keep of the local environment whilst on holiday. Some natural parks in the UK have already taken this opportunity by setting-up the visitor-payback system scheme where visitors make a free donation while visiting environmentally sensitive destinations.

---

[112] English Tourism Council, 2002

The Väinameri region in western Estonia is an important biological and multi-functional area in the Baltic Sea and coastal zone management plans were prepared by the Helsinki Commission. Since 1997, the Väinameri project has been carried out by a large network of partners in Estonia and in Sweden with WWF and SIDA as main donors. This model project proposes rural development as a tool for sustainable management of semi-natural grasslands to re-boost a very vulnerable post-Soviet agriculture and preserve valuable degraded ecosystems. At the same time, small scale economic activities such as tourism, handicrafts, bio-energy and fisheries were developed to generate income, create jobs and maintain cultural and local socio-economic values.

The objective of the eco-tourism component was to increase the attractiveness of the area, build environmental awareness and education, and develop small scale tourism based on natural values and cultural heritage.

Rational ecosystem management provides raw materials for wooden handicrafts, such as juniper and pinewood. Cattle and sheep farming allows production of labelled quality meat and artisans' use of locally produced leather and wool. The making of

Key issues:

⇨ Improvement of coastal landscape management, protection of natural values, relaunch of agricultural production, restoration of grasslands for quality beef cattle and sheep rearing.

⇨ Grassland management has been included in the Estonian CAP system as an agri-environmental measure.

⇨ Job creation in traditional handicrafts and tourism industries set up and run by local communities.

⇨ Project as a demonstration site for rural development and nature conservation and also as a model for neighbouring countries (Latvia, Finland and Russia).

wool knitwear is a traditional branch of the local handicrafts. Market research and well-informed pricing are necessary tools to make the practising of crafts profitable.

The project encourages cottage tourism through study courses, advertising and research. It has created 7 nature study trails, 4 demonstration sites and 3 different ecotourism packages for bird watching, orchid/rare species visits and family hospitality at farms. Moreover, a link to an international network has been established for marketing purposes.

Links & references:

COASTLEARN case studies web page:
http://www.netcoast.nl/coastlearn/website/tourism/casestudies_vainameri.html

The WWF Väinameri project: www.arhipelaag.ee/vainameri/

3. Tourism types regions and cohesion indicators

3.1 Tourism Types Classification, GDP per Capita and Unemployment Rates

The classification into three main tourism types provided in this study is compared with the latest available data of the economic and social indicators commonly used in cohesion policy analysis, i.e. GDP per capita and unemployment rates. Reference is to the 1999 NUTS classification. The analysis does not include the Guadeloupe, Martinique, Guyana and Réunion (the four French DOM), Canarias and Ceuta y Melilla in Spain, and Açores and Madeira in Portugal. All of them (with the exception of Ceuta y Melilla) are outermost regions. Most of them are islands visited by tourists year-long. Tourism in these regions can be a very important sector for their economy, some already strongly relying on tourism revenues.

There is only a slight direct correlation between the level of GDP and tourism development, with the exception of tourism Type 3 regions where low levels of GDP generally correspond to less visited regions. Tourism and global economic wealth, thus, do not necessarily seem to proceed together. In other terms, tourism seems to develop in other places than the major economic poles. This also means that the tourism sector does not always contribute to a real economic growth of the concerned region.

Some of the most visited regions (tourism Type 1) show low values of GDP per capita (below 16.000 €). However, it is evident that the highest values of GDP per capita (over 25.000 €) belong either to type 1 or type 2 regions, with the exception of North East Scotland and of some Finnish regions[113], all characterised by a low population density. The first type 3 regions encountered in a classification sorted by GDP/capita descending values is Brabant Wallon, in Belgium, with about 24.700 € of GDP/capita and 7.9% of unemployment rate. Most of the regions with low values of GDP per capita are located in the following areas: new Member States, New Länder of Germany, Portugal, north-west, west and south of Spain, southern regions of Italy and Greece. There are also a number of black spots in Austria, Belgium and the UK.

---

[113] Data for Finland are only available at national level

All regions with unemployment rates below 4.5% belong to type 1 or 2 regions, with only one exception (Niederoesterreich in Austria, with 3.5% unemployment rate). For unemployment rates over 10%, type 3 regions are frequent but in general it is observed that regions with high values of unemployment rates belong to any tourism type (for example Berlin as a type 1 region, with 17.5% of unemployment, Andalucia as a type 2 region, with 18.6%, and most of the Polish regions, belonging to type 3 and having unemployment rates between 16 and 26%. Some mass tourism regions and urban destinations (Type 1) also show relatively high unemployment rates, such as Nord-Pas-de-Calais (12.5%) and Reg. Bruxelles (15.6%), respectively.

3.1.1   Type 1- Most Visited Regions

A total of 92 regions (NUTS2 level) belong to this type, confirming the high profile of the European Union as a favourite destination. Almost all the regions are located within the EU 15 countries, with the exception of Malta, Cyprus and Prague. Ten regions have a GDP per capita below 16.000 €, 44 regions have GDP/capita values below 25.000 €, 28 between 25.000 and 35.000 €, and the remaining 9 regions above 35.000 €.

These regions are characterised by high tourism pressures on the environment. Most of them are coastal and middle mountain zones with the exception of regions located in Germany, Luxembourg and in the Netherlands. The French regions are characterised by the concentration of large-sized tourism accommodations, thus limiting land take values. In this sense, these regions can be considered as more sustainable than the mass tourism destinations, although problems may be related to the infrastructure built to support the tourism activity, such as marinas and golf courses, having a huge impact on the environment.

Most type 1 regions have well developed economies, but some regions in Spain, France and the UK have high unemployment rates or low GDP per capita. Among the type 1 regions with a low level of GDP per capita are: Malta, Ionia Nisia, Kriti, Attiki, Notio Aigaio in Greece, Algarve in Portugal, Calabria, Campania and Puglia in Italy, and Cyprus. Two out of the three mentioned Italian regions also have some of the highest unemployment rates (23.4% for Calabria and 20.2% for Campania). Several among the poorest regions belonging to this type are located in coastal areas, making spatial planning and environmental policy of primary importance.

Within the most visited regions are distinguished two sub-types: the densely populated regions (sub type 1.1) and the mass tourism destinations (sub type 1.2). A region may belong to both sub-types, as is the case for Inner London, or may belong to only one sub-type (Emilia-Romagna, for example, as mass tourism destination, and Ile de France as densely populated region).

3.1.2   Type 1.1. - Densely Populated Regions

A total of 45 regions belong to this sub-type. These regions include most of the urban destinations, with Prague being the only representative region of the new Member States. Tourism development in these regions does not create significant pressures.

Most of the densely populated areas in Europe are found in the United Kingdom, Germany, Belgium, the Netherlands, Italy and France. Country capitals belong to this sub-type with Athens, Lisbon, Madrid, Vienna and, as already mentioned, Prague.

Tourism establishments in the major European cities are generally of a large size. In other regions with low tourism intensity, the size of the accommodation establishments can be lower, notably in Germany that is also a densely populated country. Moreover, there is a growing tendency of spreading hotel buildings around urban areas which contributes to increasing the land sprawl of cities.

3.1.3   Type 1.2. - Mass Tourism Destinations

Some (12) densely populated regions also belong to the second sub-type of type 1, i.e. the mass tourism destinations. The mass tourism destinations are internationally re-known locations for holiday. These include 17 regions, all but one (Malta) located in the EU 15.

Most of these regions are islands and coastal areas characterised by wild climate (Liguria, Malta, Ionia Nisia), or alpine and mountain regions (Tirol, Trentino Alto Adige), i.e. fragile environments. Most of these regions are located in Italy, Austria and Greece with isolated spots in the Balearics in Spain, Cornwall & Isles of Scilly in the UK, and Malta. The islands are characterised by limited land availability and concentration of large-sized hotels.

Coastal areas show relative small-sized accommodations widely spread over the territory; competition with other industries is common, leading to some conflicts of land use. Most of the seven outermost regions[114] fall under this type.

3.1.4 Type 2 and 2.1 - Traditional Regions and New Tourism Destinations

A total of 93 regions belong to this type. They are characterised by relatively small tourism bed capacity, sometimes with numerous small-sized accommodations like the 'Beds and Breakfast' in the UK. The natural, historical and cultural assets may be of special attraction. The British and German regions dominate this group, but several are also found in France. Regions in Hungary, Czech Republic, Slovakia and Poland also belong to this type. Almost all regions have good economic conditions, the Hungarian and the Slovakian ones in particular, and very few are facing problems (only five regions belong to Objective 1 class, one – Leipzig - has a high unemployment rate, and two Scottish are sparsely populated areas).

BOX C.4 The peculiarities of the French and British regions

With similar tourism density and intensity, the values found for the third indicator "tourism land take" show very different features in France (low values) and in the UK (high values). The French regions have a low number of tourism establishments for accommodation but of large size, while in the UK there is a higher number of accommodations but of small size. The tourism activity in France is concentrated in specific locations, avoiding a dispersed impact on the territory. Such concentration should facilitate the management of tourism and the implementation of operational measures for sustainability. However, tourism in France is also more intensive than in the UK. Here, the industry is spread over the territory, with small tourism managers facing scale difficulties for the set up of sustainable practices.

Within this type, a sub-type (Type 2.1. New tourism destinations) is characterised by a relatively high value of tourism intensity, i.e. of tourism bed-places per inhabitant, indicating that the tourism sector for these regions, although small destinations, has an economic importance and there is scope for its further development. As several of these regions have a low population density, rural activities may constitute the main attractions. They encompass a total of 47 regions, all but 6 (Zachodniopomorskie in Poland, Jihozapad and Severovychod in the Czech Republic, Közep-Dunantul, Del-Dunantul, and Nyugat-Dunantul in Hungary) located in the EU 15. The new tourist destinations of the new Member States are among the poorest regions, with a GDP/capita below 7.000 €. Several of these regions are sparsely populated areas.

---

[114] with the exception of French Guyana

3.1.5 Type 3 - Less Visited Regions

They encompass a total of 59 regions, more than half (31) being located in the EU 15. Over 32% of these regions have a GDP/capita above 17.000 €. They include: Niederoesterreich in Austria, Brabant Wallon in Belgium, Vali-Suomi, Etela-Suomi, Uusimaa in Finland, Champagne-Ardenne, Haute-Normandie, Centre, Bourgogne, Lorraine and Picardie in France, Giessen, Halle, Brandenburg and Thueringen in Germany, North East Scotland and Northern Ireland in the UK, la Rioja in Spain and Molise in Italy. Among these regions, six are considered sparsely populated areas (Bourgogne, Centre, Champagne-Ardenne, Vali-Suomi, Etela-Suomi and North East Scotland), benefiting from high value-added economies but with accessibility problems.

The economy of these regions is generally driven by other sectors (agriculture or industry); thus they are either not interested in developing a tourism industry or they do not have the necessary assets to attract tourists. Although in these regions there is no particular need for a sustainable tourism regional strategy, some opportunities for sustainable tourism development may still exist. These regions show similar features, as far as tourism is concerned, to those EU regions that suffer from natural handicaps.

Almost two-third of the regions belonging to this type are poor regions, several being Objective 1 and also sparsely populated areas. All these regions suffer from structural problems, due to poorly developed economies or natural handicaps. Some of these regions cumulate negative features; the region of Extremadura (Spain), for example, cumulates low GDP values, low population density (26 inh./km2) and high unemployment rate (17.4%), besides being an external EU border region. The more densely populated regions are under industrial conversion; there is little opportunity for sustainable tourism development there, as they do not have, in general, attractive landscapes or natural assets.

All new Member State regions except 13 are among the less visited destinations in Europe. These regions have great potentials for tourism development, notably those having attractive capitals, such as Slovenia and the three Baltic countries. Moreover, Jihovychod and Stredni (Czech Republic), Pomorskie (Poland), Vychodne and Stredne (Slovakia) already show a relative importance of tourism in their economy (demonstrated by values of tourism intensity over 3) and one would expect that they could shortly become part of the new tourism destination type. Exceptions within the new Member States include Cyprus, Malta, Prague (CZ), Közép-Magyarország (HU) and Bratislava (SK), i.e. countries or country capital regions that are also the most visited regions within their respective countries (either belonging to type 1 or type 2 tourism regions). Cyprus, Malta and Prague are very popular destinations of international renown (classified as type 1, most visited regions); they benefit from natural and cultural assets that favour tourism development.

3.1.6 Sparsely Populated Regions and Peripheral Regions

Sparsely populated and peripheral regions belong to any of the above identified types, although peculiarities may be identified.

The six recognised sparsely populated areas include: the strip of territory which runs obliquely across France (Champagne, Bourgogne, Centre, Auvergne, Limousin and Midi-Pyrénées) with population density of about 50 to 60 per km[115]; Scotland, with a density of about 67; Ireland (with the exception of Dublin area) with a density below 52; Greece (with the exception of the Eastern Continental Greece and the Athens area); Central and southern Spain (Madrid excepted) and the eastern and southern regions of Portugal (Algarve, Alentejo and Centro); and Finland (with the exception of Uusimaa). All but three (Algarve, South Western Scotland and Eastern Scotland excepted) are small destinations and among the less visited areas. About two-thirds of the sparsely populated regions, are traditional regions of destination of relative small European importance, but for which tourism is taking a growing place in their economy (features of Type 2.1. regions). About half of the less visited regions are also sparsely populated regions. The factor of being a sparsely populated region does not automatically imply a low level of GDP.

The peripheral regions generally are sparsely populated areas and agriculture-oriented. These regions belong to any tourism type with a dominance of tourism type 2.1 and type 3 (like the sparsely populated areas). The most concerned regions are located in the north of Greece and the new Member States. The only conclusion is that dedicated programmes to peripheral regions must include sustainable tourism as a priority especially for the less visited regions (type 3).

---

[115] Committee of the Regions, 2002 (b)

3.2   Fostering Sustainable Tourism in the Identified Tourism Types

After comparing regional disparities and the level of tourism development, for each main tourism type, the conditions allowing a better fostering of regional policies implementation are highlighted below. Strategic actions for each type are reported under paragraph 4.2.3.

1.   Most visited regions (Type 1)

Most visited regions are characterised by high tourism pressures on the environment. Tourism can support the creation of jobs especially in those regions benefiting from natural assets. A better organisation within the tourism industry and the preservation of the environment are of major importance. In the most visited regions with low levels of GDP and often high rates of unemployment the tourism activity is important but apparently it is not enough to sustain steady economic growth. The quality of the environment must be of major concern as tourism flows can be intense. Together with a diversification of the economy, the strategy would be to develop an integrated sustainable tourism regional plan.

2.   Most visited regions located in densely populated areas (Type 1.1)

These regions are mainly characterised by urban tourism and encompass the capitals of major countries. This tourism type does not impact significantly the territory or the natural resources, anyway no more than any other industry. However, attention has to be paid to the big metropolitan area regions where there is a growing trend to build hotel-chains outside the cities centres, thus increasing the urban sprawl without contributing largely to the local economy. An integrated urban planning and the fostering of transport inter-modality in local transport systems are major policy concerns.

3.   Mass tourism destinations (Type 1.2)

This sub-group of type 1 is characterised by the highest values in all three selected indicators (tourism density, intensity and land take). The environmental and social impacts of tourism are evident in those economies highly dependant on tourism.

Strong economic, social and territorial policies in all domains must be developed taking into account the peculiarities of the tourism sector. The ESDP and Local Agenda 21 need special attention.

4.   Traditional tourism destinations (Type 2)

These regions are tourism secondary poles. It is difficult to assess if their size and organisational structure allow better management of the tourism activity towards sustainability.

5.   New tourism destinations (Type 2.1.)

Within the traditional tourism destination type, some regions show a high tourism intensity; this indicates that tourism is gaining some economic importance. Tourism may represent an alternative development activity for these regions. The risk, however, is twofold: to become too highly dependant on tourism, and to move towards unsustainable patterns while moving towards type 1 regions. This group of regions, thus, requires special attention as these are the most likely to move towards a further development of the tourism industry. Fatal and irreversible errors (already experimented in type 1 regions) should be avoided at an early stage of planning. Territorial planning within the ESDP, environmental and transport services within SGEI and TEN-T policies, cross-border cooperation, and EC funds are priorities.

6.   Less visited regions (Type 3)

Less visited regions are characterised by low values of the three indicators. They may be categorised into two main groups: regions heavily relying on other economic activities, such as industry, where the development of tourism is not possible; and regions with a potential to direct their economy more towards tourism activity in order to create added value. The latter case will be considered here.

As these regions do not usually benefit from traditional and natural assets to attract tourists, options would be to develop small-scale forms of tourism, based on the attractiveness of agricultural and forest landscapes, on the promotion of cultural and traditional heritages, theme parks and trails. Several of these regions are sparsely populated areas, often agriculture-oriented and/or peripheral, making rural tourism and accessibility two of their most important features. Economic development through the tourism sector shall be pursued further to the recognition that tourism has a potential to support the convergence of the EU regions. The socio-economic and territorial dimension of the cohesion policy should target the integration of the sustainability of tourism into strategic measures, in particular spatial planning, trans-territorial cooperation, and the environmental service infrastructures within the SGEI and the TENs. Trans-territorial cooperation in general is of particular importance to foster development opportunities for peripheral regions.

Table C.1 summarises the cohesion policies relevant for each tourism type.

Table C.1	Policy focus for each tourism type
Type 1	ESDP, SGEI on Environmental services and (local) transport services, TEN-T (local system), Environmental policy (quality of the bathing waters, EIA, SEA), PPP.
Type 1.1.	ESDP and Urban planning, SGEI (transport infrastructures), TEN-T.
Type 1.2	ESDP, SGEI on Environmental services and Transport services, TEN-T, Environmental policy (quality of the bathing waters, EIA, SEA), Trans-Territorial Cooperation.
Type 2	ESDP, SGEI (including new ICTs), TEN-T, Environmental and Cultural Policies, Funding (EC and MS).
Type 2.1	ESDP, SGEI, TEN-Trans, Funds (EC and Member States), PPP, Trans-territorial Cooperation, Environmental, Enterprises, Transport, Education and Training, Culture, R&D.
Type 3	SGEI (ICTs), TEN-Trans, Enterprise (in particular SMEs), Environment, Education and Training, R&D, Trans-territorial Cooperation

In general, the following broad conclusions may be drawn:
- for all types the ESDP policy is relevant;
- different domains of the SGEI are of relevance according to the regional context: environmental service infrastructures for the more tourism-oriented and tourism-dependent economies (type 1.2 and 2.1); local transport systems for all types; and access to ICTs for the smaller destinations to create synergies in support to their penetration into the international tourism market (types 2 and 3) in particular;
- private public partnerships and suitable forms of governance are important for the sustainability of tourism in all tourism types, especially for those having sufficiently developed economies and organisational structures. The more tourism is important within regional economies, the more PPPs have the possibility to set up and grow.

4.   Conclusions and Recommendations

4.1   Conclusions

Tourism generates economic and employment benefits for the host communities, contributes to the development of rural areas and to the increase of economic opportunities in less developed areas. It is thus able to foster a more fair distribution of economic activities and revenues over the Union's territory, especially with regard to regions that suffer from structural problems and geographical handicaps.

Tourism development needs to be guided by an integrated approach; this necessity is a direct consequence of the structural links between tourism and several other economic sectors.

The tourism sector has very specific features that need to be taken into due account while designing sustainable tourism strategies; its competitive nature, its being based on the territory's natural resources (often represented by sensitive environments), its spatial and temporal concentration.

The regions that are the most attractive for tourism development usually benefit from natural assets that need to be preserved, making sustainability the only option for their viable future.

Promoting sustainability means managing tourism so as to minimise the possible negative impacts on the environment and on the social features of destinations. Sustainable tourism shall imply preservation and promotion of the European natural and cultural heritages.

The management of sustainable tourism requires active and balanced collaboration between public (regional and local) planning authorities on one hand, and the tourism business and all other stakeholders on the other hand; decentralisation of decision making to regional and local governments is thus necessary to develop economic, social and environmentally sustainable and responsible tourism.

Sustainable tourism has a vital role to play in fostering the economic, social and territorial cohesion, in enhancing regional competitiveness and in promoting sustainable development over Europe. It is of strategic importance to reach the Union's objectives, especially since its enlargement. Sustainable tourism promotes a better reciprocal understanding among the cultural, social, economic and environmental features of regions.

A political recognition of the importance and potential of tourism sustainability is crucial. The coordination of cohesion policy with other Community policies and interventions, including competition policies, is of particular relevance.

Cross-border co-operation is an important tool for promoting sustainable tourism because tourism ignores national barriers; less advanced regions may be supported in benefiting from good practices and in developing sustainable tourism regional strategies. Trans-border networks can also support this process.

In this context, information and networks are essential to support sustainability; exchange of best practices and lessons learnt are among the most urgent actions to be developed.

The ESDP would play a major role in fostering the implementation of sustainable tourism by supporting improvements in spatial planning and transport development systems. Tourism and transport are intrinsically linked. Regional aviation and availability of other sustainable means of transport are key success factors of sustainable tourism.

4.2   Recommendations

1. Reinforce the integration of territorial cohesion policies within economic and social cohesion policies. Sustainable tourism as a driving force for promoting cohesion in Europe may become a trial to explore the concrete implementation of the Gothenburg and Lisbon goals. In this context, the new ERDF regulation shall include sustainable tourism activities in its eligibility criteria.

2. Assess the territorial impact of relevant Community policies (environmental, transport) and programmes (TENs and ESDP) and improve the knowledge of environmental trends and policy impacts, especially at local and regional levels.

This would represent a pre-requisite for the proper outlining of sustainable tourism strategies.

3. Promote Integrated Quality Management for destination managers (local and regional authorities) and Integrated Coastal Zone Management at sea destinations in order to support a sustainable spatial planning of tourism activity. The European Commission should further disseminate the concerned methodological publications to the national tourism organisations and regional authorities.

4. Promote and support the implementation of Local Agenda 21 in collaboration with all tourism stakeholders. Several experiences in this regard have already been compiled but they need to reach a larger audience[116]. Such exchange of know-how will be facilitated by the development of reliable networks that aim at supporting the local and regional authorities to concretely implement sustainable tourism at destinations.

5. Consider the carrying out of a Strategic Environmental Assessment and Environmental Impact Assessment for any tourism infrastructure project, compulsory. Legislation in this area should be reinforced.

6. Make land use planning and development control effective. Local authorities have to develop efficient land planning tools able to integrate the natural values of the terrestrial and aquatic environment. This process will also support the NATURA 2000 programme. Studies on the tourism carrying capacity of the destinations should be carried out.

7. Guide tourism in natural areas by means of integrated management plans developed by qualified experts and implemented with adequate resources. The experience of the European Charter for sustainable tourism in protected areas (EUROPARC) constitutes a good example; the adopted methodology can be implemented in other natural European areas, protected or not protected. The WWF Protected Natural Areas Network could also serve as focal point to exchange information on existing experiences.

---

[116] An interesting publication is provided by UNEP and ICLEI: Tourism and Local Agenda 21, The role of the Local Authorities in Sustainable Tourism, 2003.

8. Develop specific codes of conduct for tourism managers and tourists as well as comprehensive monitoring systems.

9. Study the potential of economic incentive tools and measures able to support the tourism contribution to the preservation of European natural and cultural heritages.

10. Integrate the sustainable tourism issue into the ESPON programme, notably referring to accessibility indicators and to urban-rural typology, impacts of policies in fields of transport, ESDP, governance and environment. In the same context, further work on sustainable tourism could be developed in cooperation with the INTERACT programme in the framework of INTERREG III.

11. Compile a best practices guide in SGEI related to local/regional public transport, water and waste management services. This guide could be particularly valuable for those regions receiving a large number of tourists compared to their population.

12. The European Commission and the regions should organise a public consultation prior to the WTO GATS decision to possibly further liberalise tourism services, as this might work against the increase of tourism development in the European regions. The rapid globalisation of the tourism market and the growing influence of big operators can encourage anti-competitive practices creating barriers to the operational capacity of local SMEs. As a consequence, economic and social benefit reductions may be expected from the tourism sector as an endogenous economic regional development path.

13. EU supported projects and cooperation programmes should be compatible with the goals of sustainable development and include the promotion of sustainable tourism to foster the implementation of regional policies. All projects should be evaluated and monitored according to sustainability criteria and indicators.

14. Awareness of EU tourists on sustainability of tourism shall be increased to encourage responsible behaviours during their travelling within and outside the

EU. Tourism codes and sustainable tourism charters should be largely distributed to citizens[117].

4.2.1 Recommendations related to the Cooperation with Border Regions

1. A recent proposal for a regulation establishing a new legal instrument in the form of a European grouping of cross-border cooperation authority– recommended to be renamed by the Committee of the Regions into 'trans-European' (EGTC) – has been adopted by the European Commission on the 14th of July 2004[118]. This new legal instrument aims to transfer to the EGTC structure the capacity to carry out cooperation activities on behalf of public authorities, local and regional but also national. This new frame should include an effective support to the sustainable tourism operations that would be initiated.

2. In this context, the idea of creating specific 'European Cooperation Areas', launched by the AEBR[119], should be implemented as far as natural geographical features and institutional capacities are concerned to set out Euroregions across national borders. The implementation of sustainable tourism could highly benefit from the creation of such cooperation zones.

4.2.2 Recommendations related to the Outermost Regions

The European Commission should carry out a cross-sectoral analysis where special attention is paid to the opportunities to support sustainable tourism within the regional strategies of the outermost regions. A detailed study on the implications of relevant Community policies[120] in these regions should be carried out; the implementation of suitable regional strategies should take into account the requests of these regions together with the governments of their respective Member States. The planned Wider Neighbourhood Action Plan[121] could include significant hints for the implementation of sustainable tourism strategies in the outermost regions.

---

[117] An example is the WorldWise Tourism campaign in the UK
[118] European Commission, 2004 (a)
[119] Committee of the Regions, 2002 (c)
[120] Such as transport, NTIC, and the trans-national and cross-border cooperation programmes
[121] European Commission, 2004 (b)

4.2.3   Recommendations related to Identified Tourism Types

Type 1, sub-type 1.1
Strategic actions for most visited regions located in densely populated areas shall include: the introduction of better management practices within the tourism industry (CSR, indicators and reporting); the development of sustainability along the whole tourism-chain, oriented to high quality environmental standards, services and products; the innovation and adaptation of the local transport system by favouring low emission buses and taxis, tramways and subways, creating car parks outside cities centres.

Type 1, sub-type 1.2
Strategic actions for mass tourism destinations shall include: the introduction of better management practices aimed to renovate destinations; the improvement of the stakeholders involvement in each destination; the development of a spatial integrated strategy at destination; and the safeguarding of the social and environmental aspects of the territory.

Type 2
Strategic actions for traditional destinations shall include the implementation of a sustainable tourism strategy involving all partners. The strategy should focus on spatial planning and on the preservation of the natural and cultural heritages, for which appropriate forms of governance and funding, at national or European level, are required.

Type 2, sub-type 2.1
Within the new tourism destinations, strategic actions shall include:
- the promotion of the diversification of tourism products and services through: new forms of tourism based on agriculture, nature and traditions; low resources consumption accommodation forms; appropriate support to micro and SMEs;
- the development of integrated sustainability tourism strategies, especially in areas that suffer from a permanent disadvantage (sparsely populated regions and poorest regions);
- the promotion of exchange of information, networking, enhancement of tourism employee skills, economy and employment development based on the promotion of European heritages;

- the funding of such strategies implementation, through EC initiatives and programmes, and the promotion of private-public partnerships.

Type 3

Strategic actions for less visited regions shall include: the facilitation of access to ICTs for micro and SMEs; the fostering of collaboration between the private and public sectors; the enhancement of quality of products and services, marketing operations, infrastructures and transport systems; the facilitation of access to funding.

SECTION D: GOVERNANCE AND SUSTAINABLE TOURISM

1. Governing Sustainable Tourism: the Background

1.1   Targeting Good Governance

Good governance is a target in all complex systems but it is also very difficult to achieve, as it requires mastering of many variables and compromises among many stakeholders. There are some basic guidelines for good governance, which are presented on section 1.1.1. However, they only constitute a basis on which one has to build specific rules, addressing the inherent features of each system studied. Hence, the specificities of Europe and its multi-level government are briefly presented on section 1.1.2, as they constitute the environment on which the good governance principles are to be applied in the case of European tourism sustainability.

1.1.1   The Definition and Basic Principles of Good Governance

"The debate on European governance, launched by the Commission in its White Paper of July 2001, concerns all the rules, procedures and practices affecting how powers are exercised within the European Union."[122].

Governance is hence an abstract concept dealing with principles, modes and ways of organisation and is increasingly important as systemic complexity increases and central structures or hierarchical governments become unable to deal with this complexity alone[123,124]. The following principles emerge as relevant for the design of a democratic and efficient development policy:

- A policy should *have a vision*, which must be long term and flexible. These two targets may be combined if an adequate mechanism including a good information system with early warning for potential change is designed, together with an inclusive and effective consultation and decision making system.

---

[122] EU Glossary web site: http://europa.eu.int/scadplus/glossary/index_en.htm
[123] Organisation for Economic Co-operation and Development, 2003
[124] Ahrens J., 2002

- A good policy must be *integrated and multi-sectoral*. Focusing in the narrow interests of a sector creates tensions with other sectors and deprives it from the potential to exploit synergies and economies of scope.

- Efficiency also requires *transparency, stakeholder involvement and accountability*. *Transparency* is important to reassure stakeholders that the management is effective and gives them the possibility to adjustments of change, if necessary. Transparency needs to be combined with *stakeholder involvement* based on the establishment of dialogue. Finally, *accountability* is also a *sine qua non* condition of good governance. One manager/organisation must be assigned with decision power; after short and efficient consultations the final decision must be taken, for which the manager/organisation must be accountable to a board or society as a whole. For the system to work efficiently, some *basic managerial principles* are also needed.

1.1.2 The Dimension of Multi-level Governance and the Subsidiarity Principle

The above mentioned principles are generic and apply to all types of governance. In the case of policy intervention, complexity is further increased by the interaction of various levels of government and suggests that the territorial additional dimension needs to be taken into consideration. The optimal level of action and interaction between the territorial, national and transnational or global level are determined by socio-economic and technical variables. Globalisation, which is characterised by ever-increasing international trade and foreign investment flows, has brought with it new forms of business co-operation and international policy coordination. After the 1980s a more advanced and complex form of internationalisation appeared that involved a degree of functional integration between internationally dispersed actors. Global coordination is needed and increasing for international trade, capital movements and environmental protection.

The national level (and the supranational in the case of the EU) remains dominant for most interventions of economic and social policy, but the sub-national level (regional and local authorities) emerges as increasingly relevant for policies for which *"proximity matters"*. The increasing global competition requests the exploitation of any cost advantage or quality improvement actors can create: agglomeration is one way of cost-sharing, hence *the relevance of the territorial level for all economic activities, which can benefit from agglomeration economies.*

Good governance has to be designed in a way that takes into account the most appropriate level of policy intervention, be it international, national, multilateral, regional or sub-regional.

The Treaty of Maastricht introduced the principle of subsidiarity as a general principle applicable to all areas of nonexclusive competence, while the global approach for its application was set by the Edinburgh European Council of 1992[125]. The subsidiarity principle "*is intended to ensure that decisions are taken as closely as possible to the citizen and that constant checks are made as to whether action at Community level is justified in the light of the possibilities available at national, regional or local level. Specifically, it is the principle whereby the Union does not take action (except in the areas which fall within its exclusive competence) unless it is more effective than action taken at national, regional or local level. It is closely bound up with the principles of proportionality and necessity, which require that any action by the Union should not go beyond what is necessary to achieve the objectives of the Treaty*"[126].

Examples of cases where it is more effective to act at a higher level refer to major infrastructure and regulatory frameworks, to the achievement of economies of scale, for example through the adoption of common standards, or of economies of scope for the creation and better exploitation of a body of knowledge through studies and evaluation, and to the introduction of checks and balances of an external monitoring procedure.

The Constitutional Treaty specifies that the EU, in certain areas - among which tourism is explicitly mentioned -, will be entitled to intervene "*to support, coordinate or supplement the actions of the Member States without thereby superseding their competence in these areas. The Union's support will essentially be financial in nature*"[127]. However, it will not be until the entry into force of the Constitutional

---

[125] Committee of the Regions, 2004 (c)

[126] EU Glossary web site: http://europa.eu.int/scadplus/glossary/index_en.htm

[127] Summary of the Union's legislation, A constitution for Europe; on article I-17: Areas of supporting, coordinating or complementary action http://europa.eu.int/scadplus/constitution/competences_en.htm

Treaty that these notions and modalities for their application will be further specified, also taking into account the finalization of European Agenda 21 for Tourism.

1.2 Structural Characteristics of the Tourism Sector: Actors and Policies in Europe

1.2.1 Key Features of the Sector and its Stakeholders

While in the past tourism was bound to certain locations, of historic relevance and/or offering special advantages for traditional holidays, today competition among regions at the global level is increasing, while new forms of tourism emerge. Travel and organisational costs lowered significantly and do not constraint any longer the number and type of destinations[128]. Transcontinental tourism is also increasing rapidly and competition both within and outside Europe is pushing hard for both quality improvements and cost reductions. In this context *agglomeration economies and externalities matter sufficiently and these can only be organised at the regional or trans-regional level, which is gaining in importance.* Territorial authorities can in fact provide for the necessary infrastructure, joined marketing and decisions for interregional cooperation.

The regional level plays a crucial role in the tourism industry for identity, strategy and implementation:

- It determines the *identity of the region/city/territory*, which acts as a unit of attraction for tourism. This identity is often determined by characteristics external to the regional strategy (climatic conditions, historical or natural heritage), but it may also be a result of an effective competitive strategy (building specific infrastructure for sports activities, festivals, environmental labels etc). More often, it is a combination of the two. In many cases the regional identity for tourism fully complies with the overall national image (e.g. most regions in Greece, Spain, Italy and Portugal market the climate and the sea for summer holidays, while most Austrian regions market skiing and the lakes, an image promoted also by the respective national authorities), but it may also offer more specialised features in the same context (e.g. the Mediterranean diet), or totally different products (e.g. specific promotion of the

---

[128] World Tourism Organisation, 2000

Natura 2000 areas in several regions in each country). In these cases, territorial authorities need to take the lead because the brand refers to the sub-national level. National governments will then not intervene and the only alliances that can be expected are trans-regional cooperation schemes.

- It determines the *internal strategy,* mainly deciding which role tourism is expected to play in the overall development of the region; in its broad scope, such strategy needs to comply with the national and European guidelines related to the sector. The need and the success of a regional strategy depend largely on the economic relevance of tourism in each region, on potential accumulated negative externalities (pollution, crowding, lack of zoning), on the effectiveness of governance structures (involvement of all stakeholders to assure long term commitment), and on the efficiency of the regional administration. The internal strategy is of paramount importance for regions where tourism is a major economic activity[129] such as in the Balearic islands, in the Aegean islands, Tirol and Salzburg, where other sources of revenue play a minor role. Regions with high regional GDP per capita, like Inner London and, on a lower scale, Madrid, are apparently less dependent on tourism, despite the contribution of the sector.

- The implementation of this internal strategy (which may be implicit or explicit, persistent or *ad hoc,* long or short term) relies on *regional funding,* which is usually insufficient and needs to be matched with national funding. Their relative share depends on the overall national governance principles (federal versus non-federal states) and the relative importance of the sector in the overall economic activity. The regional level also matters for the adoption of trans-regional initiatives, proving more and more important to offer competitive and attractive packages. The efficiency of the administration is a crucial element for a successful implementation and in this context public-private partnerships or principles of outsourcing and externalisation may be catalytic.

The national level plays an important role where scale is relevant. National tourism organisations are important in all the Member States for which tourism is a key source of contribution to GDP such as Cyprus, Malta, Austria, Spain, France, and Portugal.

---

[129] Based on GVA values per capita (Eurostat 2002 data) from the NACE branch "hotels and restaurants"

For those countries with lower average income, travel and tourism are in relative terms one of the most important sources of revenue (Cyprus, Malta, Greece, Portugal, Spain) thus making it important for the national authorities to intervene and assure the continuation and sustainability of the sector. In this case the national authorities are providing regulatory frameworks, standards and certification (type of services offered, compliance with health and other standards), the national identity and major international infrastructure (like national ports, airports and highways).

The stakeholders, who need to be consulted for an effective governance in the tourism sector, have been comprehensively identified and defined by the European Working Group D on the promotion of sustainable development and protection of the environment for the tourism sector, and include[130]:

- policy makers, namely national, regional and local tourism information offices and tourism agencies;
- social partners, namely Federations representing tourist industry sectors and trade unions;
- tourism suppliers including the accommodation industry, catering sector (restaurant, cafe, bar, etc.), transportation sector, attractions and activities, as well as tourist guide services;
- commercial intermediaries in tourism industry, namely tour operators and travel retailers;
- universities, research bodies and consultancies, which may be public, private, public-private and NGO's;
- hosts and guests.

The complex system of actors and their interactions suggest that changing or even shifting strategies may be a difficult task. Adopting a sustainable policy strategy for the tourism sector – i.e. fostering sustainable tourism - would imply the participation of the whole industry chain, from producers to consumers. A better collaboration between the private sector (local SMEs) and the public authorities is necessary to create the conditions for a sustainable management of the activity. This should imply a systematic search for new paths of development that integrate on an equal balance the economic, social and environmental dimensions. While in the long run the total impact will be positive, a certain rearrangement of costs and benefits in the short run

---

[130] Merchadou C., et al., 2001

may create friction and resistance, the interests of some stakeholders may also be affected, making alliances for the shift towards a more ambitious strategy more difficult than expected.

1.2.2 Links to European Union Policies

As previously mentioned, the EU does not have a real, long term and systematic "tourism policy" but fragmented interventions, the increasing role of the sector only very recently having been acknowledged. This increasing role relates to a broader representation of European interests in multilateral activities, such as those of the United Nations, and to the adoption of standards.

Specific European policies that directly or indirectly affect the evolution of tourism and its competitiveness include:

- *Regional development and social policies.* The increasing role of cohesion consideration and the relative share of the European budget invested in Structural Funds are relevant to tourism, which represents an important source of growth for the European less favoured regions (Objective 1) and in some cases also for regions in industrial decline (Objective 2). It is a responsibility of the regional authorities in the context of the adoption of the Regional Operational Programmes or the Single Programming Documents to decide which share of their development funds will be dedicated to tourism. In principle, the European Commission accepts the proposal of the regional governments, as long as measures and strategies comply with the EU policies and the general philosophy of the structural funds and there is an agreement on the monitoring indicators. Interventions may include important co-funding of infrastructure, individual support for private actors in accommodation and transport, and the strengthening of enterpreneurship via the creation of local cooperatives. In the same context, programmes on education and training are supported by the European Social Fund.

- *Internal market.* Provisions of the Internal Market are important in all the areas where fragmentation is avoided. In the case of tourism this applies mainly to the free movement of people and services on one hand, and to the adoption of common standards on the other. The most important example of the former refers to the mutual recognition of specific skills necessary to offer services across the

EU, as in the case of tourist guide services and hotel management. For the latter the creation of pan-European standards applies to common standards for quality control such as the HACCP[131] standard. The internal market provisions are not directly linked to sustainable tourism itself, but to tourism in general. In case more ambitious standards for sustainable tourism would be suggested in the future this might be best channelled via internal market regulation.

- *Agriculture and rural development* are strongly related to tourism as the latter may potentially co-exist, complement or replace these activities. The problems emerging from the decreasing employment in agriculture and the relevance that EU support to agriculture has within the Commission budget, have contributed to the recommendation of rural development models tackling the diversification of strategies. These, either aim at replacing agricultural activities with tourism or at complementing agricultural production with small-scale agro-tourism. For both cases the LEADER initiative has been an important source of funding.

- *Environmental policies*, which have a huge potential to mitigate negative externalities. The clean environment plays more and more a role for competitive tourism as new entrants (for examples from Asia) offer less polluted sites for leisure.

- *Enterprise policy.* Meeting the challenge to remain competitive and keep up with technology is essential for sustainable growth; the EU enterprise policy provides its contribution by fostering innovation, entrepreneurship and competitiveness in manufacturing and services. While tourism has not received major attention in the past decades, it is now explicitly recognised that *"Europe is the world's most visited tourism region. This calls for a response that does not throttle the development of a major service industry or prevent people taking the holiday of their choice, but protects natural resources and the environment, so that the development of tourist sites does not destroy the very heritage on which the industry is built"*[132].

---

[131] The Hazard Analysis and Critical Control Point was an alliance formed in 1994 in Texas including standards that assure safer meat and poultry products. It then extended to a much broader scope of food products, assuring the quality of catering. More and more tour operators request HACCP compliance.

[132] DG Enterprise web site: http://europa.eu.int/comm/enterprise/index_en.htm

- *Transport* policy has its own dynamics and rather than tourism interests, it takes into consideration other economic and social priorities. Tourism adds to the increasing demand for transport and to the problems that threaten our mobility (congestion, augmented fuel consumption, rise in pollution levels). The European Commission recognises that the present patterns of transport growth are unsustainable. The main challenges are at the EU level: how to encourage a better balance between the different modes of transport and how to make better use of existing networks (integration of Europe's fragmented patchwork of regional and national transport networks). An increasing role of the railway seems to be favoured along the promotion of combined journeys — road–rail, road–sea, rail–sea, air–rail — for both passengers and freight.

1.3 The Crucial Level of Governance for Economic Development: the Territorial Authorities

Diversity and different degrees of political will and actual means exist among territorial authorities in Europe. The characteristics of territorial authorities, their functioning and finally certain barriers to their activities are briefly described. The paragraph is finalised with conclusions on the current state of territorial policies in Europe, which can be of relevance to sustainable tourism policies.

1.3.1 Potential of the Territorial Authorities

Devolution is taking place in Europe, where there is a systematically increasing emphasis in the role played by territorial authorities. Historically, only Germany and Austria had a federal structure giving substantial regional autonomy to the Länder, while now more and more Member States proceed to a regionalisation of different degrees. The arguments behind this increasing role are political, based on an increasing perception of regional and local identity, supported by technology (local media), and economic, based on the need to exploit agglomeration economies.

The degree of regional autonomy varies considerably from one Member State to another. There are three dimensions that need to be taken into account to characterise the definition of the territorial authorities' decision making power:

- the political authority, the legal system and evolving administrative acts;

- the financial capabilities, given by the share of the budget that is managed by the territorial authorities, compared to the national budget;
- the administrative capabilities, which are determined by the available skills and the accumulated experience of territorial autonomy.

These three dimensions do not coincide at all. All Member States are somehow delegating decision making on development policies to the lower level. But the endowments differ considerably. Germany, Belgium, Austria and Spain have the most powerful territorial authorities at the level of the region: political authority, financial and administrative capabilities co-exist. The UK, the Netherlands and the Nordic countries are also making enormous progress in that respect; in their case, financial and administrative capabilities are driving forces. The UK is a special case where the devolution process for Scotland, Wales and Northern Ireland has a different degree. France, the cohesion countries and the new Member States have adopted the political principles without however endowing the territorial level with the necessary means[133].

Certain regions, municipalities and cities are more active than others within Europe, an indicator being, for example, the intensity with which they apply for and implement European initiatives like INTERREG, LIFE and LEADER, or the way in which they deal with particular strategic development problems. Although the formal distribution of powers is agreed and adopted by national legislation, also regions of the same country demonstrate a different degree of activism. Baden-Wuertenberg in Germany, the rich provinces of central Italy[134], Catalonia in Spain and Central Macedonia in Greece have succeeded in certain points of their history in considerably outperforming national averages because of efficient territorial strategies.

This proves that although the political authority is crucial, there is no doubt that capabilities do affect the degrees of freedom of intervention. In this context the particular case of tourism is analysed hereafter.

---

[133] For details of the devolution process in each Member State reference is to two recent publications by the Committee of the Regions: "Devolution process in the European Union and the candidate countries" (updated at January 2005) and "Strengthening regional and local democracy in the European Union", volume I and II, released in February 2004.

[134] Regions with active agglomeration economies becoming increasingly wealthy because of an active policy are presented in Porter M.E., 1980.

1.3.2   Functions and Role of the Territorial Authorities in the Tourism Sector

While in rhetorical terms all territorial authorities adopt the priority of sustainable development, only a subset express active interest in adopting a new strategic thinking and invest the necessary resources to reverse past trends. The difficulty for bridging theory and good will with practical applications is partly determined by limitations of resources and partly by the long versus short term impacts that create tensions among stakeholders. Since consensus is sometimes very difficult to achieve, there is an inherent danger to avoid action and let the current status prevail.

Territorial authorities may facilitate tourism development in various ways. All are entitled to intervene in respect of local marketing, local infrastructure for transport - ensuring easy accessibility to destinations -, management of waste, employment and educational policies, although only few have the means. In addition, size plays a crucial role, even if it is a double edged sword: bigger regions can pool resources together, but their interventions may become effective at the cost of intra-regional diversity. Cities, or smaller communities seldom have more responsibilities than zoning.

Federations representing tourist agency sectors are usually active at the national level[135], where they include major players. There is a considerably smaller and less influential number of federations (such as small local hotel associations) at the regional level, and those are usually more directed towards pooling resources for business improvements rather than adopting strategic positions and contributing to a development dialogue.

At the regional level, *employers* are members of local chambers. Their influence is related to the relative importance of the sector for the local economy. However, there are few cases where local federations can play a very active role influencing the tourism model. The model works best when selected opinion makers take the lead and create a partnership between the territorial authorities and local agents (collectively represented or not) to face a problem in consensus.

---

[135] At the European level the employers of the sector are represented by the European Federation of Food, Agriculture and Tourism Trade Unions (EFFAT) and the Confederation of National Associations of Hotels, Restaurants, Cafés and Similar Establishments in the EU and EEA (HOTREC).

Employees in the tourism sector usually belong to national trade unions; they include both highly qualified personnel, working in the tourism management of big hotel chains and commercial intermediaries, and less qualified staff. Only at firm level are employees unionised locally. At any rate, since tourism is one of the sectors where part-time and fixed-term contracts play an important role, because of the seasonal character of the industry, unionisation is low. In most Member States these employees have a less strong representation, a situation further emphasised by undeclared work. The sector, in fact, because of its seasonal character, often includes informal labour relations (undeclared short-term work) as well as illegal migrants, who are not represented in the labour movements.

As far as *tourism suppliers* are concerned, the smaller ones among them are usually locally organised. Smaller hotels not belonging to bigger chains, privately rented rooms, agro-tourisms and camping, as well as catering services composed by small enterprises serving local needs, or broader operations serving wider chains are lobbying at the regional level.

Finally, it is evident that consultation at the regional level is not easy and strongly depends on the capabilities of the territorial authority. In general, because of the high number of actors involved and of their vested interests it is difficult to strike new balances. It takes a strong political will, a long term agreement and at least a certain degree of consensus for a renewed strategy. It is also important to have a strong leader behind the new vision, who will accompany and adapt it for the initial period, as long as it is still vulnerable and amenable to change. This strong leader does not have to be part of the political authority but can emerge from any of the stakeholders. However, the agreement and embracing of the new ambitious policy by the territorial authority is a *sine qua non* condition of success.

1.3.3   Barriers to a more pro-active Role of Territorial Authorities

Evidence suggests that the territorial authorities have an important role to play[136,137], however even disposing of size, legally supported power and capabilities, they are not in a position to act alone.

---

[136] Storper M., 1995
[137] Sternberg R., 1994

Experimenting a longer tourism season in Rhodes, Greece

BP_6

Greece, is one of the major tourism destinations in Europe and tourism is a key contributor to national GDP. The country suffers from the short tourism season, which inhibits economies of scale and quick amortization. Most islands have high occupancy rates only between May and September.

The national tourism organisation has never promoted Greece as a place for extended tourism because part of the country is characterised by a period of bad weather conditions; hence, there is no tourism in Greece over about five months each year and hotels, shops and restaurants are closed. Consequences include temporary unemployment and congestion during the summer.

Some islands however, further in the south, have a longer period of good weather. Rhodes is one of them and is a typical mass destination resort. Although in between October and March the weather is not as good as in the spring and summer, the business sector would benefit substantially from a better distribution of visits over the year, which would increase local income without increasing congestion.

Key issues:

⇨ Partnership between the territorial authorities and local agents to face a problem in consensus.

⇨ Attempt to reduce the seasonality of the tourism activity and its extreme consequences (congestion during summer and unemployment during the off-season).

In 2003 the hotel, restaurant, shop and bar owners of Afantou Beach, one of the most popular beaches on the island of Rhodes decided to keep their premises open 12 months a year. The Major of Afandou adopted the idea and acted as coordinator. The target was the extension of the tourism period from November to February, knowing that in the short term this would not trigger particularly encouraging results but adopting a longer term, consensus-based strategy. The result was very encouraging as in the third season of this operation, international charter air traffic off season is doubling.

Links & References:

This best practice is based on interviews.

National Sustainable Development Policy in Ireland

The principal goals and polices defined in the 1997 publication 'Sustainable Development: A Strategy for Ireland' outline the development and delivery of policies and programmes in the area of environmental protection and sustainable development. The integration of environmental considerations into other policy areas is a key way for securing a balanced development. The strategy also adopts a multi-level compliance, since it is connected to the targets of the Rio de Janeiro Earth Summit.

Tourism has a prominent place in this overarching strategy with a broader partnership of national and local authorities. The action programme towards sustainable tourism envisages, among others:

- due consideration given to tourism while preparing land use policy guidelines for planning authorities, developers and the public;
- planning authorities to ensure that over-development does not occur
- good environmental management ensured by the Department of Arts,

Key issues:

⇨ Balanced development targeted through the integration of environmental considerations into other policy areas.

⇨ Strategy adopting a multi-level compliance.

⇨ Tourism has a prominent place in this overarching strategy.

Culture and the Gaeltacht for historic properties and other tourist attractions falling under its jurisdiction;
- prevention of damage to beaches, sand dunes and seashore ecosystems through the provisions of the Foreshore Acts;
- provision of training emphasising the sustainable use of resources and highlighting natural products;
- development of codes of conduct and practice for tourists, to raise awareness on the potential impact of damaging behaviours on sensitive areas and sites.

Links & references:

The Irish Department of the Environment, Heritage and Local Government web site:
http://www.environ.ie/DOEI/DOEIPol.nsf/wvNavView/Sustainable+Development:+A+S trategy+for+Ireland?OpenDocument&Lang=

Government of Ireland, The Department of the Environment, 1997. Sustainable Development - A strategy for Ireland.
http://www.antaisce.org/environment/docs/Sustainable_Development_Strategy.pdf

Beside the lack of capabilities, serious limitations, which impose negotiations between the territorial and national authorities, are:

- the national competence on taxation: this not only deprives means from territorial authorities but does not allow them to use taxation as a policy instrument for sustainability, in case they would choose to do so;
- the distribution of tax revenue among regions and among different sectors or types of policy intervention; in most Member States the share between national and regional resources remains strongly in favour of the former;
- major transport routes, international airports and ports need national decision making and funding;
- the adoption of standards at the national or even supranational level do not allow for a more severe legislation at local level, even if this were applied to support sustainability, since it would be considered as acting as a barrier to trade and to the Single Market.

To deal with these problems territorial authorities need to lobby at the national level. Trans-regional lobbying is more effective in these cases and national governments cannot easily ignore it.

In addition to the distribution of power among political authorities the strength and degree of involvement of major stakeholders may act as a barrier for specific activities:

- stakeholders from regions where tourism is important influence decision making and national strategies much more than those coming from emerging regions;
- short-term interests (like the need to amortise low quality investments or avoid the cost of new investments) diminish the potential for longer term strategies;
- alternative means of transport or supplies may also end up with decisions in favour of the stronger actors, instead of the long term benefits of the overall development.

1.4 Conclusions on the Principles of Good Governance in the Tourism Sector and its transformation into a Sustainable Strategy

There is not a single model of good governance in any sector, thus not in the tourism sector either.

Good governance may have different institutional set ups but the following principles need to be respected: integration, multi-sectoral vision, transparency, involvement, accountability and efficiency.

The role of territorial authorities is very important in order to assure economies of agglomeration and act as control mechanisms for the respect of good governance principles.

There is a significant role for higher levels of governance in the tourism sector as far as standards, European values and pan-European marketing are concerned.

The consultation process at the regional level should include mainly tourism suppliers and local employees' centres, as only these are likely to be locally represented.

The interaction between the territorial and national level is affected by the legal, budgetary and administrative powers of both levels and the way they intermingle. Legal responsibility (e.g. major revenue taxation decisions, standards) lies almost exclusively with the national level. The territorial level has only some influence in the local taxation and this with limited degrees of freedom. Budgetary responsibilities are mixed; some countries are giving more autonomy to the regions than others and budgetary authority is usually more limited than what rhetoric suggests. What seems to be most important in the case of the design of a sustainable tourism strategy regards the administrative capabilities of the lower level: unless they are appropriate either the national level retains responsibilities in areas where it is sub-optimal to do so, or responsibilities are transferred but regional policy effectiveness is low.

When it comes to the limits of the legal competencies of the territorial authorities, lobbying at the national and EU level is necessary; in this case gaining allies and lobbying trans-regionally increases the potential of success.

1.5   Recommendations

Based on these conclusions, three basic recommendations emerge to territorial authorities wishing to be involved in sustainable tourism development policies:

1. Adopt a strategic vision, based on local advantages and measured with global competitive pressures, incorporating sustainable tourism principles, as analysed in Section B of this study, and analysing them in the context of local advantages and disadvantages.

2. Sensitise and mobilise regional stakeholders, without whom the public sector alone cannot succeed. Similarly the market forces alone are insufficient as well. Hence, the best way to exploit synergies is their coordination and commitment to mutual benefit. This means, concretely, that the local authorities will adopt plans for clean (or in the cases of damages from the past actively cleaning the) environment; in this context they will need to negotiate with the national authorities, if necessary, the means for achieving this goal; hotels and catering should adopt the necessary standards for quality and environmental respect; agents promoting the new strategy and tools for that should be made available.

3. Organise the position of lobbying within the higher levels of governance. Since the adoption of new balances needs transregional and often national investments, local stakeholders will need to coordinate and promote the local positions in their national federations. Examples are local hotels earmarking the position of the region in the national hotel federations or tour operators being mobilised to market the region as one valuing sustainable tourism.

2. Models of Governance in European Tourism

While there are certain principles and good practices in the case of European governance, the actual situation depends on sectoral features and is characterised by diversity. Hence, there is not a single model, which should be recommended as an overarching development strategy, but strategies and policies are very much path dependent. But the "*history matters*" does not preclude the possibility to group regions together into clusters with similar characteristics, abstracting from details, and thus recommend policies appropriate for each group.

The first paragraph is dedicated to experimenting with such typologies, while the second presents the findings. Two types of specific cases are discussed after that: the theoretical merits of public private partnerships and real cases of good governance in the selected types of regions. Conclusions and recommendations follow.

2.1 Experimenting with Typologies

In an effort to group regions together into a reasonably operational number of clusters, which would request similar strategies and efforts from the side of the territorial authorities, the following three dimensions are considered as the most relevant ones:

- the level of autonomy enjoyed by the territorial authorities in each Member State;
- the relevance of the tourism sector for territorial development as well as for Europe as a whole;
- the potentially accumulated damage for sustainability.

A major barrier to a smooth processing is that, in practice, perfect indicators to match the notions that need to be captured do not exist; moreover, statistics are either not available or are not detailed at the regional level. Inevitably, it is necessary to refer to *proxies*. A better statistical coverage and/or internal regional debates using qualitative statements and positioning regions or sub-regions in different or more refined categories constitute an interesting extension of this first crude approach.

2.1.1 A Classification based on the Level of Decision-making Autonomy and Capabilities

Tourism governance cannot be independent of the principles guiding the articulation of central and territorial power in each Member State. The type of autonomy (regional or even sub-regional) is affected by:

- *general principles*, like subsidiarity or national political discourse about the relevance of the territorial level; these set the frame but do not create the real operational environment, which is shaped by the factors mentioned hereafter;
- *legal and institutional terms* at the national level, namely the formal provisions for autonomy, which are composed of legal acts and institutional practices;
- *real transfer of the decision making process and implementation*. Legal transfer is a prerequisite but the real transfer itself depends on the share of the public budget managed locally, compared to the budget managed nationally, but also on the administrative skills and the political weight of local politicians and stakeholders. Ideally, the level of decision making could be measured by a *combined indicator* reflecting at the same time the formal and real transfer of power in the tourism sector or in the overall development process, if there are no specific provisions for tourism. This combined indicator would be based on a scale of legal transfer of power, the number of regional public servants compared to the size of budget or to the number of national civil servants, their formal educational level and the share of regional budget for development. Lobbying power should also be quantified;
- the *level of consultation with stakeholders and the institutionalisation of their involvement,* since this reflects good internal governance that can reinforce real autonomy. This, needs qualitative data not easily obtainable, unless specific surveys are introduced.

Alternative weightings for the individual components of such a combined indicator[138] should be tested. However, such an indicator does not exist, not even a proxy for it at the European level. The only alternative is therefore to use the formal structure

---

[138] This indicator would be the combined ranking of the following components: (a) the share of local budget compared to the national budget; (b) regional civil servants divided by the local budget; (c) the average educational level compared to the educational level of civil servants at the national level; (d) the share of regional budget used for development versus administration; (e) the number of (active) representatives of stakeholders in the regional council.

combined with general knowledge about the budget relevance. This proxy leaves us with the following three broad groups:

- Member States composed of one region only (at NUTS2 level), namely Luxembourg, Cyprus, Malta, Slovenia, Denmark and the Baltic republics. In this case the national and regional levels coincide and thus the strategy adopted depends on the organisational set up rather than the level of decision making.
- Federal States and Member States where there is a longer or shorter tradition of entrusting the territorial level with development initiatives. In this case the regional and local authorities have both the administrative competence and sufficient means (compared to the overall means available, not necessarily to the means needed) to intervene for local tourist development. Regions in Germany, Austria Spain, the UK and Belgium belong to this category and so do territorial authorities in the Netherlands, Sweden and Finland. Apparently, the time elapsing between formal autonomy and real autonomy is not very long, if the means are sufficient, as pointed out by the rapid maturity achieved by Belgium within two decades.
- Member States where there is a tradition of strong central power but overall European policies are pressing towards more regional autonomy. The problem in these regions is that regional and local authorities usually lack the financial and administrative skills to pursue active policies and the degree of completion of the transfer of power within this group varies considerably from one country to another. It should also be mentioned that in this fluid situation the personalities and determination of local councils and engaged stakeholders can act as a leverage to give more real power to one region compared to another in the same Member State; effective public-private partnerships, for instance, can be crucial. Regions in the following countries belong to this category: France, Ireland, Portugal, Greece, Italy, Poland, Hungary, the Czech and Slovak Republics. However, here the degrees vary substantially with France and Ireland being sometimes closer to the second category.

2.1.2 A Classification based on Tourism Relevance

Tourism is an important and increasing source of wealth in Europe and particularly so for some of its regions. However, it is important to distinguish two dimensions in the economic relevance of tourism, which are not mutually exclusive, but do not coincide either:

1. *The relevance of the region for European tourism*, which may be high or low. A good way to distinguish this dimension is to break the number of European regions into two groups - top and bottom regions - using simply the ranking of total revenue gained from tourism. Top regions are relevant for wealth and employment overall, well marketed and known within and outside Europe and in that sense they are European or national assets. However, tourism is not necessarily of high regional relevance, since in these regions other sources of wealth creation may be more important; development policies may wish to face new opportunities or be threatened. So, being an important region for European tourism does not necessarily imply that territorial authorities would need to be active in tourism policy.

2. *The relevance of tourism for local development,* indicating the role played by tourism in overall local wealth creation. It is clear that when the contribution of the sector to local activities is important, its sustainability becomes an important parameter and policies in this case may need to be pro-active or not. However, when the share of tourism is low this does not mean that it should remain low in the future and further categorisation is needed. A good indicator for relevance is regional GVA generated by tourist activities total or per capita

The crossing of the two dimensions is presented in the following table. In the scheme, the correspondence with the tourism typologies identified under section B is also highlighted. The acronym RST refers to Regional Strategy for Tourism.

Category I and II are regions for which tourism is important but at different scales.

Category III includes regions which became winners through the market mechanism, while *Category IV* includes regions of two kinds: those regions which are generally very poor/rural or both and can find an interesting development strategy in specialising in tourism emerging niches, and regions where tourism should not become a priority of territorial policies because the economy is driven by other activities and other needs are more pressing. For *Category IVa* regions, on the other hand, active and long term sustainable tourism policies are needed and are among the most appropriate tools for their development.

Table D.1 Classification of regions on the basis of tourism relevance

	Regions ranking high in European tourism	Regions ranking medium to low in European tourism
Regions for which tourism is a vital share of local wealth creation	**Category I: High RST** Corresponding to mass tourism destinations (type 1, sub-type 1.2). Very relevant regions with a need for territorial support in priority. Example: Balearic Islands	**Category II: Tailored RST** Corresponding to traditional tourism destinations (type 2) Regions which depend on tourism but are of limited relevance to Europe Example: Voreio Aigaio
Regions for which tourism is less important as a share of local wealth creation	**Category III: Irrelevant RST** Corresponding to densely populated regions (type 1, sub-type 1.1). Very relevant regions but probably with no need for territorial support in priority. Example: Inner London	**Category IV: New/Nil RST** **Category IVa: New tourism policy focus.** Corresponding to new tourism destinations. (type 2, sub-type 2.1) Regions which are generally very poor/rural or both; in tourism they can find an interesting development strategy in emerging niches where they can become competitive. Example: Slovenia. **Category IVb: No need for a ST strategy.** Corresponding to a sub-group of the less visited regions (type 3) Regions where tourism should not become a priority of territorial policies because the economic landscape is well served by other activities Examples: Niederoesterreich, Brabant Wallone, Lorraine.

2.1.3   Path Dependencies: introducing the Level of Sustainability

Past strategies and path-dependencies are the third dimension for classifying regions in regard to the need and type of regional interventions. In a number of regions, tourism policy in the past has neglected the dimension of sustainability and has promoted (or left to the market) a model of mass tourism without investing in sustainability. The result is a high number of destinations where mass tourism (usually with a low contribution to GVA per incoming tourist) has resulted in the deterioration of the environment. The lack of preventive investment and regulation refers to zoning, investments in the quality of the air and the water, waste disposal and recycling. This has in turn triggered a negative image of the region and made it unattractive as a tourism destination, leaving it with a cost leadership instead of a differentiation advantage. Reversing a negative trend is both more costly and institutionally more difficult, as vested interests are expected to oppose change. Thus, for regions with accumulated problems, a sustainable strategy will be more difficult to adopt and implement than for regions starting a more pro-active policy now.

Since sustainability became a key concept with increasing emphasis in the last two decades only, "late coming regions" can benefit from starting at the beginning with the building of a more modern image, which includes services, clean environment, and marketing niches.

Three categories are thus suggested:

- Many of the regions/destinations which emerged as mass tourism in the past have done so at the cost of their environment. Damage in terms of pollution and zoning may be irreparable in the short term. These regions need a **strategy reversal** which is more difficult than the creation of a promotion strategy to introduce tourism as a key activity (for example some Italian and Spanish coastal regions, and Northern Crete). Some regions can demonstrate already successful strategies in that respect and constitute best practices.
- Few regions organised tourism with sustainability considerations and the corresponding investments from the very beginning. Usually, these regions serve high income tourists and some typical examples can be found in Switzerland, top ski resorts in Austria and France, luxury sea agglomerations in Sardinia, Eastern Crete and Southern France. These agglomerations are usually organised at municipal, rather than regional level. These can now benefit from natural resources which are still attractive. They also constitute good practices examples for regions conceiving tourism strategies at a later stage.
- Regions with **no accumulated damages** in either the environment or their reputation because they have had no mass or low quality tourism or other environmentally damaging production.

Distinguishing the three categories based on objective indicators will be very difficult, as it would involve qualitative appraisals, linking the level of pollution to incoming tourism plus surveys investigating the international image of each region. Such an appraisal would be even more complicated by the fact that brand names are sometimes referring to regions and others to smaller areas or even individual hotel facilities within a territory.

2.2   Main Conclusions on the Clustering Process

The effort to create a "governance map" based on a classification of decision making and implementation relevance did not produce any significant results, since the only proxy available was the legal status of the regions. Serious constraints are also faced in quantifying the impact of past strategies and path-dependencies on the level of sustainability.

Within the scope of this study, it is thus only possible to suggest policy interventions (or Regional Strategies for Tourism) for the theoretical types identified within the classification based on tourism relevance. As mentioned, this classification may be linked to the classification of tourism types outlined in section B of this study, the correspondence being specified in table 1.

2.2.1   High Regional Strategies for Tourism

In the High RST category, where tourism is already strongly present and is important not only for the region but also for the country and even for Europe as a whole, strategies at the regional level are usually insufficient, because the scale of the industry goes beyond the capabilities of a lower level of governance. Thus, the territorial authorities need to:

- focus on their vision and incorporate sustainability in it, specifying the extent to which the local model complies fully with the national image or has specific added value to offer;
- make sure the necessary local skills and funding may be mobilised. The territorial authorities are the most appropriate agent to judge on the adequacy (or not) of these capabilities;

- for whatever is beyond the local potential, organise the necessary links to assure assistance at the national and the European level. Stakeholder involvement is relevant both for the regional strategy and for broader lobbying, in particular because some of the actors will have a broader coverage themselves (such as the bigger hotel chains);
- often, these destinations have been abused in the past and suffer from congestion and environmental damages. Extra resources for a strategy reorientation need to be earmarked;
- a good strategy to rapidly improve the local image and assure higher level support is the creation of broader trans-regional alliances (see Box D1), or national (as the Irish Sustainable Development described in the previous chapter) or even European scale partnerships (e.g. a broader initiative on agro-tourism).

Neither of the above suggestions, including a successful and well marketed trans-regional strategy, are, however, sufficient without the design and implementation of a solid monitoring system.

> **Box D.1 Declaration of Seville**
>
> Mediterranean towns and local authorities declared together in Seville, in 1999, that they intended to maintain their identity and respect the "eco-region" leading to a stable economy. Their target was to link national and regional and sub-regional levels of government in a common effort while stressing the intensification of local democracy and participation. Environmental protection is explicitly mentioned in the Declaration. The Declaration is furthermore accompanied by an action plan envisaging, among other points:
>
> - high involvement of all practitioners of the Mediterranean Basin through partnerships and joint actions;
> - participatory processes by all possible means and implementation of local action plans for sustainable development, such as local Agenda 21;
> - exchanges of knowledge among practitioners;
> - respect the cultural and ethnic diversity of the Mediterranean Basin.

2.2.2 Tailored Regional Strategies for Tourism

Tailored RST are appropriate for smaller scale activities, which are relevant for the region but not so much for the country or Europe as a whole. For this type of strategy territorial authorities need to rely more on their own forces.

For regions trying to exploit specific advantages there is a need to maintain and promote natural and cultural sites; while most cities and regions have traditionally undertaken this type of activity, natural sites are often neglected and emphasis is given to the promotion rather than the sustainability aspects. The regions disposing of Natura 2000 sites, for instance, can benefit from promoting them. Regions facing traffic congestion problems, need to promote a model of alternative transport means and the enhancement of public transport.

In general, the territorial authorities need to:

- focus on their vision and incorporate sustainability in it, trying to promote specific niches and an image compatible with the evolving needs of tourism. A good management and monitoring system is again a prerequisite for success;
- ensure that the necessary local skills and funding are mobilised. Support from local actors and small private-public networks are important elements that can help to fill gaps in resources;
- tourism-focused support from resources offered by the national or European authorities is less likely, unless they are provided in the context of other policies: environmental protection, regional development aid or integrated transport design. Thus, the territorial authorities need to keep contact with all these types of national/European policies to exploit emerging opportunities;
- in this category some destinations have also been abused in the past and suffer from congestion and environmental damages. Extra resources for a strategy reorientation need to be earmarked.

> **Box D.2 Viabono, a new type of tour operator with emphasis on sustainable niche markets**
>
> The German umbrella brand "Viabono" for sustainable tourism products was established in Germany 2001 with the support of public financing. Later, it started being financed from the fees raised from issued licenses. Applicants may include hotels, campsites, tourism villages, bed and breakfast, nature parks, holiday apartments and cabins. Applicants have to meet tough environmental criteria and submit written proof of their statements. Among the criteria are waste reduction and recycling, energy efficiency and savings, noise pollution reduction, client comfort, respect of nature and country side, synergy with the local economic structure. The brand name uses its own standards and the internet as effective tools to market sustainability all over Germany. It is an example of market forces promoting sustainable measures.

Creating a good strategy, marketing it and, based on good governance principles, sharing the vision, the risks, the funding and the implementation with the private sector, is the most appropriate way to proceed. In this case the necessary resources are of lower scale. Broader agreements can help market such a strategy. The Viabono Initiative in Germany suggests a good practice (see Box D.2).

2.2.3   New Regional Strategies for Tourism

Regions that lack other types of attractions and have for this reason not been considered a traditional tourism destination, may adopt a new element in their development strategy and focus on sustainable forms of tourism (small hotels, or agro-tourism), or in specific other types of new activities (themes, sports etc). The difficulty of starting from scratch is compensated by the advantage of being free of accumulated damages for their sustainability or image. Steps to follow would be:

- focus on the vision and incorporate sustainability into it, trying to promote specific niches and an image compatible with the evolving needs of tourism. Stakeholder involvement would include actors with no experience in tourism;
- make a clear "business plan" for the targets and expectations of the new policy;
- try to attract some of the national actors (hotel chains, existing brand names, tour operators);
- make sure that consensus has been achieved and that they can mobilise the necessary local skills and funding.

2.3   Funding Needs, Constraints and the Relevance of Public-Private Partnerships

One of the major constraints, while trying to adopt a new, more demanding and long term strategy, is funding. Funds are necessary both for small-scale investments and for larger, indivisible projects, for physical and for intangible investments.

Table D.2   Investments' general classification

	Small scale	Indivisible
Tangible	Accommodation Catering Specific sites Means of transport	Airports, road, ports, cleaning the environment (all types of waste)
Intangible	Marketing hotels and restaurants, skill enhancement	Marketing the country, region, locality; regional training activities

All these investments can take sustainability into consideration or not, but as a general rule it should be kept in mind that:

- investments in sustainable activities are more costly than in others;
- regions in need of new tourism strategies require considerable investments.

Small-scale investments are usually undertaken by the private sector and include the building/operating of accommodations, catering, means of transport and entertainment. They are also connected with intangible investments like marketing, technological and organisational improvement and personnel training. Such investments, in particular in poorer areas or risky markets, are often supported by financial incentives in the form of grants or tax exemptions. Often these incentives are dictated by short-term needs and avoid the political cost of requesting a sustainability vision. Regional and national authorities need to connect public support with the compliance of private investments with sustainability.

Indivisible investments require large sums of funding, which poorer regions cannot afford. The more these infrastructures are demanding with high environmental standards, the more costly they are and the higher is the likelihood that regional authorities will compromise for quality/sustainability in order to reduce the total cost.

It is evident that in certain cases the creation/reorientation of tourism strategies is important and that both in regions which are less favoured and in regions where the past has created damages to sustainability there is a need for considerable indivisible tangible and intangible investments. The rule is that such regions do not dispose of the means to heavily invest in indivisible infrastructure, which has a long-term benefit. Thus, they are often caught in a vicious circle of underdevelopment, not because of lack of strategy or vision but because of lack of funds.

The solution may be found through public-private partnerships, which encompass many types of alliances based on both private and social returns of investment. Such partnerships may include partnering of the regional authorities with collective representations or individual actors to promote the region (e.g. jointly financed portals for instance), broader regulatory agreements (e.g. opening hours and special labour market arrangements, as often tourism is associated with more flexible employment structures) and, more recently, the particular case of privately financed initiatives[139].

In smaller partnerships and networks the public sector either offers grants or takes the role of the intermediary and/or regulator to increase trust relationships between the members of the network. In the case of PFIs the target refers to major tangible, indivisible investments, whereby the public sector gives a private consortium a concession to construct and then operate a major project for a limited period of time. The consortium, usually composed of big, multinational companies, is in a position to borrow from the capital and money markets and share the cost of the initial investment with the public. The investment amortisation and the

> **Box D.3 Major Privately Financed Initiatives (PFIs) in Attica**
>
> Attica, the region surrounding Athens, has been a less favoured region with major problems of sustainability attributed to its metropolitan character, attracting manufacturing investment and inward migration, but also to a very high share of tourism visiting the classical archaeological sites. By the end of the 20th century the traffic and pollution problems had considerably deteriorated the quality of life in the city of Athens. However, national and regional authorities did not address the problem, despite regional support funding from the EU. In connection with the preparation of the Olympics the decision was made to undertake three major public works with a PFI mode:
> - a new international airport
> - a ring-road motorway and
> - a subway.
>
> The three projects made quite a difference in the daily life of the citizens, reduced pollution and made the city more attractive for tourism.

profits of the consortium are financed by the operation of the project. In Box D.3 the case of Attica is presented, where the decision to build three major projects by PFIs changed the landscape of the region. The crucial element for successful PFIs is the existence of a future market and the skills to negotiate a mutually beneficial agreement, where both the private sector will make reasonable profits and the public will benefit from large social returns on investment. The share of initial funding and the time horizon of the concession are the crucial elements in the negotiation.

2.4   Conclusions

No data is available for a detailed and systematic analysis of tourism policy at the regional level. There is thus a necessity to strongly lobby in favour of improving available statistics.

---

[139] More details on PFIs are provided in section E of this study.

Since sustainability has a long-term horizon and is costly, it will never be obtained by market forces alone; there is a need for a vision and strategy, with persistence and political commitment. But it is also a typical area where long term private and social return on investment coincide and thus the public sector and tourism stakeholders can and should share this cost.

Regions, which need to adopt a sustainable tourism strategy or re-orient their strategies towards a new brand name, need to invest heavily to implement and market their new strategy. To do that they should (with different emphasis depending on the types of region):

- make explicit strategic plans and match them with resources and a good management and monitoring system;
- clarify the role of stakeholders and share with them some of the funding and risks;
- organise trans-regional, national and international alliances accordingly;
- link support to individual companies with sustainability considerations;
- promote public-private partnerships and PFIs.

The urban governance and development in Banská Štiavnica, Slovak Republic

Banská Štiavnica, the oldest mining town in Slovakia, is an historic centre and an outstanding example of advanced medieval urban design. It is located in south-central Slovakia on the steep slopes of the Glanzenberg and Paradajz mountains. The wealth generated by a mineral and mining economy supported the development of crafts and fine arts up to the 19th century, when with the gradual exhaustion of the mines, decline started. The town lost its administrative importance, the University and significant research institutions. The population dropped by one third and deterioration of the historic centre and of several architectural and technical monuments occurred.

Restoration and conservation activities date back to the 1950s when the town was declared one of the first Urban Conservation Areas in Slovakia. A strategy based on awareness raising of its cultural and technical values and on gaining international recognition is more recent. In 1993, Banská Štiavnica was

Key issues:

⇨ Since 1993, the historic town was included in the UNESCO World heritage list.

⇨ International recognition and improved local governance were driving forces to re-boost economy while becoming a tourism destination.

inscribed on the UNESCO World Heritage List. It became the district administrative centre and the headquarters of two nation wide institutions, university education returned after 80 years, more than 30 architectural monuments were renovated, several sites were preserved, more than 2,000 jobs were created. In the past ten years it has also sought for destination of tourism. As such, it has been studied as a pilot demonstration project for promoting sustainable tourism in Central and Eastern Europe.

It is also registered in the UN-Habitat "Best practices database in improving the living environment".

Links & references:

UNESCO World Heritage web page on Banská Štiavnica: http://whc.unesco.org/pg.cfm?cid=31&id_site=618

UAKOM Unit, Matej Bel University: http://www.uakom.sk/bs/bans_hist.html

BfN, 2002. Biodiversity and tourism in the framework of the convention on biological diversity. The case of the natural and cultural heritage of Banská Štiavnica, Slovak Republic. Garbe C., et al. (Eds). http://www.bfn.de/09/banska.pdf

UN – Habitat, Best Practice Database in Improving the Living Environment : http://www.bestpractices.org/database/

3.   The Role of ICT in Sustainable Tourism

3.1   Key Features of the ICT revolution

The Information & Communication Technology (ICT) revolution refers to the application of a broad scope of new products and services, which are transforming all kinds of interaction in business. The major changes emerge from services using digital electronic methods and tools to gather, process, share and distribute information. Digital electronic methods and tools can be software applications and components, data, formal specifications, standards or devices. These means are becoming increasingly powerful, cost-effective and diversified in the last decades, combined, since the early '90s, with the secular changes brought up by the Internet, which cancelled the costs of distance in communication. The revolution introduced by the Internet consists mainly on the ability to use ICTs real time and interactively among independent users, be it intentionally (closed networks with defined relations as in electronic data interchange), targeted (electronic marketing) or fuzzy (peer to peer).

While the diffusion pace of these technologies is faster than for any other technology in the past, it is still in a process of growth. Although technologies themselves are broadly and cheaply available, matters of organisation, standards, skills and, last but not least, social resistance, delay their ubiquitous adoption.

One major characteristic of the ICT sector is that it is highly pervasive, thus triggering a new techno-economic paradigm. This makes it important for every aspect of economic and social life, ranging from business transformations to wider welfare effects related to electronic health services and transport safety.

In economic activities the *concept of e-business* is adopted, meaning "doing business electronically". This denotes ICT applications in the business sector helping to increase and improve the content of information and at the same time to reduce its cost. This applies to any type of information affecting the internal organisation of a company (value chain) as well as its contacts with its environment, both upstream and downstream (value system)[140]. Thus, the impact on individual companies affects the whole industry via the changes it triggers to the value system.

---

[140] Porter M.E.,1985

At the same time these processes can facilitate the government in becoming less bureaucratic and more efficient in its role as regulator and in the interaction with citizens/consumers. The corresponding concept to e-business is *e-government*, where information and interaction are increasingly exchanged electronically.

The crucial features of the diffusion of e-business/e-government, which affect all economic activities, may be summarised in the following points:

- Information becomes more widespread and less costly; thus economic activities operate closer to what economists call a perfect market squeezing rents to an industry average in commoditised markets.
- However, at the same time, the possibility to increase information flows and customise them, allows firms to adopt *strategies of differentiation*[141] thus profiting from increased rents attributed to niche or captive markets. This feature is of particular interest to peripheral market segments, which traditionally did not benefit from economies of scale or scope and remained marginal.
- Besides the effect on the facilitation of access to information, e-business is characterized by a considerable decrease of information processing costs. This affects the cost structure in all industries but particularly in those where information plays a crucial role (such as financial markets, retail trade, marketing and tourism).
- As a result, it is clear that in this period of business restructuring and re-adjustment the adoption of new strategies and visions will determine the success or failure of individual actors in the years to come.

In the following paragraphs an effort is made to identify the way and extent with which these features apply to the tourism industry and how they can contribute in fostering sustainable tourism.

3.2   The Influence of ICT on Tourism

The analysis of the application of crucial e-business features in tourism implies a systematic review of the ways these applications are integrated into the business. The following paragraphs provide a quick overview of the diffusion of these technologies,

---

[141] Porter M.E.,1985

as well as an effort to identify how this affects the various stakeholders and the balance of power among them.

3.2.1   The Role of ICT for Tourism: Ways of Influence

Tourism, being among the most information-dependent industries, is highly influenced by the introduction of ICT services. The term 'e-tourism' is being used more and more widely referring to e-business in the field of travel and tourism, i.e. the use of ICT to enable tourism providers and destinations to operate more efficiently, and to reach and serve consumers more effectively with facilities to search, compare and book tourism products. After an initial period of ICTs used to market tourism, the sector now uses the Internet for interactive services.

The following steps in the value chain are influenced by the adoption of ICTs[142]:

- front office: reservations, check-in, payments;
- back office: accounting, payroll, human resources management, marketing;
- customer entertainment and service;
- communication with consumers and partners;
- marketing research;
- reaction and management of unexpected events;
- flexible and dynamic pricing through yield management;
- differentiation and personalization of products;
- monitoring performance indicators and building feedback mechanisms;
- control of business processes and personnel.

ICT applications may be considered as playing a variety of roles:

- *Marketing/informing of firms:* initially, it was larger companies and bigger chains only which offered information and marketing via the Internet, but as cost for home pages reduces, most companies even of very small scale, are offering individual information and often the possibility to book on-line. *Ceteris paribus*, regions where a high share of firms uses Internet facilities are likely to attract more tourists than others.

---

[142] World Tourism Organisation, 2003

- *One way access to regional information*, mainly the provision of the basic features of the place to visit, is also facilitated. This is an easy part, where technologies are broadly available (although systematically progressing) and the exploitation of this function is largely a matter of decision, design and diffusion. This simple model consisting of a web site is by now fairly easy and inexpensive that every region, city or locality can afford it. But as technological capabilities improve and users become experienced and demanding, higher value added and better content is required. Web sites of this type may be created by individual actors (hotels, catering) or whole countries, regions or smaller territorial units. The broader the population covered, the more likely the need for a portal rather than a simple site. Overlapping sites may end up by doing more damage than good.

- *Transaction oriented sites* are the most important tools offered by ICT applications and through the facilitation of direct contacts between clients and service providers they may be altering the structure and power of the stakeholders. This will be analysed in more detail in the next paragraph. Although technologies are available here as well, diffusion is often limited through problems of data security and the cost of maintenance. Here again the unit of promotion can be individual actors or pooled resources in broader geographical areas. Web sites used for transactions have created a new kind of intermediaries, electronic ones, that offer the possibility to book on-line and charge the tourism actors a fee for this service.

- Help to change the *strategy and vision of regions*, enabling new forms of tourism, if the adequate infrastructure is provided for (e.g. health tourism through e-health, business and education facilities through access to broadband and wi-fi's). ICTs in that sense offer the possibility to create new niche markets and build competitive advantages instead of relying on comparative advantages[143].

---

[143] The modern theory of international economics accepts the reasoning that competitive production in a geographical location does not need to rely on given comparative advantages (climate, natural resources) but can be systematically built.

Firms, territorial and national authorities are well aware of this enabling technology as well as of the dangers associated with it, if they neglect them. However, the pace of diffusion differs and the type of ICT adoption as well: hardware enabling access to information is increasing rapidly, created by market opportunities in core regions and Community support framework funding in less favoured regions. One way flow of information, namely the creation of web sites and e-mail, are common tools, while interactive services, covering the whole range of transactions, are not as frequent, as they are most costly and need organisation, scale and maintenance. Issues of security, interoperability and electronic payment are inhibiting rapid adoption.

3.2.2   Evidence on ICT Penetration in the Tourism Industry

The Internet will become a major sales channel and will affect all parts of the value chain. Since its creation, national tourism offices, regional agencies, major chains and intermediaries offered sites with information and marketing for their localities. In the United States and Europe this is now commonplace. However, as technology spreads, being present in cyberspace is insufficient: design and user friendliness need to improve along users demand of more interactive services to be able to complete all their transactions on the web.

The following features are relevant [144]:

- So far, only the major players and half of the tourism SME companies have incorporated the Internet into their day-to-day activities. SMEs still have a lot of work to do in this area. The majority still takes the order via the phone or fax. Only 37% of the micro-enterprises, i.e. those with less than 10 employees, are selling via their own web sites. And only 22% of them are linking themselves with the web sites of other business/organisations. This indicates that they do not yet sufficiently anticipate the value of this new technology as an enabler for business success. The funding of the necessary platforms (portals, communication platforms) will not be a barrier for SMEs, because the major players will want to invest in them.
- Because of the growing competition between these major players, *it is likely that prices of tourism products will decrease and more technology will be used* in order to reduce costs and remain competitive. The major tourism

---

[144] World Tourism Organisation, 2003

stakeholders and companies will therefore invest in the Internet as a way to reduce distribution costs (e.g. booking services, e-marketing). SMEs will need to benefit from these investments.

- However, the on-line market has arrived in Europe, even with some lags compared to the United States. The WTO projects that about 1 additional percentage point of the whole market is going electronic by 2006, thus forecasting that 6% of the whole market will be on-line by then. Certain features are of interest in this process:

  - 64% of Internet sales are direct sales;
  - UK sales represent 34% of Western European sales;
  - airlines are 60% of total sales and half of this is from low-cost airlines.

Figure D.1 ICT, Hotels and campings with 10 or more employees, 2004*, percentage

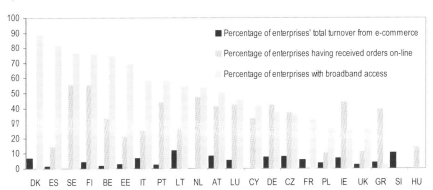

* Data for FI, LU and FR refer to 2002; data for GR refer to 2003   Source: based on data from Eurostat

On average, at EU level, 5.29% of the hotel and camping enterprises' total turnover is from e-commerce. According to 2004 data from Eurostat Lithuania accounts for the highest rate (11.5%) while Spain shows the lowest (1.2%). The five declaring countries among the new Member States have an average which is higher than the EU average (6.94%), a further demonstration of the dynamism of tourism enterprises in these regions. Figure D.1 shows a diversified penetration of ICTs in the hotel business in Europe.

It is clear that as Internet home penetration increases tourism destinations, which will not offer interactive facilities, will be losing out to electronically better-endowed ones.

Regional tourism associations will have an important role in this area because economies of scale and scope will play a role. They will further develop their web-offering, enabling SMEs not only to be accessible, via regional portals, to their potential consumers, but also to have access to experiences and best practices from other SMEs from their region or beyond it. This type of knowledge sharing will be an important enabler for innovation.

3.2.2.1   *The case of ICT in the transport sector*

The transport sector is characterised by a high fixed-cost base, and maximising load factors whilst reducing the cost of operating planes, trains or coaches is the key to maximising profits (e.g. low cost airlines). One of the most important structural changes is the adoption of e-booking. Many companies have successful and sophisticated web sites. Automated booking systems enable 'around-the-clock' access for customers and reduce administration and call-centre costs as well as commission rates.

One of the most rapidly applied services in the early days of e-commerce was the online travel industry, which "took off" in the United States as millions of consumers booked their own travel reservations. Travelocity, Orbitz, Priceline and Expedia served as models - showing other industries innovative ways to use the Internet to bring better service and pricing options directly to customers. Even while the US travel industry as a whole staggered, following the terrorist attacks of 11 September, the online segment recorded huge gains. This year, nearly one-third of US travel will be booked online, with online agencies accounting for nearly half of that total.

There is plenty of scope in most transport modes to utilise technology to make travelling conditions easier and to facilitate inter-modal transfers. Integrated ticketing between different modes facilitates a seamless journey and makes public transport more attractive. Better baggage handling, too, between different transport modes, including during transfers, encourages using these modes.

3.2.3   Striking a Balance between Centralised and Decentralised Systems

ICTs do not only facilitate transactions and make them more cost effective, but they considerably affect the power and articulation of the stakeholders.

The actual market is evolving towards one where business networking, system integration and customer relation building will become key for all operations in the industry. New business models emerge, intermediaries are reorganised, consumers get more information without additional cost and increase their own scope of choice, smaller actors can easily pool resources and benefit from economies of scope, which allow them to compete with bigger actors more effectively than in the past.

In the past, economies of scale were the determining factor of cost and information and thus the travel organisers and intermediaries (namely travel agencies and tour operators) dominated the industry. Tour operators, especially in the UK and Germany, have experienced rapid vertical and horizontal integration, thus bringing all the tourism sector enterprises under one umbrella. This consolidation is limiting the number of medium sized tour operators in the market. In a study, it was found that by 1997, a 35% market share of the tourism sector was controlled by the 5 largest tour organisers (term referring to tour operators and travel agents together). By 2002, this figure had increased to 70%[145].

The interrelation of travel products is complex and the role of the travel organiser is varied and evolving. Traditionally, tour operators have had a wholesaling role, packaging products such as airline seats, hotel rooms and coach transfer facilities in bulk for sale to the travel agent. Agents act as retailers in the chain, selling travel services or packaged trips to the customer; they carry no stock and act as intermediaries between the traveller and supplier. Tourist guides and tourist information services play a supporting role to the tourism product, offering information and services, usually at the tourism destination. However, the traditional delineation is blurring as tour operators are increasingly selling their packages direct to customers, cutting out the intermediary. In other cases, the providers, such as hotels and airlines, are selling direct to customers, bypassing travel organisers altogether[146].

Because of ICTs, barriers to entry are diminishing and new actors are emerging, as is the case of intermediaries having much lower fixed costs and working on commission. The case of Expedia (Box D.4) is of interest and so is Tiscover, which started in a small city in Austria ten years ago and expanded to become a multinational player.

---

[145] Leidner R., 2003

[146] European Commission, Directorate General for Enterprise, 2003

However, a full decentralisation and an annulment of economies of scale are by far not generalised. Three online firms now control over 55% of all online travel bookings[147]. In the case where standards and cyber-security play a crucial role, only centralized systems (Galileo, Amadeus) can operate.

The major challenge introduced by the ICTs is the degree with which actors will take advantage of them:

- Bigger actors can reduce their cost, improve their marketing and become even more competitive, through better internal organisation;
- However, at the same time, smaller actors or collective representations (government, semi-government or private) can pool resources and exploit economies of scope they could not exploit in the past.

> **Box D.4   Major European travel sites**
>
> Expedia is the most visited multi-category travel site in Europe, closely followed by Lastminute.com. The findings are from a Nielsen/NetRatings report, also highlighting that the number of European women visiting travel sites has increased more significantly than men in the past year.
>
> Multi-category travel sites attracted 2.2 million more women to their web sites in February 2005 compared to a year ago, a trend reflecting the experience of the United States. Women account for 44% of visitors, compared to 36% at the same time last year. Italy saw the largest growth at 50%, while women in the UK and Sweden lagged behind with just a 3% increase over one year.
>
> Top 10 multi-category travel sites in Europe as at February 2005, in terms of unique audience (000s) and active reach (%) are: Expedia 4,448 (3.96%); Lastminute.com 3,976 (3.54%); voyages-sncf.com 3,304 (2.94%); Opodo 2,193 (1.95%); Yahoo! Travel 1,748 (1.56%); TUI 1,726 (1.54%); Ebookers 1,276 (1.14%); eDreams 1,217 (1.08%); Virgin Travel 1,190 (1.06%); Hapag-Lloyd 1,096 (0.98%).

The future is still open, but the need to reinforce the pooling of resources is clear. This leads to the reinforcement of the dynamics of the SME segment. This enterprise group represents a high number of companies and employees and has always been the backbone of the tourism industry.

3.3   Influence on Sustainability and Networks

In selecting the most crucial features in order to understand the role of ICTs in sustainable tourism, it is important to keep in mind that ICTs allow for the marketing of smaller scale activities and niche markets; as environmental issues are in the minds

---
[147] World Tourism Organisation, 2003

of consumers, direct marketing may benefit this market segment. Very small activities, like agro-tourism or small traditional hotels can strongly benefit from the opportunities offered by ICTs to pool resources, market and sell very small scale tourism products.

What ICTs seem to contribute to is this increased potential of information. The new challenge with this is who will manage this information and who will be accountable for it. This question brings us back to the levels of governance but also to good governance models, namely:

- Which level is the most appropriate to gather tourism information and spread it in the public domain? There are many cases[148] where more actors tried to become the official source of information for a particular territory.
- Who is accountable for this information? What about abuse, fraud or limited reliability and lack of update? As there are no standards for benchmarking in the internet yet, there does not seem to be any solution to the problem, and this is not unique to the tourism sector but everywhere.
- What about potentially controversial information? Who has the right to impose his view? In particular, when dealing with digital images and information on cultural/natural heritage, who should control the content?
- What about replication of costs? If the local and regional levels are the most appropriate ones to manage official sites, then they would need to pay for the same platform as many times as territorial authorities would decide to create a site. The more interactive and reliable the platform, the higher the cost.

These questions give a first idea of the problems associated with the potential offered by ICTs. While there is no uniform answer on how to deal with this problem, and since diversity confirms that there is more than one model which can work well, the only arising recommendation is that territorial authorities could label one site as "the official site" of the region. But to do that they should be sure to have the resources to maintain and improve it, as well as the stakeholders' agreement.

---

[148] In Crete, a region highly dependent on tourism, the creation of a regional site was strongly delayed in the late 1990s because there was disagreement between the regional authority (who had created a special development company for this purpose, and this never really operated) and major stakeholders. As long as the debate lasted, a variety of individual sites emerged.

There are several initiatives supported by the Commission in the tourism sector to promote e-business. Their complete list and description is available through the ISPO web site[149].

Examples on how Internet and/or Networks can support Sustainable Tourism include the Network for the Sustainable Development of Tourism Destinations in Europe[150], and the ECOSERT Partnerships Projects (INTERREG)[151].

3.4   Conclusions and Recommendations

The introduction of ICTs and the Internet are deeply affecting the future of tourism creating both threats and opportunities. Features analysed above from the point of view of regional development policies for sustainable tourism may be summarised as follows:

- In the future, on-line tourism market will increase significantly and soon regions without a good site/portal offering good information and interactive services will be losing out compared to those regions that can offer them.

- ICTs offer an opportunity to create new regional tourism strategies, which will make regions competitive in selected niche markets; the marketing tool bringing them close to consumers reduces tremendously the cost and time to see return on investing in such a strategy.

- Sustainability can benefit from the introduction of ICTs because of a better operation and monitoring of all tourism-related activities.

- Sustainability can further benefit from the possibility to pool resources and promote small actors, remote places and agro-tourism.

---

[149] Information Society Promotional Office, Tourism:
http://europa.eu.int/ISPO/ecommerce/books/aecev2/1_4_2.htm
[150] The network web site: www.tourism-site.org
[151] ECOSERT web site: www.ecosert.org.gr

However, the introduction of ICTs increases market transparency and competition, thus threatening regions that are unable to benefit from the introduction of modern techniques.

The important lessons for action by territorial authorities may include:

- to adopt explicit strategies and visions taking the new enabling technologies into consideration and positioning their tourism strategy in this context;
- to dedicate resources to use these technologies not only for marketing but also for interactive services;
- to assure quality of design and service as well as accountability.

In this context, the streamlining of activities and the selection of alliances and complementarities with national authorities and the private sector are crucial.

A network for e-tourism, the case of Austria

CS_6

The Austrian Federal Ministry of Economic Affairs and Employment - with the support of the Federal Provinces of Lower Austria, Salzburg and Tyrol - created and developed 'anet', a competence network on e-tourism. The network aims to facilitate the take up of the new opportunities created in the tourism industry by the rapid developments of technologies. Among the network's main objectives are the enhancement of the national tourism-oriented IT industry and the strengthening of the tourism economy through the improved competitiveness of tourism SMEs.

The network has three competence centers in Krems (Tourism Research Center), Salzburg (eTourism Center) and Innsbruck (eTourism Competence Center Austria) and a common umbrella organization in Innsbruck. Each center is supported by business and research partners. In particular, the eTourism Center aims to develop an innovation process leading to the optimization of the value chain through the use of information technologies and to deliver to the industry end-products enabling better planning, services, and marketing. Within a project timeframe of 4 years and a budget of € 5.74 Million - of which 40% from the Austrian Federal

Key issues:

⇨ Integrated strategy at national level to face the challenges of e-commerce developments within the tourism industry

⇨ Participation of private and public stakeholders

⇨ Specific target to maintain high the competitiveness level of Austrian SMEs within the tourism industry, with the twofold aim to reduce the costs for providers and increase the quality of services.

Ministry for Economy and Labour, 20% from the State of Salzburg, 40% from the Industry Partners, the following key objectives will be tackled: improvement in the quality of services for the guest through ICT; costs reduction for the service provider and increased visibility on the market; standardization of information systems and processes

In 2004, 2219 Austrian enterprises belonging to the NACE category 'Hotels, camping sites and other providers of short-stay accommodation' had Internet access, representing 96.4% of the total, this value being well above the national average of 93.7% (Statistics Austria) for total industry enterprises.

Links & references:

Austrian Network for e-tourism ('anet') web site: http://www.anet-network.at/english/network.html

eTourism Center web site: http://www.etourism-center.at/html/index_e.html

Statistics Austria web site: http://www.statistik.at/

SECTION E:
FUNDING SUSTAINABLE TOURISM IN THE EUROPEAN UNION

1.   The Structural Funds

A number of tourism projects have received support from the EU despite the absence of a specific budget line dedicated to tourism activities. In fact, tourism project proposals can be submitted to "horizontal", i.e. not sector-based, programmes, actions or instruments. The single, largest source of funding for tourism, particularly in the less developed regions, are the Structural Funds, aiming at achieving greater economic and social cohesion and reducing disparities among the EU Member States.

Structural Funds are non reimbursable grants, co-funded by public and private sources, and channelled through three instruments:

· **Objective 1[152], 2[153] and 3[154] Mainstream Programmes,** negotiated between the European Commission and the responsible authorities in the Member States, the latter being also responsible for local programme implementation. More specifically, they finance the European Regional Development Fund (ERDF), the European Social Fund (ESF), the Financial Instruments for Fisheries Guidance (FIFG), and the European Agricultural Guidance and Guarantee Fund (EAGGF). They account for 94% (183.56 billion €) of the total Structural Funds allocation (EU 15);

· **Innovative Measures**, targeting experimentation on regional development through innovative actions implemented by public and private partnerships at regional level; 0.5% (1 billion €) of the total Structural Funds allocation is earmarked under this heading (EU 15);

· **Community Initiatives,** whose general objectives are decided at the Community level and proposed by the Commission to the Member States. They are

---

[152] Objective 1 regions have GDP per capita below the 75% threshold of the EU 15 average and absorb 70% of the overall budget for Structural Funds. Before enlargement, they covered some 50 regions with 22% of the overall EU 15 population.

[153] Objective 2 regions are those undergoing economic and social restructuring. They account for 18% of the EU 15 population and receive 11.5% of the Structural Funds' budget.

[154] A sectoral Objective targeting job creation and training systems and covering the whole EU with the exception of Objective 1 regions (where sectoral measures are already part of the programmes). It receives 12.3% of the budget.

implemented through operational programmes in partnership with the concerned regional and local authorities. 5.35% (10.44 billion €) of the total Structural Funds allocation for the period is set aside under this instrument (EU 15).

In 1995, the Community Action Plan to Assist Tourism[155] attributed a budget of 10,5 billion € of which 20% for 'tourism and environment' (pilot projects and soft tourism). In recent years, the Structural Funds have provided an average of 800.000 € per year for direct measures to tourism development, many of which related to quality improvement. From the year 2000 onwards, Structural Funds were expected to give more emphasis on the issues of sustainability in tourism. The overall allocation for the 2000-2006 period, covering two Objectives areas (Objective 1 and 2) as well as the sectoral Objective 3, was 195 billion € for the EU 15 Member States and 22 billion € for acceding countries (period 2004 – 2006).

In the next programming period, 2007-2013, Structural Funds will represent about one third of the EU 25 budget for a total of 336.1 billion €. The majority of this amount will be spent in less-developed Member States and regions and will focus on the three priorities of convergence, competitiveness and co-operation.

1.1   Objective 1, 2 and 3 Mainstream Programmes

1.1.1   European Regional Development Fund (ERDF)

The ERDF is the major source of funding for tourism development. Many of the Member State programmes include special measures for tourism development. In the previous programming phase (1994-1999), 4.2 billion € was allocated to 367 tourism projects through the ERDF. Priority was given to the improvement in the quality of tourism supply, the reduction of the seasonal character of tourism, the development of the exploitation of the cultural patrimony of Europe, promotion of rural tourism and of training within the tourism industry. To mention some examples, in Spain the development of non-intensive tourism in the Aragon region has been co-financed under the Structural Fund 5b objectives[156]. In the programming period 2000-2006, Greece and Portugal developed programmes on culture and tourism. In Greece, the

---

[155] Council of the European Union, 1992
[156] European Environment Agency, 1999

ERDF invested 415 m€ to promote tourism potentials, preserve archaeological heritage and modernise infrastructures and tourism related services[157].

Despite this large contribution from ERDF, the exact financial figures channelled specifically to tourism activities, i.e. not indirectly benefiting the sector, are difficult to extract. As Rodriguez-Pose and Fratesi[158] state " *...In the continental regions of Portugal, and during the second programming period, an average of 10% of Objective 1 Funds has been targeted to business and tourism support. However, it is not easy to distinguish the specific share allocated to tourism neither the kind of projects supported. It is reasonable to advance that funds were mostly addressed to support infrastructures development, and not sustainable tourism projects...*".

In Corse, an example of indirect, but vital, contribution to tourism development is the Ajaccio airport project, with ERDF contributing 7.9 m€ out of 17 m€. Completed in 1999, the airport doubled its capacity to respond to the increased flux of visitors and the infrastructural design was improved to minimise landscape impact.

1.1.2   European Social Fund (ESF)

This entity provides funding for developing human resources and aid for employment in the tourism sector through Objective 3 measures and the EQUAL Community Initiative.

1.1.3   Financial Instruments for Fisheries Guidance (FIFG)

The main instrument for Community aid to the fisheries sector applies only to coastal regions and aims at re-boosting the economy in areas dependent on fisheries and aquaculture through socio-economic measures. Tourism projects might be eligible provided they meet relevant criteria, e.g. training of fishermen and diversification of activities.

---

[157] European Commission, Directorate General for Regional Policy, 2002
[158] Rodriguez-Pose A., Fratesi U., 2002

The overall Structural Funds allocation for Spain (2000-2006) is 46.768 billion € of which 94 m€ for the Objective 2 areas of the Balearic islands region. In total, almost 550 m€ are mobilised, including 96 m€ from public authorities and 350 m€ from the private sector. The programme targets the creation of some 5.000 new jobs and the maintenance of around 23.000 existing ones. It includes five priority areas: competitiveness, employment and productive fabric; environment and water resources; knowledge society; transport and energy networks; local and urban development.

The Balearics benefit from different sources of Structural Funds: Objective 2, Objective 3, Cohesion Fund, INTERREG III, EQUAL, LEADER +, FIFG (outside Objective 1). The population of the archipelago, currently standing at 900.000 residents, has among the highest annual income of the country (over 21.000 €/per capita) and an employment rate well below the average. Three quarters of the jobs are concentrated in services and around half are driven by tourism. Excluding construction, industry is highly fragmented and employs 12% of the active population.

Key issues:

⇨ Main target of diversifying the economy and decrease dependence on tourism.

⇨ Cohesion Funds used for environmental protection projects with indirect advantages for the tourism industry.

⇨ Synergies between Mainstream Programmes and Community Initiatives funded projects.

The primary sector is marginal. The region is often quoted as an example of mass tourism with high environmental costs, approaching a final phase of decline. A recent study by Aguiló et al. (2005) takes into account the model of sustainable development and analyses three hypotheses addressing economic and social variables. In general, it is accepted that the Balearics need to diversify the economy to decrease the excessive dependence on tourism. Investments in innovation concern for two thirds the ICT sector, and for one fifth the environmental sector. With public concern and awareness raising regarding the depletion of natural resources, tourism enterprises with credentials for sustainable and compatible environmental impact have potentials to gain an increasing market share.

Links & references :

Finestra Turistica web site, CITTIB (Centre d'Investigació i de Tecnologies Turístiques de les Illes Balears): http://www.finestraturistica.org/fintur/quees/index.en.jsp

Govern de les Illes Balears, Conselleria d'Economia, Hisenda i Innovació: http://www.caib.es

Brochure on Structural Funds: www.mcrit.com/euram/documents/bale_funds.pdf

Aguiló E., Alegre J. and Sard M., 2005. The persistence of the sun and sand tourism model. Tourism Management, Volume 26, Issue 2: Pages 219-231

The "Schaufenster" project in Bremerhaven[159] (Germany), with an EC contribution of 3.7 m€ (out of 12.17 m€) allowed the restructuring and modernisation of the old harbour quarter and came up with an integrated approach to economic development, including tourism, cultural attractions and vocational training specifically targeting fisheries. Restructuring of the fishing sector taking into account tourism potentials is also represented by the fishing port of Peniche in Portugal, where some ships where equipped and converted to tourism sailing and fishing[160].

1.1.4   European Agricultural Guidance and Guarantee Fund (EAGGF)

This is the Community instrument to support the agriculture and forestry sector and provides an indirect contribution to the development of rural tourism through its Guidance Section. The Community Initiative LEADER+ is funded under this heading and supports a number of initiatives directly or indirectly related to sustainable tourism.

1.2   Innovative Measures

A number of Innovative Measures deals with tourism, in particular with the application of information and communication technologies and promotion of networking and best practices. A vast library of projects is available through the DG Regional Policy portal[161].

An example is provided by the 3I (Innovation in the Ionian Islands) programme in the Ionian islands[162], promoting business innovation and world-class tourism practices. The main goal is to make businesses and technology intermediaries aware of global trends in technology, innovation, and marketing, and implement some of the most advanced practices in these fields. Specific objectives on sustainable tourism development are: to blend digital services into traditional services providing innovative services in the tourism sector, such as weekend travelling roadmaps, hotel selections and booking, virtual cultural routes, senior citizen off-season travelling,

---

[159] Schaufenster" web site: http://www.schaufenster-fischereihafen.de/
[160] European Commission, Directorate General for Regional Policy, 2001
[161] European Commission, Directorate General for Regional Policy, 2004 (a)
[162] Innovation in the Ionian Islands web page: http://hermes.westgate.gr/3i/page_en/index.htm

cultural event travelling planner; to develop quality standards and benchmarking in large tourist operations; to create new services and innovative start-ups capitalising on the local resources of tourism, culture, local agricultural products and artefacts; the protection of the rural environment from the expanding need of enlargement of the urban areas and the monitoring and control of clean salt water conditions, especially in the resorts that are certified as 'blue flags".

1.3   Community Initiatives

During the period 2000-2006, four Community Initiatives are operational: EQUAL, INTERREG III, LEADER+, URBAN II. They differ in their programming and funding mechanisms from the Mainstream Programmes but derive their finance from the same Community budget allocation. In fact, INTERREG and URBAN are financed under the ERDF, LEADER+ under the EAGGF and EQUAL under the ESF.

1.3.1 INTERREG   III: trans-European   co-operation   for   balanced development

INTERREG III is made up of 3 strands and has a total budget of 4,875 billion € (1999 prices):

- INTERREG IIIA: <u>cross-border cooperation</u>, i.e. between adjacent regions (i.e. all NUTS III areas situated along the internal and external land borders of the EU and certain NUTS III maritime areas) aims to develop cross-border social and economic centres through common development strategies. Only this strand offers direct financial support for individual enterprises. Tourism is the only economic sector explicitly mentioned in the guidelines as a target for development. In the period 1994-1999, approximately 200 m€ was allocated to tourism projects with INTERREG IIA[163]. Within the 17,5 % of the budget allocated to mountain areas, about 45 % has been spent on tourism projects, most of them in the Pyrenees and Bohemian Massif.

- INTERREG IIIB: <u>transnational cooperation</u>, seeks to involve national, regional and local authorities to promote better integration within the EU through the creation of macro-regions. The proposed case study (CS_7) is an example of

---

[163] European Commission, 2001 (e)

combined funding between this programme and PHARE to promote high quality tourism in the Baltic area.

- INTERREG IIIC: interregional cooperation, seeks to improve the effectiveness of regional development policies and instruments through large-scale information exchange and sharing of experience (networks). For instance, the SUstainable and VOcational Tourism (SUVOT) project, a 3-year INTERREG IIIC project recently launched, aims at reinforcing the action lines of the Network of Cities for Sustainable Tourism (NCST). It consists of 16 local authorities that signed a common charter committing themselves to the promotion of sustainability in coastal areas. The project also aims at advising local governments in other tourism areas to define strategies for sustainable quality; or the ECOSERT (European Co-operation for Sustainable Environmental Regional development through Tourism) project[164] aiming at enhancing economically isolated and depressed regions through the development of sustainable tourism strategies. The main objective of the project is to establish a methodology for the preparation of coordinated and cross-sectoral Regional Environmental Sustainable Tourism Plans. The methodology is expected to be applicable to other regions, so as to become a common tool to "*systematically plan environmental upgrading through eco/cultural tourism at a regional level*"[165].

1.3.2 URBAN II: Economic and Social Regeneration in Urban Areas

Areas and sites selected under this programme do not qualify for tourism support. However, implemented measures can indirectly influence the quality of a larger area or of adjacent tourist destination(s).

One of the most interesting features of URBAN II is the exchange of good practices across Europe, funded under a specific programme, the "European Network for Exchange of Experience", or "URBACT"[166]. Total cost of the project is 24.760 m€, ERDF contribution is 15.9 m€. Within this specifically targeted programme, the

---

[164] ECOSERT project web site: http://www.ecosert.org.gr/
[165] ECOSERT project web site: http://www.ecosert.org.gr/
[166] URBACT web page: http://www.urbact.org/srt/urbact/home

Partners4Action network[167] deals, through a series of working groups and studies, with the use of PPPs to tackle economic, social and environmental problems within deprived urban neighbourhoods across Europe. Partner cities seek to identify best practices on how public authorities, mainly city councils, can work effectively in partnership with the private sector to ensure both new investments and long term sustainability.

1.3.3 LEADER+: Links between Actions for the Development of the Rural Economy

LEADER+ targets natural and cultural heritage. Tourism is not directly mentioned as a priority sector, but it is possible to develop tourism-related proposals, especially of a sustainable nature, if the criteria are fulfilled.

Under LEADER II, the previous phase, almost 40% of the budget was channelled to measures for rural tourism. In Leader + rural tourism projects are eligible if they match one of the following three strands:

- support for integrated development strategies of a pilot nature for rural territories relying on a bottom up approach and horizontal partnership;
- co-operation between rural areas (both inter-territorial co-operation and transnational co-operation);
- creation of networks of actors and the setting up of a European observatory of rural areas, responsible for the animation of the network.

The case of nature tourism development in the National Park of Peneda Gerês, Portugal, represents the type of initiative that can be funded under a LEADER project[168]. Tourism demand in this area has existed for a long time, mainly in relation to the spa of Gerês, but it clearly increased with the creation of the Park in 1971. Today it receives nearly one million visitors per year, being the fourth most popular tourism destination in Portugal. The LEADER Program covers the Park territory and four Development Associations, implementing LEADER Local Action Plans since the programme phase I. These Associations have been acting to promote local

---

[167] The Partners for Action is a project funded by the URBACT programme. It is a network of cities aiming at identifying best practices to create partnerships with the private sector to tackle urban renewal.
[168] Cristóvão A., 2002

development based on endogenous resources, giving particular importance to environment, tourism and local products, such as: the creation of rural tourism housing in the mountain villages; the promotion of a particular label, the Village Tourism ("Turismo de Aldeia"); and the preservation of the cultural heritage, namely traditional agricultural constructions used in the past to store cereals or to manage water resources (the so called "espigueiros", "azenhas" and "moinhos").

1.3.4 EQUAL - Development of Human Resources

This Initiative is open to all sectors and tourism projects for training and employment can be eligible. In particular, the "Enterpreneurship" field targets business and job creation in urban and rural areas. A useful project database is available on the EQUAL portal[169] and provides users with a search tool interface to screen funded and ongoing initiatives by country and theme.

To quote an example of funded action, the CIT - Competence in Tourism - project in the Allgaeu-Oberland region (Germany) aims to improve the occupational abilities of people, not yet integrated into the labour force, through the tourism sector. It will accomplish this target by creating qualification standards, streamlining marketing strategies, offering consultant work and supporting existing activities. The degree of accomplishment will be measured by successful re-integrations into the work force, self-employed workplaces supporting or sustaining livelihood, as well as stable employment. An obstacle is the poor reputation of jobs in the hotel and restaurant industry in this region. Many highly qualified professionals relocate to neighbouring Austria due to the fact that there jobs are held in higher esteem and are better remunerated. Businesses are forced to rely on foreign labourers, often insufficiently qualified, and limited by residence permits, generally issued for a total of three months.

---

[169] EQUAL portal: https://equal.cec.eu.int/equal/jsp/index.jsp?lang=en

Since 1999, INTERREG and PHARE funds have been used to promote high quality tourism in four regions of the Baltic area. All partner regions are characterised by extended protected areas. The first INTERREG IIC/PHARE project, '*High quality tourism – sustainable development in sensitive areas in four regions around the Baltic Sea*' was implemented in Cesis District (Latvia), Suwalki (Poland), Mecklenburg Lake District (Germany) and Östergötland (Sweden) over the period 1999-2000. The project focus was on *accessibility, marketing and synergy between tourism and other economic activities.* The successful cooperation among the partners brought the approval of a new INTERREG IIIB/PHARE project on 'Sustainable Regional Development – High Quality Tourism 2' (2002-2005) focusing on the development of thematic tourist routes and areas, of guidance and information services, as well as on the marketing and distribution of regional products. The project's objective is '*to strengthen the integrative role of spatial approach within a high quality, sustainable tourism development*'.

Overall, all regions were targeting the enhancement of their economies (in

Key issues:

⇨ Interregional cooperation among four regions aimed at promoting sustainable tourism in sensitive areas (protected areas, natural parks).

⇨ High quality tourism as driver of sustainable regional development.

⇨ "bottom up" approach to encourage local initiatives and involvement, also taking into account the viewpoint of the locals and the regional values.

particular, raising employment opportunities) and higher visibility as destinations at national and international level. Both projects were to look for strategies emphasising the tourism potentials of these territories in a sustainable manner, by also deciding on suitable locations for development.

The Local Government Information Network – an information clearinghouse whose aim is to support the enhancement of the skills of local government officials of Central and Eastern European countries - has classified the involvement of the Cesis District Council within several sustainable development activities as "best practice".

Baltic Sea Region INTERREG III B web site:
http://www.spatial.baltic.net/programm/project.php?id=10169&start=0

High Quality Tourism Project web site: http://www.baltic-area.net/

Cesis District best practice document:
http://www.logincee.org/libdoc/20040706_{D41C32A6-500E-4F11-8D83-63D453298F7D}.doc

REGIOnal No. 3, December 2000. Neue Impulse für die Region: Das Projekt *High Quality Tourism* im Rahmen des EU-Programms Interreg IIc http://www.region-seenplatte.de/download/heft3.pdf

2.   The Cohesion Fund

The Cohesion Fund finances projects designed to improve the environment and develop transport infrastructure in Member States whose per capita GDP is below 90% of the Community average. As such, it is an indirect source of funding for sustainable tourism initiatives. Since 1993, the Member States qualifying for assistance are Ireland, Greece, Spain and Portugal. The budget for the 2000-06 period amounts to 18 billion €. Projects must belong to one of the two below categories, receiving half of the budget each:

- Environment projects, i.e. projects helping to achieve the objectives of the Community's environmental policy. In accordance with the Directives on the environment in force today, the Fund gives priority to drinking-water supply, treatment of wastewater and disposal of solid waste. Re-afforestation, erosion control and nature conservation measures are also eligible. In Spain, the Cohesion Fund supported the reduction of harmful tourism effects in national parks as well as a 32.5 m€ water desalination plant project in Mallorca, benefiting 345.000 inhabitants and tourists during the summer season.
- Transport infrastructure projects, i.e. projects to establish or develop transport infrastructure within the TEN, or projects providing access to the TEN. In Portugal, major interventions on inter-modality transport network were funded

Based on the new European Commission proposal[170] on Structural Funds' reform, adopted in July 2004, the Cohesion Fund will be more integrated into the operation of the mainstream Structural Funds applying in 2007-2013, with an expected allocation of 63 billion € and decentralised management to local authorities. The assistance will not only cover major transport and environmental protection infrastructures, but also projects in the fields of energy efficiency, renewable energy and inter-modal, urban or collective transport. Hence, indirect actions in favour of sustainable tourism development can be wider in number and typology. Moreover, as a result of the enlargement process, the number of eligible Member States has increased and will cover the 10 new Member States as well as Greece and Portugal (i.e. Spain and Ireland are no longer in the list).

---

[170] DG Regional Policy, proposal for new regulations web page:
http://europa.eu.int/comm/regional_policy/sources/docoffic/official/regulation/intronewregl0713_en.htm

3.   Other Financial Instruments

3.1   Pre-accession Instruments: PHARE, ISPA, SAPARD

These three programmes benefit formerly acceding countries (now EU Member States), plus Bulgaria and Romania, scheduled to enter the EU in 2007.

PHARE, with some 1.560 m€/year, was the main instrument for assisting candidate countries to meet EU accession criteria. Originally created in 1989 to assist Poland and Hungary, it was later extended to other 8 accession countries (Czech Republic, Estonia, Latvia, Lithuania, Slovakia and Slovenia, as well as Bulgaria and Romania). The beneficiaries are institutions and organisations that play a role in the implementation of EU legislation and policies, including not only national administrations but also NGOs and business associations. In the Baltic countries, Poland, Hungary, Romania and Bulgaria, tourism was included in national PHARE programmes, while in the Czech Republic and Slovenia, tourism projects were included in the PHARE *Cross-border Co-operation Programmes* with neighbouring EU Member States; while tourism is no longer covered by national PHARE programmes it is still very often addressed in the *PHARE Cross-border Co-operation*. In order to avoid overlapping with the ISPA and SAPARD programmes, PHARE does not support large-scale investment projects in transport, environment or agriculture, with the exception of regulatory infrastructure not eligible under ISPA or SAPARD. In the new Member States, contracting of PHARE tenders can continue until the end of 2005, and disbursement of payments until the end of 2006.

ISPA – Instrument for Structural Policies for Pre-Accession, established in 1999, was designed to address environmental and transport infrastructure priorities identified in the ten applicant countries. Its focus on environmental and transport infrastructure has allowed PHARE to focus on other aspects of Economic and Social Cohesion. Contribution to tourism activities are of an indirect – but essential – type, given the importance of rational transport infrastructure and environmental protection for the sustainable development of tourism.

SAPARD – Special Accession Programme for Agriculture & Rural Development, established in 1999, aimed to support acceding countries with the problems of the structural adjustment in their agricultural sectors and in rural areas, as well as in the implementation of the *acquis communautaire* concerning the Common Agricultural Policy and related legislation. Rural tourism activities can be supported if they have a driving role in economic and social development.

3.2   CULTURE 2000

Culture 2000 was set up as a single financing and programming instrument for cultural co-operation. The following objectives of the programme are related to tourism in the EU:

- promoting cultural dialogue and mutual knowledge of the culture and history;
- sharing and highlighting the common cultural heritage of European significance;
- taking into account the role of culture in socio-economic development;
- improving access to and participation in culture for as many citizens as possible.

Tourism can benefit if its development or the conservation of cultural heritage are integrated into the local planning or into a master plan. In 2003, 12 projects on cultural heritage, 4 projects on cultural heritage laboratories and 2 multi-annual co-operative projects were supported.

Besides the initiatives funded under Culture 2000, DG Regional Policy portal provides a useful database of some 500 examples of projects dealing with economic or social development implemented in recent years with the support of the Structural Funds and the Cohesion Fund. In particular, it is possible to search for specific success stories, under the theme "Tourism and Culture"[171].

3.3   LIFE III

Subdivided into three strands (Nature, Environment and Third Countries), LIFE III is the Community financial instrument for the implementation of the European Environmental policy as defined by the 6th Action Programme for the Environment. It can also apply to countries outside the EU (LIFE Third countries strand). Although the

---

[171] DG Regional Policy, Success Stories database:
http://europa.eu.int/comm/regional_policy/projects/stories/index_en.cfm

programme was due to terminate at the end of 2004, a 2-year extension was granted until the end of 2006. From 2007 onwards, the new programme, "LIFE+", would become the EU's single financial instrument targeting only the environment. LIFE+ will closely support the priorities of the 6th Environment Action Programme (2002-2012), namely to combat climate change, to halt the decline in bio-diversity, to minimise negative environmental effects on human health, and to deal with natural resources and waste in sustainable ways. The Commission has proposed to commit a total of 2.19 billion € from 2007 to 2013.

Until the end of 2004, LIFE III Environment was mainly guided by the priority fields of the 5th Environmental Action Programme, which includes tourism. The extension for 2005 and 2006 foresees to focus mainly on the priorities of the 6th Environmental Action Programme, which does not include tourism anymore. During its different phases, this strand funded a number of initiatives on rural and sustainable tourism; a sample is shown in the table below. LIFE III Nature aims at the conservation of natural habitats of the wild fauna and flora of the Community and (for candidate countries only) of international interest. Development of sustainable tourism is very marginal and it is not mentioned as a priority; although sometimes it is included as a side objective (see example in the table below).

The portal of DG Environment provides a comprehensive database of funded LIFE projects[172]. The following table lists a selected sample of projects dealing with sustainable tourism and funded under different phases of this programme.

Table E.1 Selected sample of LIFE projects

Project title/acronym and source of funding	Title/Objective(s)
LANDSCAPE LAB - Tourist Destinations as Landscape Laboratories - Tools for Sustainable Tourism LIFE III Environment	The project sees tourist destinations as landscape laboratories, where tools for sustainable tourism are developed and demonstrated. The actual test ground is the Ylläs-Levi area in Finnish Lapland.
Restoration of clear water lakes, mires and swamp forests of the Lake Stechlin LIFE III Nature	Besides the conservation measures, another aim is a comprehensive visitor management scheme for making better use of the site's potentials for sustainable tourism.
TOURFOR - Integrated tourism with the development of forest resources LIFE II Environment	A joint initiative to encourage and promote sustainable management with the creation of a community wide recognised award system.

---

[172] DG Environment LIFE project database: http://europa.eu.int/comm/environment/life/project/[...]

Green Flag for Greener Hotels LIFE II Environment	To assess the feasibility of an ecological label in hotels.
LANDSTATE LIFE II Environment	Sustainability of tourism and agriculture through total consumer involvement.
Partnership in Sustainable Tourism on Kefalonia and Ithaca LIFE II Environment	To integrate environment in the tourist development on the islands of Kefalonia and Ithaca.
Integrated Cooperation on Sustainable Tourism Development and Recreational Use in the Wadden Sea Area LIFE II Environment	To prepare, test and implement models of communication and co-operation among authorities and organisations involved in the development of the Wadden Sea area.
Tourism Eco-labelling LIFE I Environment	To demonstrate the protection of environmental quality by transforming it into a marketable economic asset.
Evaluation and development models on tourist activities in sensitive areas LIFE I Environment	Definition of models for the development of specific forms of tourism in ecologically protected areas.

3.4 RTD Framework Programmes (FPs)

This is the Community financial instrument to fund Research and Technology development projects and programmes (RTD). Managed by DG Research, it is built into the nature of the FPs to support innovative actions and projects of an experimental and foresight nature. Dating back to 1984, the FPs have supported a number of research projects dealing with sustainable tourism; some recent examples are reported in the following table. The ongoing Sixth FP covers the period 2002-2006 with an overall allocation of 17.5 billion €.

Table E.2 Selected sample of projects funded within the FPs

Project acronym and source of funding[173]	Title/Objective(s)
HARMONISE IST - Fifth Framework Programme	Tourism Harmonisation Network, to improve quality of tourism information for Internet users through harmonisation of information.
GREEN HOTEL EESD - Fifth Framework Programme	Integrating Self Supply Into End Use For Sustainable Tourism - Target Action.
HI-TOUCH IST - Fifth Framework Programme	E-organisational methodology and tools for intra-European sustainable tourism.
SWAMP EESD - Fifth Framework Programme	Sustainable Water Management and wastewater Purification in tourism facilities.

[173] Extracted from the CORDIS database: www.cordis.lu

SUT-GOVERNANCE EESD - Fifth Framework Programme	Sustainable Urban Tourism: involving local agents and partnerships for new forms of Governance .
SPRITE LIFE QUALITY - Fifth Framework Programme	Supporting and promoting integrated tourism in Europe's lagging rural regions.
VMART IST - Fifth Framework Programme	Virtual Market place for Rural Tourism sales, development and ICT services and Applications.
OPTOUR LIFE QUALITY - Fifth Framework Programme	Determination of the opportunities for and barriers to advocating tourism as an agent of rural diversification and development in a range of EU countries and Accession states.
Mobile Tourism Guide IST - Fifth Framework Programme	To promote the development and deployment of innovative 2.5G and, eventually, 3G wireless applications & services for mobile tourists at a pan-European level, thus promoting the use of 2.5G/3G cellular networks.
ALMA INCO 2 - Fifth Framework Programme	Arabic linguistic multilingual applications in the context of data exchange on " sustainable environment and tourism".
STEPS FOR ISLANDS ENV 2C - Fourth Framework Programme	Sustainable Tourism's Environmental Practice System For Islands
EMPOST-NET ENV 2C - Fourth Framework Programme	The Emerging Paradigm Of Sustainable Tourism - a Network perspective.
(Ski Area) Management Information System ENV 2C - Fourth Framework Programme	A cost effective application of remote sensing to environmental aspects of ski regions.
Cultural and policy determinants of sustainable tourism development ENV 2C - Fourth Framework Programme	To assess the relationship between tourism as an economic and social activity, and the environment.
Tourism and leisure policies in European rural regions, current trends and future prospects - a thematic study on sustainable development TMR -Fourth Framework Programme	Improving the sustainable tourism competitiveness and the quality of life in the European rural territories, especially those included in the less-favoured regions.

3.5   Others

In addition to those described above, there are a number of other Community programmes, run by different Commission Directorate Generals, that can provide alternatives for funding, such as SAVE and ALTERNER (energy sector) and LEONARDO (vocational training and education).

The following table lists some examples of already completed projects in the tourism sector.

Table E.3 Selected sample of tourism projects funded within other funds

Project acronym and source of funding	Title/Objective(s)
REST ALTENER 2	Renewable Energy and Sustainable Tourism
INVEST LEONARDO DA VINCI 1	Innovation in Vocational Education for Sustainable Tourism
TINNPE - LEONARDO DA VINCI 1	Continuing training in tourism-related SMEs to take account of the challenges set by the European charter for sustainable Tourism in the Natural and National Parks of Europe

Tourism is also included in the 'industry, services and agriculture' funds provided by the European Investment Bank (EIB) for a sustainable and balanced development. In 1995, industry and services received 4617.1 m€, of which 137.1 m€ were specifically earmarked for tourism, leisure and health (corresponding to 0,8 % of total EIB financing). For comparison, Trans-European networks received 6.6 billion €; environment protection was allocated 6 billion €; and the energy-supply sector 3.4 billion €.

A complete and comprehensive list of funding mechanisms in the tourism sector are provided in "EU support for Tourism Enterprises and Tourist Destinations – An Internet Guide[174] and through the Directorate General for Enterprise portal[175].

In addition, the Commission report on Community measures affecting tourism[176], presents a list of existing European Structural Funds and initiatives that are of interest in support to the establishment of sustainable tourism.

---

[174] European Commission, Directorate General for Enterprise, 2004
[175] European Commission, Directorate General for Enterprise web page "funding and instruments available": http://europa.eu.int/comm/enterprise/services/tourism/policy-areas/instruments.htm
[176] European Commission, 2002

4. Public Private Partnerships: Merits, Challenges and Opportunities

4.1 The Concept and Critical Factors of PPP Success

In the orthodox economic theory, the public and the private sectors have separate roles to play in economic development. Modern theories, however, recognise the limited potential of the public sector to mobilise the financial resources needed to construct the necessary infrastructure rapidly and effectively. They thus look for alliances between the public and the private sector that will enable both private and social returns on investment[177].

The basic notion of Public Private Partnership (PPP) includes a co-operation agreement between a public organisation with a (or more often a consortium of) private enterprise(s) to undertake a specific investment together and share the costs and profits in a way formally agreed in advance. By definition, the public sector is expected to attend to community interest, stewardship and solidarity. The private sector is thought to be creative and dynamic, possessing capital, managerial efficiency, professional knowledge and entrepreneurial spirit. So governments at different levels, political parties, financial institutions and all the industries involved in public services or facilities of any sort (education, health care, utilities, mass transportation) seek new synergetic forms of collaboration to satisfy expectations and interests[178]. The notion of Public Private Partnerships is found in the literature both as a generic concept[179] to describe this new form of alliance and as one particular form of co-operation. Many models of PPPs are reported[180], the following three types being the most frequently encountered:

- *Private Finance Initiative (PFI) of procurement[181]*: in this scheme the public sector must secure value for money, while the private sector service providers

---

[177] The PPP concept is very old but in the past it was only occasionally used. Historically, the first partnerships for financing public infrastructure appear in the 17th century with the construction of French canals and bridges, followed by the Suez Canal, the Trans-Siberian railway, US rail and power companies.

[178] Scharle P., 2002

[179] Akintoye A., Hardcastle C., Beck M., Chinyio E., Asenova D., 2003

[180] Merna T., Smith N., 1999

[181] Introduced by the British government in the 1980s, it has offered a solution to the problem of securing necessary investment at a time of severe public expenditure restraint.

must genuinely assume responsibility for project risks. Establishing a PFI is a particularly complex process as it involves a variety of actors.

- *Public Private Partnerships (PPP)*: they derive from the PFIs but with a different set of priorities and emphasis. The concept implies that complex and expensive projects are managed efficiently - delivering on time and on budget; risk is managed effectively - so the consumer can benefit from enhanced services without the taxpayer having to shoulder the burden of failures or fluctuations in demand; the reservoir of potential in public sector ideas, assets, and brands are exploited and public sector workers are not restricted by outmoded structures or restricted working practices[182].

- *Build-Operate-Transfer (BOT)* schemes are of increasing interest with the growing thrust towards privatisation infrastructure projects in both developed and developing countries. A BOT is a project based on the granting of a concession by a client to a consortium or concessionaire who is required to "build" (including financing, design, management of implementation, procurement and construction), "operate" (including managing and operating the facility or plant, carrying out maintenance, delivering product/service and receiving payments to repay the financing and investment costs and to make a margin of profit) and "transfer" the facility or plant in operational condition and at no cost to the client at the end of the concession period[183]. *BOO* (Build-Operate-Own) is a variation of BOT, where the concessionaire *owns the site and does not transfer it*. An intelligent allocation of risks is a prerequisite to success and this is a particularly difficult task given the many variables and unknowns to be assessed for such *projects, which are typically long term and complex*. Not all projects can be undertaken successfully using BOTs. A particularly co-operative PPP is a precondition for BOTs. The host government shall provide the necessary support, prepare an adequate legal framework, ensure the right political and commercial environment and provide minimal guarantees to maintain a balanced risk-return structure[184]. Several BOT ventures have run into trouble due to cost overruns, unrealistic price and income projections, and legal disputes. In virtually all these cases it has been the government and the general public – not the private operators - who have ultimately shouldered the cost of failure[185].

[182] Smith A., 2001

[183] Kumaraswamy M.M., Zhang X.Q., 2001

[184] Kumaraswamy M.M., Zhang X.Q., 2001

[185] Kumaraswamy M.M., Zhang X.Q., 2001

The increasing number of PPPs, in their various forms, has contributed to their empirical study and the identification of *critical elements of success,* which have to be kept in mind, if such type of funding is adopted. The most important among them are:

1. Make sure that the project will be **beneficial for both sides**. If not, the private sector will not respond to calls as it has often been observed[186].
2. Make sure that the **culture of the participants is supportive** to the project. Imposing technical solutions top down, without mutual respect, trust and co-operation is likely to result in frustrating results[187].
3. Organise the necessary **legal environment**. The key elements that need to be addressed by the legal system refer mainly to laws allowing a sound project-specific concession agreement (land acquisition and expropriation may be a crucial aspect in many cases), dispute resolution (neutral international arbitrator) but no over-regulation. Similarly, the jurisdiction may impose certain rules of interpretation that are binding.
4. Make sure to have the **appropriate skills for execution**. The crucial elements appear at all stages of the cycle: negotiation and contract but also implementation, operation and potential transfer stages. The governments should continue to play an active role throughout the project cycle to ensure quality, efficiency and satisfaction. The externalisation of such management tasks through the support of consultants is one way to resolve the problem, however the client still needs to be able to understand/dialogue with his selected consultant to be able to gain from the project.

The most important element that accompanies the projects throughout their lives is the *distributions of risks and profits.* A risk assignment mechanism is necessary in order to assign the risks to those best placed to control them. Some risks should remain within the public sector, mainly macro and micro level risks, i.e. site availability and political risks. The majority of risks, namely those associated with the project itself, should be allocated to the private sector. Relationship risks, "*force majeure*", and risks by legislation changes should be shared by both parties. However, there are some risks where unilateral allocation is not always obvious like the level of public support, project approval and permits, contract variation and lack of experience, so they should

---

[186] In the second half of the 1990s, for instance, the Turkish government planned 179 BOTs of which only four materialized.

[187] Kwan A.Y., Ofori G., 2001

be handled on a case-by-case basis[188]. Financial risks in particular are eliminated in well functioning national capital markets. Transferring risks to the private sector frees the taxpayer from unnecessary burden, creates a greater incentive for the private sector to deliver according to the budget and on time, and when they do, benefits the citizen - the consumer of public services.

Evidence on generalised success or failure is inconclusive. According to some sources PFIs have delivered substantial cost savings in project schemes[189], while other have serious reservations about the potential of accumulated benefits.

4.2   Areas and Role of PPPs in Europe

The complexity of the PPP agreements, the limited experience and the number/complexity of crucial success factors have as yet limited the number of PPPs implemented, compared to their promising nature. A selection of the best known projects financed in European countries is presented in the table below:

Table E4. Selection of PPPs projects financed in Europe

Title	Cost
Vasco da Gama Bridge, Portugal	$ 1000 million
ORLYVAL, France	no cost data
Eurotunnel, France-UK	undisclosed, <15000 million
M1 Motorway, Hungary	$ 300 million
M5 Motorway, Hungary	$ 400 million

Source: extracted from Scharle P., 2002

The European Investment Bank loans for PPP projects, over the period 1990-2003, total 14.688 m€, distributed as follows: 62% to roads and motorway, 17% to urban development, renovation and transport, 7% to airports, 7% to traditional and high speed trains, 4% to social infrastructure (education and health), 2% to power generation, transmission an distribution, and 1% to drinking and wastewater treatment[190].

---

[188] Bing L., Akintoye A., Edwards P.J., Hardcastle C., 2004
[189] Private Finance Panel, 1996
[190] European Investment Bank, 2005

It is thus evident that project focus is on transport infrastructure, the main reason being that it represents a fairly secure source of revenue for the private sector, since flexibilities can be calculated, fees can be agreed *ex-ante* and the risk is often considered lower as when dealing with regulators. However, there are some projects, in particular in the UK, which involve energy and the environment, such as the Scotland Baldovie Waste to Energy Plant, the Esk Valley Purification System, and the Scottish Highland Sewerage. In 1997, for example, East of Scotland Water invited tenders to take the Esk Valley project forward using Private Finance Initiative funding; this project is one of the three major PFI projects currently being implemented in its territory, as part of a £820m investment programme over 5 years to meet environmental legislation. Besides nationally funded initiatives, the European programme URBACT for the exchange of good practice in urban areas specifically deals with PPPs in urban areas (reference is to paragraph 1.3.2. of this section).

Hence, from the evidence gathered as yet:

1. PPPs can be used and are often called upon to finance transport infrastructure, which indirectly, may improve sustainable tourism significantly, since it can help improve access without increasing or even by limiting emissions.
2. Sustainability is directly addressed via energy plants, which are already operational under PPPs. However, the extent to which such projects are of interest to the private sector depends heavily on the public power regulatory framework in each Member States. Other utilities, which can benefit from PPPs are wastewater treatment plants.
3. There is no evidence of PPP projects related to sustainable tourism directly, such as support of natural heritage. This is probably associated to the high elasticity of demand for such parks, where high entrance fees would discourage visitors, hence stakeholders apparently calculated that it is easier to give grants or finance such endeavours entirely by public funds, rather than go through the cumbersome procedure of PPP tendering with an ambiguous response from the private sector, which may not be seeing the clear benefit, one of the crucial success factors of PPPs. However, this does not mean that such a potential is excluded with theoretical arguments, if a cost benefit analysis proves beneficial, the case can still be made. Developments in environmental economic assessment can prove particularly useful in this regard.

4.3   Areas and Role of Local and Regional Authorities in Developing and Implementing PPP and PFI

The above considerations point out that experience up to now shows that there is a *minimum scale*, which is necessary for the promotion of PPPs in order to amortise the high cost of the whole procurement cycle. Hence territorial authorities should keep in mind that only major projects are likely to be addressed with PPPs. It is possible that as experience is increasing, legal environments improved and risk-sharing rules standardised, the minimum scale for successful projects will be reduced. However, *although there is no simple quantitative barrier or prescription, for the time being and in regions/countries with a less* suitable culture and legal environment, the case remains difficult and should be addressed with caution.

A first point of relevance for territorial authorities, when assessing the potential of PPPs is *the knowledge of all the actors that need to be involved*: the public body responsible for the project and its consultants, the bidders, the selected contractors, financial institutions and facilities management organisations.

An analysis undertaken, based on 68 interviews with stakeholders involved, suggests that the achievement of best value requirements through PFI should hinge on: *detailed risk analysis and appropriate risk allocation,* drive for faster project completion, curtailment in project cost escalation, encouragement of innovation in project development and maintenance cost being properly accounted for. Factors that continue to challenge the achievement of best value are: high cost of the PFI procurement process, lengthy and complex negotiations, difficulty in specifying the quality of the service, pricing of facility management services, potential conflicts of interest and the public sector clients' inability to manage consultants[191]. Beside the risk, the *managing of complex projects* is another issue to be considered.

In general the key issues for the application of PPPs by territorial authorities are:

1. Many of the success features (notably legal environment and culture) are nationally embedded/regulated and thus if inappropriate, territorial government should not act pre-maturely. The only role where they can limit themselves is in

---

[191] Akintoye A., Hardcastle C., Beck M., Chinyio E., Asenova D., 2003

lobbying for the national government to improve the regulatory framework before they act; acting without an appropriate national legislation may lead to failures.

2. If the national scene allows for that, there are still two important conditions for local authorities to intervene successfully in favour of sustainable tourism: carefully study the scale of the project they wish to launch and make sure that it is sufficiently large to generate the necessary profits to make it attractive to the private sector; and assure the necessary skills (even if hiring consultants, the public service will need to interact and guide the consultants) for a right balance of costs and benefits between the public and the private sector.

3. Finally, it seems that for this type of intervention, areas affecting sustainable tourism indirectly, like transport, health and educational infrastructure, are more frequent than others.

5.   Conclusions and Recommendations

5.1   Funding Instruments

It is widely recognised that external funding, in addition to public and private finance, can play an important role in boosting the tourism industry, especially in weak economies[192]. In this sense Community support can be pivotal in directing and stimulating development of sustainable tourism throughout the EU. The following recommendations are suggested to guarantee a synergic approach and maximise the benefits to the widest range of stakeholders:

1.   Given the wide scope and cross-sectoral nature of many sustainable tourism projects and initiatives, a rationale for the set-up of a stand-alone funding instrument cannot be suggested. However, within the legislative proposals by the European Commission for the reform of cohesion policy (2007-2013), and considering the importance of the tourism sector in economic, social and cultural terms, it seems appropriate to create specific measures for the development of "cross-border and transnational programmes and networks" on sustainable tourism, under the "European territorial cooperation objective"[193]. In addition to this, the maximum coherence within all EU funded programmes and close co-ordination among the responsible Commission Directorates should be guaranteed so as to ensure that a sustainable tourism process is widely and evenly developed on a pan-European scale.

2.   The use of charters, quality marks and certification schemes are recognised as useful instruments in ensuring informed decision-making, and support through instruments such as LIFE, LEADER and other programmes should continue.

3.   The evaluation and monitoring of tourism related projects receiving EU funds should focus on the sustainability criteria built into the projects and should ensure compliance of commitments to sustainability.

4.   A comprehensive enquiry into the issue of green taxes for the tourism industry should be carried out at European level. It should take into account both the

---

[192] Hurley A., Archer B., Fletcher J., 1994
[193] European Commission, Directorate General for Regional Policy, 2004 (b)

opportunity for punitive taxes via the "polluter pays" principle and tax breaks for certified good practice, so as to provide incentives to the move towards a sustainable tourism industry. It should also be analysed if the cash flows generated by green taxes levied on tourists and tourist operators, is earmarked and used by the concerned authority to support further sustainable tourism initiatives or if they merely represent an income for the government central board of revenue.

5. Implementation of ICZM should be fostered through LIFE and INTERREG. The release of Structural Funds to Member States for use in coastal areas should be made dependant on the elaboration of an integrated territorial master plan developed according to the principles of the ICZM strategy.

6. To achieve greater private sector involvement in the use of Structural Funds, simpler and faster application processes should be put in place by the local authorities responsible for mainstreaming national and regional programmes. Moreover, match funding by private operators, particularly small entrepreneurs/firms, should be facilitated through an easier access to favourable credit schemes and venture capital.

7. New forms of funding through private-public partnerships (PPPs) need to be set up, making this issue of crucial importance for less-developed regions.

5.2   Public and Private Partnerships

The principle of public and private sector partnering for the rapid and efficient creation of public infrastructure is a case worth considering for development purposes both at national and regional level. The above means that once a need is identified and prioritised, stakeholders should review the potential of promoting the investment via some kind of partnership.

The following basic points should be verified:

•   unless a minimum framework and culture at the national scale exists, territorial authorities should, in general, refrain from PPPs (exceptional cases of very beneficial projects, including all elements described hereafter may however exist);

- the bigger the scale, the more likely the private sector will be interested in responding;
- the less regulated the sources of income to be generated from the exploitation of the investment, the more likely the partnership will be successful;

If projects responding to the above mentioned conditions are identified at the regional/local level, then one public organisation should be selected to have ownership of the project and prepare it according to the general principles recommended for successful PPP. It should be noted that exceptional administrative capabilities are needed to set up efficient projects; if the capabilities and culture are unfavourable it might be better to abandon the idea.

Projects indirectly affecting sustainable tourism, like transport, health, and educational infrastructure are more often encountered than those more directly linked to sustainability. Energy investments and waste treatment already exist as case studies but in a very limited number of cases. Moreover, there are no cases of direct funding of sustainable tourism sites, like parks and natural heritage, probably because the income generation is not considered adequate; with the current state of knowledge and consumer preferences, grants or tax breaks are probably a more appropriate means of funding of natural resorts.

Given the above remarks what can be done to facilitate the introduction of PPPs at the territorial level is:

1. In countries where the legal framework and culture are unfavourable, national authorities should start working towards the creation of the necessary institutional set up, as well as towards the training of civil servants to enhance their skills to identify and implement successful PPPs. They should also start with cases with the highest likelihood of success to slowly build up a conductive environment. As national legislation is needed for the set up of successful concessions, it is unlikely that *regional authorities alone will be in a position to go into such partnerships, without a clear agreement and support of the national political authorities.* The European Commission is expected to issue a communication within the end of 2005, following a consultation process, launched in April 2004, on public procurement and public-private partnerships. The aim was to assess if there was a need to improve EU law in this area. Possible measures to increase fair

competition include legislation, interpretative communications, initiatives to improve the co-ordination of national practice and exchange of good practice between Member States.

2. Since one of the major constraints is lack of skills, a scheme of certification of consultants in this field could be created for regional authorities to rely on. Also, specific training courses organised centrally to help regional policy makers understand the principles and stakes of PPPs are specific ways to raise awareness and improve capabilities.

3. Regions with serious accumulated environmental damage should consider the idea of applying PPPs for more environmentally friendly energy resources or waste treatment by giving generous fees to the bidders; while this would require high fiscal disadvantages for the territorial authorities to attract the private sector (publicly generated income), the need to reverse accumulated damage makes the case a priority.

RECOMMENDATIONS

This chapter summarises the recommendations provided in the study sections.

Section B: Concepts and Principles of Sustainable Tourism

B1.   A Community methodology on indicators and monitoring system for sustainable tourism based on low cost and reliable time series data should be developed, recognizing the need to balance the three dimensions of sustainable development: environment, economic and social. A specific study on this issue should be carried out, to be coordinated and monitored by the existing group on tourism statistics within Eurostat.

B2.   The European Commission should reinforce its support to the diffusion and exchange of best practices on sustainable tourism development for tourism destination managers and businesses (in particular SMEs). Guidelines, indicators and tools, and useful methodological examples are needed to foster the concrete and operational implementation of sustainable tourism in the regions of destination. Attention should be paid to the creation of a network of pilot territories that are leaders in implementing a specific domain of sustainable tourism.

B3.   The cooperation between, on one hand, local and regional public authorities and, on the other hand, all the tourism stakeholders, including industry and representatives of the consumers, should be promoted further. Stronger collaboration is essential especially for spatial and territorial planning, strategic environmental assessment and environmental impact assessment. A discussion platform could be set up, chaired by the Committee of the Regions, or within the Sustainable European Regions Network.

B4.   Communication on the preparation of the Agenda 21 for European Tourism should be improved, internally, within the concerned Directorates General, and externally, with federations representing the various stakeholders of the tourism sector. Local public and private tourism managers and tourism small-sized suppliers shall be sufficiently represented within the EC Sustainable Tourism Group.

B5.   To ensure the follow-up and monitoring of the implementation of the Agenda 21 at local, regional and national levels, it is suggested to establish a *"Committee 21"* for European Sustainable Tourism. Its long-term activity would maintain the consultation process among the representatives, allowing for further improvements and adaptations along the development of sustainability.

B6.   Indicators and good practice exchanges are crucially lacking: a European Observatory on Sustainable Tourism, acting as a technical body of the *"Committee 21"*, could be in charge of collating and disseminating the necessary information. This observatory could also be part of a Network of Regions of Tourism Destinations.

Section C: Sustainable Tourism and Territorial Cohesion

C1.   Reinforce the integration of territorial cohesion policies within economic and social cohesion policies. Sustainable tourism as a driving force for promoting cohesion in Europe may become a trial to explore the concrete implementation of the Gothenburg and Lisbon goals. In this context, the new ERDF regulation shall include sustainable tourism activities in its eligibility criteria.

C2.   Assess the territorial impact of relevant Community policies (environmental, transport) and programmes (TENs and ESDP) and improve the knowledge of environmental trends and policy impacts, especially at local and regional levels. This would represent a pre-requisite for the proper outlining of sustainable tourism strategies.

C3.   Promote Integrated Quality Management for destination managers (local and regional authorities) and Integrated Coastal Zone Management at sea destinations in order to support a sustainable spatial planning of tourism activity. The European Commission should further disseminate the concerned methodological publications to the national tourism organisations and regional authorities.

C4.   Promote and support the implementation of Local Agenda 21 in collaboration with all tourism stakeholders. Several experiences in this regard have already been compiled but they need to reach a larger audience. Such exchange of know-how will be facilitated by the development of reliable networks that aim at supporting the local and regional authorities to concretely implement sustainable tourism at destinations.

C5. Consider the carrying out of a Strategic Environmental Assessment and Environmental Impact Assessment for any tourism infrastructure project, compulsory. Legislation in this area should be reinforced.

C6. Make land use planning and development control effective. Local authorities have to develop efficient land planning tools able to integrate the natural values of the terrestrial and aquatic environment. This process will also support the NATURA 2000 programme. Studies on the tourism carrying capacity of the destinations should be carried out.

C7. Guide tourism in natural areas by means of integrated management plans developed by qualified experts and implemented with adequate resources. The experience of the European Charter for sustainable tourism in protected areas (EUROPARC) constitutes a good example; the adopted methodology can be implemented in other natural European areas, protected or not protected. The WWF Protected Natural Areas Network could also serve as focal point to exchange information on existing experiences.

C8. Develop specific codes of conduct for tourism managers and tourists as well as comprehensive monitoring systems.

C9. Study the potential of economic incentive tools and measures able to support the tourism contribution to the preservation of European natural and cultural heritages.

C10. Integrate the sustainable tourism issue into the ESPON programme, notably referring to accessibility indicators and to urban-rural typology, impacts of policies in fields of transport, ESDP, governance and environment. In the same context, further work on sustainable tourism could be developed in cooperation with the INTERACT programme in the framework of INTERREG III.

C11. Compile a best practices guide in SGEI related to local/regional public transport, water and waste management services. This guide could be particularly valuable for those regions receiving a large number of tourists compared to their population.

C12. The European Commission and the regions should organise a public consultation prior to the World Trade Organisation GATS decision to possibly further liberalise tourism services, as this might work against the increase of tourism development in the European regions. The rapid globalisation of the tourism market and the growing influence of big operators can encourage anti-competitive practices creating barriers to the operational capacity of local SMEs. As a consequence, economic and social benefit reductions may be expected from the tourism sector as an endogenous economic regional development path.

C13. EU supported projects and cooperation programmes should be compatible with the goals of sustainable development and include the promotion of sustainable tourism to foster the implementation of regional policies. All projects should be evaluated and monitored according to sustainability criteria and indicators.

C14. Awareness of EU tourists on sustainability of tourism shall be increased to encourage responsible behaviours during their travelling within and outside the EU. Tourism codes and sustainable tourism charters should be largely distributed to citizens.

Cooperation with Border Regions

C15. A recent proposal for a regulation establishing a new legal instrument in the form of a European grouping of cross-border cooperation authority– recommended to be renamed by the Committee of the Regions into 'trans-European' (EGTC) – has been adopted by the European Commission on the 14th of July 2004[194]. This new legal instrument aims to transfer to the EGTC structure the capacity to carry out cooperation activities on behalf of public authorities, local and regional but also national. This new frame should include

---

[194] European Commission, 2004 (a)

an effective support to the sustainable tourism operations that would be initiated.

C16. In this context, the idea of creating specific 'European Cooperation Areas', launched by the AEBR[195], should be implemented as far as natural geographical features and institutional capacities are concerned to set out Euroregions across national borders. The implementation of sustainable tourism could highly benefit from the creation of such cooperation zones.

Outermost Regions

C17. The European Commission should carry out a cross-sectoral analysis where special attention is paid to the opportunities to support sustainable tourism within the regional strategies of the outermost regions. A detailed study on the implications of relevant Community policies[196] in these regions should be carried out; the implementation of suitable regional strategies should take into account the requests of these regions together with the governments of their respective Member States. The planned Wider Neighbourhood Action Plan[197] could include significant hints for the implementation of sustainable tourism strategies in the outermost regions.

Tourism Types

C18. Type 1, sub-type 1.1. Strategic actions for most visited regions located in densely populated areas shall include: the introduction of better management practices within the tourism industry (CSR, indicators and reporting); the development of sustainability along the whole tourism-chain, oriented to high quality environmental standards, services and products; the innovation and adaptation of the local transport system by favouring low emission buses and taxis, tramways and subways, creating car parks outside cities centres.

C19. Type 1, sub-type 1.2. Strategic actions for mass tourism destinations shall include: the introduction of better management practices aimed to renovate

---

[195] Committee of the Regions, 2002 (c)

[196] Such as transport, new ICTs, and the trans-national and cross-border cooperation programmes

[197] European Commission, 2004 (b)

destinations; the improvement of the stakeholders involvement in each destination; the development of a spatial integrated strategy at destination; and the safeguarding of the social and environmental aspects of the territory.

C20. Type 2. Strategic actions for traditional destinations shall include: the implementation of a sustainable tourism strategy involving all partners. The strategy should focus on spatial planning and on the preservation of the natural and cultural heritages, for which appropriate forms of governance and funding, at national or European level, are required.

C21. Type 2, sub-type 2.1.Within the new tourism destinations, strategic actions shall include:
- the promotion of the diversification of tourism products and services through: new forms of tourism based on agriculture, nature and traditions; low resources consumption accommodation forms; appropriate support to micro and SMEs;
- the development of integrated sustainability tourism strategies, especially in areas that suffer from a permanent disadvantage (sparsely populated regions and poorest regions);
- the promotion of exchange of information, networking, enhancement of tourism employee skills, economy and employment development based on the promotion of European heritages;
- the funding of such strategies implementation, through EC initiatives and programmes, and the promotion of private-public partnerships.

C22. Type 3. Strategic actions for less visited regions shall include: the facilitation of access to ICTs for micro and SMEs; the fostering of collaboration between the private and public sectors; the enhancement of quality of products and services, marketing operations, infrastructures and transport systems; the facilitation of access to funding.

Section D: Governance and Sustainable Tourism

<u>Involvement of territorial authorities in sustainable tourism development policies</u>

D1. Adopt a strategic vision, based on local advantages and measured with global competitive pressures, incorporating sustainable tourism principles, as analysed in Section B of this study, and analysing them in the context of local advantages and disadvantages.

D2. Sensitise and mobilise regional stakeholders, without whom the public sector alone cannot succeed. Similarly the market forces alone are insufficient as well. Hence, the best way to exploit synergies is their coordination and commitment to mutual benefit. This means, concretely, that the local authorities will adopt plans for clean (or in the cases of damages from the past actively cleaning the) environment; in this context they will need to negotiate with the national authorities, if necessary, the means for achieving this goal; hotels and catering should adopt the necessary standards for quality and environmental respect; agents promoting the new strategy and tools for that should be made available.

D3. Organise the position of lobbying within the higher levels of governance. Since the adoption of new balances needs transregional and often national investments, local stakeholders will need to coordinate and promote the local positions in their national federations. Examples are local hotels earmarking the position of the region in the national hotel federations or tour operators being mobilised to market the region as one valuing sustainable tourism.

Regional Strategies for Tourism

D4. Type 1.2: Territorial authorities need to:

- focus on their vision and incorporate sustainability in it, specifying the extent to which the local model complies fully with the national image or has specific added value to offer;
- make sure the necessary local skills and funding may be mobilised. The territorial authorities are the most appropriate agent to judge on the adequacy (or not) of these capabilities;
- for whatever is beyond the local potential, organise the necessary links to assure assistance at the national and the European level. Stakeholder involvement is relevant both for the regional strategy and for broader lobbying, in particular because some of the actors will have a broader coverage themselves (such as the bigger hotel chains);

- often, these destinations have been abused in the past and suffer from congestion and environmental damages. Extra resources for a strategy reorientation need to be earmarked;
- a good strategy to rapidly improve the local image and assure higher level support is the creation of broader trans-regional alliances, or national or even European scale partnerships (e.g. a broader initiative on agro-tourism).

D5. Type 2: Territorial authorities need to:

- focus on their vision and incorporate sustainability in it, trying to promote specific niches and an image compatible with the evolving needs of tourism. A good management and monitoring system is again a prerequisite for success;
- ensure that the necessary local skills and funding are mobilised. Support from local actors and small private-public networks are important elements that can help to fill gaps in resources;
- tourism-focused support from resources offered by the national or European authorities is less likely, unless they are provided in the context of other policies: environmental protection, regional development and or integrated transport design. Thus, the territorial authorities need to keep contact with all these types of national/European policies to exploit emerging opportunities;
- in this category some destinations have also been abused in the past and suffer from congestion and environmental damages. Extra resources for a strategy reorientation need to be earmarked;
- Creating a good strategy, marketing it and, based on good governance principles, sharing the vision, the risks, the funding and the implementation with the private sector, is the most appropriate way to proceed. In this case the necessary resources are of lower scale. Broader agreements can help market such a strategy.

D6. Type 2.1: Territorial authorities need to:

- focus on their vision and incorporate sustainability into it, trying to promote specific niches and an image compatible with the evolving needs of tourism. Stakeholder involvement would include actors with no experience in tourism;

- make a clear "business plan" for the targets and expectations of the new policy;

- try to attract some of the national actors (hotel chains, existing brand names, tour operators);

- make sure that consensus has been achieved and that they can mobilise the necessary local skills and funding.

<u>Information and Communication Technologies</u>

D7. Adopt explicit strategies and visions taking the new enabling technologies into consideration and positioning their tourism strategy in this context.

D8. Dedicate resources to use these technologies not only for marketing but also for interactive services.

D9. Assure quality of design and service as well as accountability.

D10. In this context, the streamlining of activities and the selection of alliances and complementarities with national authorities and the private sector are crucial.

Section E: Funding Sustainable Tourism in the European Union

E1. Given the wide scope and cross-sectoral nature of many sustainable tourism projects and initiatives, a rationale for the set-up of a stand-alone funding instrument cannot be suggested. However, within the legislative proposals by the European Commission for the reform of cohesion policy (2007-2013), and considering the importance of the tourism sector in economic, social and cultural terms, it seems appropriate to create specific measures for the development of "cross-border and transnational programmes and networks" on sustainable tourism, under the "European territorial cooperation objective"[198]. In addition to this, the maximum coherence within all EU funded programmes and close co-ordination among the responsible Commission Directorates

---

[198] European Commission, Directorate General for Regional Policy, 2004 (b)

should be guaranteed so as to ensure that a sustainable tourism process is widely and evenly developed on a pan-European scale.

E2. The use of charters, quality marks and certification schemes are recognised as useful instruments in ensuring informed decision-making, and support through instruments such as LIFE, LEADER and other programmes should continue.

E3. The evaluation and monitoring of tourism related projects receiving EU funds should focus on the sustainability criteria built into the projects and should ensure compliance of commitments to sustainability.

E4. A comprehensive enquiry into the issue of green taxes for the tourism industry should be carried out at European level. It should take into account both the opportunity for punitive taxes via the "polluter pays" principle and tax breaks for certified good practice, so as to provide incentives to the move towards a sustainable tourism industry. It should also be analysed if the cash flows generated by green taxes levied on tourists and tourist operators, is earmarked and used by the concerned authority to support further sustainable tourism initiatives or if they merely represent an income for the government central board of revenue.

E5. Implementation of ICZM should be fostered through LIFE and INTERREG. The release of Structural Funds to Member States for use in coastal areas should be made dependant on the elaboration of an integrated territorial master plan developed according to the principles of the ICZM strategy.

E6. To achieve greater private sector involvement in the use of Structural Funds, simpler and faster application processes should be put in place by the local authorities responsible for mainstreaming national and regional programmes. Moreover, match funding by private operators, particularly small entrepreneurs/firms, should be facilitated through an easier access to favourable credit schemes and venture capital.

E7. New forms of funding through private-public partnerships (PPPs) need to be set up, making this issue of crucial importance for less-developed regions.

E8. In countries where the legal framework and culture are unfavourable, national authorities should start working towards the creation of the necessary institutional set up, as well as towards the training of civil servants to enhance their skills to identify and implement successful PPPs. They should also start with cases with the highest likelihood of success to slowly build up a conductive environment. As national legislation is needed for the set up of successful concessions, it is unlikely that *regional authorities alone will be in a position to go into such partnerships, without a clear agreement and support of the national political authorities.* The European Commission is expected to issue a communication within the end of 2005, following a consultation process, launched in April 2004, on public procurement and public-private partnerships. The aim was to assess if there was a need to improve EU law in this area. Possible measures to increase fair competition include legislation, interpretative communications, initiatives to improve the co-ordination of national practice and exchange of good practice between Member States.

E9. Since one of the major constraints is lack of skills, a scheme of certification of consultants in this field could be created for regional authorities to rely on. Also, specific training courses organised centrally to help regional policy makers understand the principles and stakes of PPPs are specific ways to raise awareness and improve capabilities.

E10. Regions with serious accumulated environmental damage should consider the idea of applying PPPs for more environmentally friendly energy resources or waste treatment by giving generous fees to the bidders; while this would require high fiscal disadvantages for the territorial authorities to attract the private sector (publicly generated income), the need to reverse accumulated damage makes the case a priority.

ANNEXES

1. Bibliography

Agence Française de l'Ingénierie Touristique, 2000. Sites Naturels, contribution du tourisme à leur gestion et à leur entretien, Les Cahiers de l'Afit, Guide de savoir-faire, Paris, 2000. http://www.afit-tourisme.fr

Ahrens J., 2002. Governance and Economic Development: A Comparative Institutional Approach. New Thinking in Political Economy, Edward Elgar Publisher.

Akintoye A., Hardcastle C., Beck M., Chinyio E., Asenova D., 2003. Achieving best value in private finance initiative project procurement. Construction Management and Economics, 21, pp. 461-470

Ambiente Italia, 2001. Valutazione della capacita' di carico per lo sviluppo turistico della provincia di Rimini, Rapporto intermedio, Rimini 15 July 2001.

Assembly of European Regions, 2003. Regions and Tourism: new strategies for a sustainable quality tourism (First AER Seminar, Porec, Istria-HR, 26-27 June 2003). Final Conclusions.
http://www.are-regions-europe.org/PDF/CC-
Main_Texte/Documents%20adoptes/Tourisme/GB_Baresconclusione_11_02.doc

Assembly of European Regions, 2004. AER Hearing on the possible impact of EU guidelines on the co-operation of regional airports and low-cost airlines: is regional development at stake? Main conclusions adopted in Bari, 13 May 2004.
http://www.are-regions-europe.org/Doc2004/Com%20C/Bari/Docts%20adoptes%20Bari/Regionalairport/GB-BarcelonaCCL.doc

Association of European Border Regions, 2000. Practical Guide to Cross-border Cooperation. European Commission, DG Regional Policy.
http://www.aebr.net/publikationen/pdfs/lace_guide.en.pdf

Baltic 21 Tourism Group, 1998. Agenda 21 – Baltic Sea Region Tourism. Baltic 21 Series No 7/98. Agenda 21 for the Baltic Sea Region.
http://www.baltic21.org/attachments/report_no_7_98__tourism.pdf

Belau D., 2003. The impact of the 2001-2002 crisis on the hotel and tourism industry. International Labour Organisation.
http://www.ilo.org/public/english/dialogue/sector/papers/tourism/impact.pdf

Bing L., Akintoye A., Edwards P.J., Hardcastle C., 2004. The allocation of risk in PPP/PFI construction projects in the UK. International Journal of Project Management.

Brundtland, G. (ed.), 1987. Our common future: The World Commission on Environment and Development. Oxford University Press.

Committee of the Regions, 1998. Resolution on a 'European Charter of regional and local authorities for a progressive and sustainable transport policy'. OJ C 251, 10.8.1998.
http://europa.eu.int/eur-lex/pri/en/oj/dat/1998/c_251/c_25119980810en00070010.pdf

Committee of the Regions, 2001. Environmentally sound transport planning in Europe. Transport Study.

Committee of the Regions, 2002 (a). Opinion of 13 March 2002 on Strategies for promoting cross-border and inter-regional co-operation in an enlarged EU - a basic document setting out guidelines for the future, Brussels, 26 March 2002.

Committee of the Regions, 2002 (b). Territorial Cohesion in Europe, CoR Studies E-6/2002, Brussels.

Committee of the Regions, 2002 (c). Trans-European cooperation between territorial authorities: new challenges and future steps necessary to improve cooperation.

Committee of the Regions, 2004 (a). Opinion on the Commission Communication Basic orientations for the sustainability of European tourism. Cdr397-2003, 21 April 2004.

Committee of the Regions, 2004 (b). Own-initiative Opinion on Low-cost airlines and territorial development. Cdr63/2004 fin, 7 July 2004.

Committee of the Regions, 2004 (c). Implementation and monitoring of the principles of subsidiarity and proportionality: issues and prospects for the Committee of the Regions. Report of the general secretariat of the Committee of the Regions, drawn up for the first Conference on Subsidiarity, Berlin, 27 May 2004.
http://www.cor.eu.int/document/de/const_107en.pdf

Committee of the Regions, 2004 (d). Opinion of the Committee of the Regions of 18 November 2004 on the Communication from the Commission A stronger partnership for the outermost regions COM(2004) 343 final. COTER-025, 2 December 2004.
http://www.cor.eu.int/alde/martin%20menis%202%20EN.pdf

Conference of the Parties, 2004. Decision VII/14 on "Biological diversity and tourism". Seventh Ordinary Meeting of the Conference of the Parties to the Convention on Biological Diversity Kuala Lumpur, Malaysia (9 – 20 February 2004).
http://www.biodiv.org/decisions/default.aspx?m=COP-07&id=7751&lg=0

Council of Europe, 1995. Recommendation No. R(95)10 of the Committee of Ministers to Member States on a sustainable tourist development policy in protected areas.
http://www.coe.int/T/E/Cultural_Co-operation/Environment/Nature_and_biological_diversity/Biodiversity/tourism summary.asp

Council of the European Union, 1992. Decision of 13 July 1992 on a Community action plan to assist tourism, 92/421/EEC.
http://europa.eu.int/eur-lex/lex/LexUriServ/LexUriServ.do?uri=CELEX:31992D0421:EN:HTML

Council of the European Union, 1995. Directive 95/57/EC on the collection of statistical information in the field of tourism. Official Journal L 291 , 06/12/1995 P. 0032 – 0039.
http://europa.eu.int/smartapi/cgi/sga_doc?smartapi!celexapi!prod!CELEXnumdoc&lg=EN&numdoc=31995L0057&model=guichett

Council of the European Union, 2002. Resolution of 21 May 2002 on the future of European tourism, 2002/C 135/01.
http://europa.eu.int/eur-lex/pri/en/oj/dat/2002/c_135/c_13520020606en00010003.pdf

Cristóvão A., 2002. Rural development initiatives and institutional arrangements in the national park of Peneda Gerês, Portugal. Paper to the Thessaloniki seminar, 17-18 March 2002.
http://www.mtnforum.org/resources/library/crisa02a.htm

E-business W@tch, 2005. The European e-Business Market Watch. Electronic business in tourism is taking off – with strong impact on intermediation. March 2005.
http://www.ebusiness-watch.org/resources/tourism/SUM06_Tourism.pdf

English Tourism Council, 2001. Tourism and transport, The issues and the solutions. English Tourism Board.

English Tourism Council, 2002. Visitor attitudes to sustainable tourism.

European Commission, 1999. ESDP - European Spatial Development Perspective. Towards Balanced and Sustainable Development of the Territory of the European Union. Office for Official Publications of the European Communities.
http://europa.eu.int/comm/regional_policy/sources/docoffic/official/reports/pdf/sum_en.pdf

European Commission, 2001 (a). A Sustainable Europe for a Better World: A European Union Strategy for Sustainable Development. COM(2001) 264 final, 15.5.2001. Office for Official Publications of the European Communities.
http://europa.eu.int/eur-lex/en/com/cnc/2001/com2001_0264en01.pdf

European Commission, 2001 (b). White Paper. European transport policy for 2010: time to decide. COM(2001) 0370, 12.09.2001. Office for Official Publications of the European Communities.
http://europa.eu.int/comm/energy_transport/library/lb_texte_complet_en.pdf

European Commission, 2001 (c). Green Paper Promoting a European framework for Corporate Social Responsibility, COM(2001) 366 final, 18.07.2001.
http://europa.eu.int/eur-lex/en/com/gpr/2001/com2001_0366en01.pdf

European Commission, 2001(d). Working together for the future of European tourism. COM(2001) 665 final, 13.11.2001.
http://europa.eu.int/eur-lex/en/com/cnc/2001/com2001_0665en01.pdf

European Commission, 2001 (e). Community measures affecting tourism (1997/1999), COM(2001) 171 final, 28.03.2001
http://europa.eu.int/eur-lex/en/com/rpt/2001/com2001_0171en01.pdf

European Commission, 2001 (f). Green Paper on Integrated Product Policy. COM(2001) 68 final, 07.02.2001.
http://europa.eu.int/eur-lex/en/com/gpr/2001/com2001_0068en01.pdf

European Commission, 2002. Community measures affecting tourism (2000), SEC(2002) 300, 15.3.2002.
http://europa.eu.int/comm/enterprise/services/tourism/tourism-publications/documents/commmeas_en.pdf

European Commission, 2003 (a). Basic orientations for the sustainability of European tourism. COM(2003) 716 final. 21.11.2003.
http://europa.eu.int/comm/enterprise/services/tourism/tourism-publications/coms/sustainability.pdf

European Commission, 2003 (b). Green paper on services of general interest. COM(2003) 270 final, 21.05.2003.
http://europa.eu.int/comm/secretariat_general/services_general_interest/docs/com_2003_270_fi_en.pdf

European Commission, 2004 (a). Proposal for a regulation of the European Parliament and of the Council establishing a European grouping of cross-border cooperation. COM(2004) 496 final, 14.07.2004.
http://europa.eu.int/eur-lex/en/com/pdf/2004/com2004_0496en01.pdf

European Commission, 2004 (b). Communication from the Commission: A stronger partnership for the outermost regions. COM (2004) 343 final, 26.5.2004.
http://europa.eu.int/comm/regional_policy/sources/docoffic/official/communic/rup/com2004343_en.pdf

European Commission, Directorate General for Enterprise, 1998. Facts and Figures on the Europeans on holidays: 1997-1998. Executive Summary, March 1998.
http://europa.eu.int/comm/enterprise/services/tourism/tourism-publications/documents/eubarholi0398.pdf

European Commission, Directorate General for Enterprise, 2003. Structure, performance and competitiveness of European tourism and its enterprises. Office for Official Publications of the European Communities.
http://europa.eu.int/comm/enterprise/services/tourism/studies/pwc/pwc_en.pdf

European Commission, Directorate General for Enterprise, 2004. EU Support for Tourism Enterprises and Tourist Destinations – An Internet Guide. European Communities.
http://europa.eu.int/comm/enterprise/services/tourism/tourism-publications/documents/internet_guide_en04.pdf

European Commission, Directorate General for Regional Policy, 2001. Structural policies and European territory. Islands and coastal areas.

European Commission, Directorate General for Regional Policy, 2002. Cooperation without borders. Inforegio Panorama n° 6, January 2002. European Communities.
http://europa.eu.int/comm/regional_policy/sources/docgener/panorama/pdf/mag6_en.pdf

European Commission, Directorate General for Regional Policy, 2004 (a). List of Homepages of the Regional Programmes of Innovative Actions (Situation on 4 May 2004).
http://europa.eu.int/comm/regional_policy/innovation/pdf/library/links.pdf

European Commission, Directorate General for Regional Policy, 2004 (b). Cohesion policy: the 2007 watershed. Inforegio factsheet 2004.
http://europa.eu.int/comm/regional_policy/sources/docgener/informat/reg2007_en.pdf

European Commission, Directorate General for Regional Policy, 2004 (c). Third report on economic and social cohesion, A new partnership for cohesion convergence competitiveness cooperation.
http://europa.eu.int/comm/regional_policy/sources/docoffic/official/reports/cohesion3/cohesion3_en.htm

European Consultative Forum on Environment and Sustainable Development Secretariat, 1999. Comments and recommendations on The European Spatial Development Perspective.
http://europa.eu.int/comm/environment/forum/spatreport_en.pdf

European Environment Agency, 1999. Environment in the European Union at the turn of the Century. Environmental assessment report No.2.

European Environment Agency, 2001. Environmental signals 2001. Environmental assessment report No 8.

European Environment Agency, 2003. Europe's environment: the third assessment. Environmental assessment report No 10.

European Environment Agency, 2005. EEA Core Set of Indicators Guide, Technical Report n°1/2005.
http://reports.eea.eu.int/technical_report_2005_1/en

European Golf Association Ecology Unit, 1995. Pilot Scheme. Jointly funded by the European Commission (DG XI - 94/C/68/12) and the EGA Ecology Unit.
http://www.golfecology.com/publics/manage/redpart.htm

European Investment Bank, 2005. Evaluation of PPP projects financed by the EIB. Synthesis Report.
http://www.eib.org/Attachments/ev/ev_ppp_en.pdf

European Partners for the Environment, 1996. Tourism, leisure, nature protection and agri-tourism: principles, partnerships and practice. Workbook, Tourism Research Group, University of Exeter, Exter, U.K., April 1996.

Hurley A., Archer B., Fletcher J., 1994. The economic impact of European community grants for tourism in the Republic of Ireland. Tourism Management, Volume 15, Issue 3: Pages 203-211.

Ireland's Presidency of the European Union, 2004. Discussion Paper. Conference on Territorial Cohesion: Meeting New Challenges in an Enlarged EU. 25 - 27 May 2004, Galway, Ireland.

Kumaraswamy M.M., Zhang X.Q., 2001. Government role in BOT-led infrastructure development. International Journal of Project Management.

Kwan A.Y., Ofori G., 2001. Chinese culture and successful implementation of partnering in Singapore's construction industry. Construction Management & Economics. Volume 19, Number 6 / October 1, 2001.

Lanquar R. et al., 1995. Tourisme et environnement en Méditerranée - Enjeux et prospective. Les fascicules du Plan bleu No. 8. Economica, May 1995. Blue Plan/UNEP/MAP.

Leidner R., 2003. The European Tourism Industry. A multi-sector with dynamic markets - Structures, Developments and importance for Europe's economy. European Commission, DG Enterprise.
http://europa.eu.int/comm/enterprise/library/lib-tourism/doc/european_tourism_industry.pdf

Merchadou C., et al., 2001. European Working Group D on the Promotion of sustainable development and protection of the environment for the tourism sector: Towards a European Agenda 21 for tourism. Contributors : Pelletreau, A., Vourc'h A. European Commission, Directorate General for Enterprise.
http://europa.eu.int/comm/enterprise/services/tourism/workinggroups/finalreportd_june2001_fr.pdf

Merna T., Smith N., 1999. Privately Financed Infrastructure in the 21st Century, Proceedings of the Institution of Civil Engineers, No 132, Nov1999.

Organisation for Economic Co-operation and Development, 2000. Tourism and Travel Patterns: Part I, Tourism Travel Trends and Environmental Impacts, Paris, 16-17 May 2000. ENV/EPOC/GEEI(2000)5.

Organisation for Economic Co-operation and Development, 2003. Strengthening Good Territorial Governance - Conclusion of Session 2. High Level Meeting of the Territorial Development Policy Committee.
http://www.oecd.org/dataoecd/48/15/3666623.pdf

Pils M., Eltschka-Schiller G., 1999. Sustainability indicators for tourism. International friends for nature, Vienna, December 1999.

Porter M.E., 1980. The Competitive Advantage of Nations.

Porter M.E., 1985. Competitive Advantage, Creating and Sustaining Superior Performance. Free Press.

Private Finance Panel, 1996. Risk and Reward in PFI Contracts: Practical Guidance on the Sharing of Risk and Structuring of PFI Contracts, HMSO, London.

Rechatin C., Dubois G., Pelletreau A., 2000. Tourisme, environnement, territoires: les indicateurs. French Institute for the Environment (IFEN), Orléans, December 2000.

Rodriguez-Pose A., Fratesi U., 2002. Unbalanced development strategies and the lack of regional convergence in the EU. Paper presented to the 2002 ERSA congress, Dortmund, 27 -31 August 2002.
http://www.lse.ac.uk/collections/geographyAndEnvironment/research/Researchpapers/rp76.pdf

Scharle P., 2002. Public-Private Partnership (PPP) as a Social Game. Innovation, Vol. 15, No.3. Garfax Publishing.

Schmidt, H., 2002 (a). Dynamic Regional Tourism. Eurostat Statistics in Focus Theme 4 - 14/2002– Industry, trade and services - Office for Official Publications of the European Communities.
http://epp.eurostat.cec.eu.int/cache/ITY_OFFPUB/KS-NP-02-014/EN/KS-NP-02-014-EN.PDF

Schmidt, H., 2002 (b). Tourism and the Environment. Eurostat Statistics in Focus Theme 4 - 40/2002– Industry, trade and services - Office for Official Publications of the European Communities.
http://epp.eurostat.cec.eu.int/cache/ITY_OFFPUB/KS-NP-02-040/EN/KS-NP-02-040-EN.PDF

Schmidt, H., 2005. Tourism in the enlarged European Union. Eurostat Statistics in Focus 13/2005– Industry, trade and services - Population and social conditions - Office for Official Publications of the European Communities.
http://epp.eurostat.cec.eu.int/cache/ITY_OFFPUB/KS-NP-05-013/EN/KS-NP-05-013-EN.PDF

Smith A., 2001. Speech by Chief Secretary Andrew Smith at the OGC PUK Conference, 23 October 2001.
http://archive.treasury.gov.uk/speech/cst/cst231001.htm

Sternberg R., 1994. Supporting peripheral economies or industrial policy in favour of national growth? An empirically based analysis of goal achievement of the Japanese 'Technopolis' Program". Environment and Planning C: Government and Policy 1995, volume 13, p. 425-439.

Storper M., 1995. Territorial Development in the Global Learning Economy. Review of International Political Economy 2, 3: pp. 394-424.

Sustainable European Regions Network, 2004. Cohesive Thinking Towards a Sustainable Future.
http://www.sustainable-euroregions.net/documentbank/sd_regions_synthesis-e.pdf

Task force on Methodologies linked to Tourism Statistics, 2002. Proposals to Update the Community methodology, 15 May 2002 (meeting on 30-31 May 2002, Eurostat, Luxembourg).

Treaty establishing a Constitution for Europe, 2004.
http://europa.eu.int/constitution/en/lstoc1_en.htm

Treaty establishing the European Community, 1957. Consolidated version.
http://europa.eu.int/eur-lex/en/treaties/dat/C_2002325EN.003301.html

United Nations Commission on Sustainable Development, 1999. Decision of the General Assembly and the Commission on Sustainable Development. Report on the 7th session, New York, 19-30 April 1999.

United Nations Environment Programme, 1995. Environmental Codes of Conduct for Tourism.
http://www.uneptie.org/pc/tourism/library/codes_of_conduct.htm

United Nations Environment Programme, 2001. Tourism focus n°13 - Soft mobility: making tourism in Europe more sustainable. Division of Technology, Industry and Economics.
http://www.uneptie.org/pc/tourism/documents/newsletters/tourism13.pdf

UNEP, MAP, MCSD-BLUE PLAN, 1999. Report of the workshop on tourism and sustainable development in the Mediterranean. Antalya, Turkey, 17-19 September 1998.
http://planbleu.org/publications/mtrs126_1.pdf

World Tourism Organisation, 2000. Tourism 2020 Vision. Vol.4. WTO, Madrid.

World Tourism Organisation, 2002. The Italian Ecotourism market, Special report No13, February 2002, Madrid.

World Tourism Organisation, 2003. E-tourism, Electronic Commerce Strategies for Development. Conference paper, Regional High-level Conference for Africa, Tunis, 19-21 June 2003.

World Tourism Organisation, 2004. World Tourism Barometer, Volume 2, No.3, October 2004.

World Travel & Tourism Council, 2004 (a). Travel & Tourism forging ahead - The 2004 Travel & Tourism Economic Research. Country Reports.
http://www.wttc.org/2004tsa/frameset2a.htm

World Travel & Tourism Council, 2004 (b). A practical manifesto from the Travel & Tourism private sector.
http://www.wttc.org/publications/pdf/WTTC%20EU%20Manifesto.pdf

2.   Other Internet links and sources

Agenda 21 for the Baltic Sea Region http://www.baltic21.org/

Ecological Tourism in Europe http://www.oete.de/eng/index.htm

ECOSERT, European Co-operation for http://www.ecosert.org.gr/aims.htm
Sustainable Environmental Regional
development through Tourism

English Tourism Council (ETC) http://www.englishtourism.org.uk

European Centre for Eco Agro Tourism http://www.eceat.nl
(ECEAT)

European Commission, DG Enterprise, 2002. http://europa.eu.int/comm/enterprise/
European Tourism Forum, Agenda 21 – services/tourism/tourism_forum/docu
Sustainability in the European tourism sector. ments/background_en.pdf
Background document.

French Institute for the Environment (IFEN) http://www.ifen.fr/

Green Certificate (Latvia) http://www.eco.traveller.lv

ICLEI, Local Governments for Sustainability http://www.iclei-
europe.org/index.php?about_us

Industry as a Partner for Sustainable http://www.uneptie.org/outreach/wss
Development: Tourism Report d/docs/sectors/final/tourism.pdf

Muscat Declaration on Built Environment for http://worldheritage-
Sustainable Tourism, 2005. forum.net/en/log/58

Network for the Sustainable Development of http://www.tourism-site.org/
Tourism Destinations in Europe

Nordic Council of Ministers Tourism Ad Hoc Working Group: Towards a sustainable Nordic Tourism, 1999	http://www.norden.org/naering/sk/sustainable_nordic_tourism.doc
PAN Parks - European network of wilderness protected areas	http://www.panda.org/about_wwf/where_we_work/europe/what_we_do/pan_parks/about.cfm
Quebec Declaration on Ecotourism, 2002.	http://www.world-tourism.org/sustainable/IYE/quebec/anglais/declaration.html
Sustainable Tourism and NATURA 2000. Based on the Lisbon Seminar December 1999	http://www.odra.org.pl/natura-tourism/content.html
The European Blue Flag Campaign	http://www.blueflag.org/
The European Destinet Sustainable Tourism Information Portal	http://destinet.ewindows.eu.org
The European Eco-label for tourist accommodation service	http://www.eco-label-tourism.com/frameset/frameset.html
The Sustainable European Regions Network	www.sustainable-euregions.net
The VISIT Initiative	http://www.yourvisit.info/
Tour Operators Initiative	http://www.toinitiative.org/
The Global Reporting Initiative (focusing on large enterprises)	http://www.globalreporting.org/
World Charter for Sustainable Tourism, 1995. Declaration of Lanzarote	http://www.insula.org/tourism/charte.htm

WTO Global Code of Ethics for Tourism, 1999	http://www.fijibure.com/uncode.pdf
WTO-UNCTAD Sustainable Tourism – Eliminating Poverty (ST-EP) initiative	http://www.world-tourism.org/step/menu.html
WTTC publication Corporate Social Leadership for the Travel and Tourism Industry, 2002	http://www.wttc.org/promote/pdf/CSLREPORT.pdf

3.   List of Presented Best Practices and Case Studies

BP_1	The Tour Operator Initiative	Section B
BP_2	The Local Agenda 21 of Storstrøm County, Denmark	Section B
BP_3	Sustainable Mobility in the Tourism sector, Austria	Section C
BP_4	The scheme of cycling roads and green tracks in France	Section C
BP_5	Ecotourism in Estonia: the WWF Väinameri project	Section C
BP_6	Experimenting a longer tourism season in Rhodes, Greece	Section D
CS_1	National Tourism Strategy and Monitoring System: the British case	Section B
CS_2	The sustainable development programme of Varese Ligure, Italy	Section B
CS_3	Cultural routes and sustainable tourism in Europe	Section C
CS_4	National Sustainable Development Policy in Ireland	Section D
CS_5	The urban governance and development in Banská Štiavnica, Slovak Republic	Section D
CS_6	A network for e-tourism, the case of Austria	Section D
CS_7	European Structural Funds (2000-2006) in the Balearics	Section E
CS_8	Promotion of High Quality Tourism through INTERREG and PHARE	Section E

4. Metadata

dataset name	**Tourism bed places**
source	Eurostat web site
release date	February 2005
table name	t_3r
geo coverage	EU 25 countries
geo level	NUTS2
data frequency	annual
year	2003, with the following exceptions: Greece (2002), Hamburg (2002, activity B100), Finland and Dytiki Makedonia (2001)
unit	Number
activity	Hotels and similar establishments (A100) + Other collective accommodation establishments, Total (B100)
notes	data for Finland refer to old NUTS classification

dataset name	**Tourism establishments**
source	Eurostat web site
release date	February 2005
table name	t_3r
geo coverage	EU 25 countries
geo level	NUTS2
data frequency	annual
year	2003, , with the following exceptions: Bremen and Greece (2002), Finland (2000)
unit	Number
activity	Hotels and similar establishments (A100) + Other collective accommodation establishments, Total (B100).
notes	data for Finland refer to old NUTS classification

dataset name	**Total area**
source	Eurostat web site, EEA (2003) for Malta and Cyprus
release date	February 2005
table name	d3area
geo coverage	EU 25 countries
geo level	NUTS2, national level for Malta and Cyprus
data frequency	annual
unit	km²
notes	data for Finland refer to old NUTS classification

dataset name	**Population at 1st January by sex and age**
source	Eurostat web site
release date	February 2005
table name	d2jan
geo coverage	EU 25 countries
geo level	NUTS2
data frequency	annual
year	2002, with the following exceptions: Greece and Italy (2001), Portugal and the United Kingdom (2000), Finland and Trentino Alto Adige (1999)
unit	number, total
notes	▪ data for Finland refer to old NUTS classification ▪ 2002 data for France are provisional

dataset name	**Gross value added at basic prices - ESA95**
source	Eurostat web site
release date	February 2005
table name	e2vabp95
geo coverage	24 EU countries: no data for Germany, Finland and Trentino Alto Adige
geo level	NUTS2, but data at national level for Finland
data frequency	annual
year	2002, with the exception of Ireland (2001)
unit	currency, million of euro (from 1.1.1999)
activity	NACE branch - H Hotels and restaurants
notes	data for Finland refer to old NUTS classification

dataset name	**Gross domestic product**
source	Eurostat web site
release date	April 2005
table name	e2gdp95
geo coverage	EU 25 countries
geo level	NUTS2, but data at national level for Finland
data frequency	annual
year	2002
unit	euro per inhabitant
notes	data for Finland refer to old NUTS classification

dataset name	**Number of Blue Flag beaches and marinas awarded by the International Jury in 2004**
source	Blue flag official web site: http://www.blueflag.org/blueflag
release date	February 2005
geo coverage	18 EU countries (no records for Austria, Czech Republic, Hungary, Luxembourg, Malta, Poland and Slovak Republic)
geo level	national level
data frequency	annual
year	2004
unit	number
notes	The award of a European Blue Flag beach is based on compliance with 27 criteria covering: water quality, environmental education and information, environmental management, safety and services. More information on criteria are available at: http://www.blueflag.org/Criteria/EuropeanBeaches

dataset name	**Nationally protected areas**
source	World Database on Protected Areas: http://sea.unep-wcmc.org/wdbpa/
release date	February 2005
geo coverage	EU 25 countries
geo level	national level
data frequency	annual
year	2002
unit	% of terrestrial and sea area
notes	Protected areas refer to International Union for the Conservation of Nature Categories I-VI. Definitions are available at: http://sea.unep-wcmc.org/wdbpa/

dataset name	**Density of road and railway networks**
source	European Union Road Federation: http://www.erf.be/ United Nations Economic Commission for Europe: http://www.unece.org/
release date	First quarter of 2005
geo coverage	EU 25 countries
geo level	national level
data frequency	annual
year	Roads: 2000 Railways: 2001, with the following exceptions: Netherlands, Italy, United Kingdom, Sweden and Germany (2000)
unit	km rail/100 km²; km road/100 km²
notes	Railways: the figure related to the United Kingdom does not include Northern Ireland data.

Committee of the Regions of the European Union

SUSTAINABLE TOURISM AS A FACTOR OF COHESION AMONG EUROPEAN REGIONS

Luxembourg: Office for Official Publications of the European Communities

2006 — 241 pp. — 16 x 23 cm

ISBN 92-895-0378-5

Price (excluding VAT) in Luxembourg: EUR 25